POSTERITY IS NOW

POSTERITY IS NOW

Practicing Museum Anthropology, Collections Care, and Collaborative Research with Indigenous Peoples

JENNIFER A. SHANNON

UNIVERSITY OF WYOMING PRESS
Laramie

© 2025 by University Press of Colorado

Published by University of Wyoming Press
An imprint of University Press of Colorado
1580 North Logan Street, Suite 660
PMB 39883
Denver, Colorado 80203-1942

All rights reserved

 The University Press of Colorado is a proud member of Association of University Presses.

The University Press of Colorado is a cooperative publishing enterprise supported, in part, by Adams State University, Colorado School of Mines, Colorado State University, Fort Lewis College, Metropolitan State University of Denver, University of Alaska Fairbanks, University of Colorado, University of Northern Colorado, University of Wyoming, Utah State University, and Western Colorado University.

ISBN: 978-1-64642-738-3 (hardcover)
ISBN: 978-1-64642-739-0 (paperback)
ISBN: 978-1-64642-740-6 (ebook)
https://doi.org/10.5876/9781646427406

Library of Congress Cataloging-in-Publication Data

Names: Shannon, Jennifer A. author
Title: Posterity is now : practicing museum anthropology, collections care, and collaborative research with Indigenous peoples / Jennifer A. Shannon.
Description: Laramie : University of Wyoming Press, [2025] | Includes bibliographical references and index.
Identifiers: LCCN 2025013276 (print) | LCCN 2025013277 (ebook) | ISBN 9781646427383 hardcover | ISBN 9781646427390 paperback | ISBN 9781646427406 ebook
Subjects: LCSH: Indigenous peoples—Research | Museums and Indigenous peoples | Indians of North America—Museums | Anthropological museums and collections | Museums and community | Ethnological museums and collections
Classification: LCC GN380 .S53 2025 (print) | LCC GN380 (ebook) | DDC 305.80074—dc23/eng/20250625
LC record available at https://lccn.loc.gov/2025013276
LC ebook record available at https://lccn.loc.gov/2025013277

Cover illustration by John G. Swogger

To Cécile Ganteaume, for being one of the first people I worked for in the museum field and for giving me meaningful research assignments that got me hooked on this whole museum thing; to Cynthia Chavez Lamar, who trusted me enough to send me into the field to do community-based research early on; to Ann McMullen, who encouraged me to get a PhD and become a curator; and to Susan Rowley, who shared a classroom with me and showed me how to teach the next generation to do this kind of work. These women inspired me and gave me opportunities to grow and learn earlier in my career, and for that I am grateful. This book is also dedicated to all my students who went along for the ride with me as we learned from each other; I experimented with and honed the ideas in this book over the course of fifteen years of teaching anthropology and museum studies including as a graduate student at Cornell University, as a postdoc at the University of British Columbia, and as a professor for twelve years at the University of Colorado. Finally, this book is dedicated to the many Indigenous community members who shared their time, thoughts, and experiences with me and shaped my teaching and practice over the years.

Contents

List of Figures	xi
Preface	xiii
Acknowledgments	xix
INTRODUCTION	**3**
1. Posterity Is Now	4
2. Teachings from Native Communities	5
3. Frameworks for Action and Accountability	8
4. A Culture of Learning	9
5. Being a Model for Others	13
6. A Companion to Practice	15
Introduction Notes	16
PART 1: COLLABORATION IS THEORY IN MOTION	**19**
7. Decolonizing/Indigenizing	20

viii | CONTENTS

8. Language and Power ... 23
9. Multiple Ways of Knowing ... 25
10. Relationality ... 27
11. For Example: Mesa Verde National Park ... 29
12. Questions to Guide Practice and Additional Resources ... 38
    Part 1 Notes ... 39

PART 2: MUSEUM ANTHROPOLOGY ... 41

13. Anthropology of Museums ... 42
14. Anthropology in Museums ... 47
15. Collecting Practice and Policy ... 53
16. Repatriation Law ... 56
17. Collections Research ... 65
18. Exhibition Development ... 68
19. Interpretation and Display ... 75
20. Community Engagement across the Museum ... 80
21. Acknowledgment and Compensation ... 82
22. Teaching Museum Anthropology ... 83
23. For Example: Collections Research Course in Cultural Anthropology ... 85
24. Questions to Guide Practice and Additional Resources ... 99
    Part 2 Notes ... 101

PART 3: COLLECTIONS ACCESS AND CARE ... 105

25. Community Visits to Collections ... 107
26. Collections Housing ... 114
27. Cultural Care ... 118
28. Collections Visits to Communities ... 124
29. Conservation ... 126
30. Repatriation Consultation ... 129
31. Catalogs and Online Databases ... 138
32. Associated Documentation and Archives ... 142
33. Digitization and Digital Return ... 143

34. Researcher Access to Collections — 146
35. Collections Management Policy and Shared Stewardship — 148
36. A Welcoming Workplace — 151
37. Teaching Museum Studies and Professional Development — 153
38. For Example: Bougainville Primary Source Book — 160
39. Questions to Guide Practice and Additional Resources — 165
   Part 3 Notes — 166

PART 4: COLLABORATIVE RESEARCH — 169

40. Values-Centered Research Practice — 171
41. Collaborative Research Design — 175
42. Grant Writing for Collaborative Projects — 182
43. Research Review and Informed Consent — 188
44. Interviewing and Recording — 192
45. Sharing Research Results — 197
46. Teaching Collaborative and Public Anthropology — 198
47. For Example: Community-Engaged Comics — 204
48. Questions to Guide Practice and Additional Resources — 212
   Part 4 Notes — 213

CONCLUSION: REIMAGINING ANTHROPOLOGY AND THE MUSEUM — 215

   Epilogue — 221
   Conclusion Note — 223

APPENDIXES — 225

Appendix A: Sample Project Newsletter — 226
Appendix B: Example Policies and Guidelines for Inspiration — 228
Appendix C: Workshop Your Project — 229
Appendix D: Sample Infographic and Grant Proposal — 232
Appendix E: Job Searching and Professional Development — 247
Appendix F: Guide to Thinking about Collaboration for Exhibit Planning — 248
Appendix G: Guide to Creating Community-Engaged Comics — 254

References	259
Index	269
About the Author	277

Figures

1.1.	Relationality	18
1.2.	Excerpt from the *Chapin Mesa Museum Exhibit Design Reference Guide*	37
2.1.	Repatriation	40
2.2.	California population over time	63
2.3.	Kalinago (Island Carib) population over time	63
2.4.	Catlin Cubes, Denver Art Museum	77
3.1.	Collections stewardship	104
3.2.	Video still, *Everything Was Carved*	107
3.3.	Viewing items in cabinets	111
3.4.	Viewing items on a table	111
3.5.	Red felt and sweetgrass in drawer	121
3.6.	Editing collections information system records together	134
3.7.	Preparing to wrap items in red cloth to return home	136

3.8. Presenting Bougainville Primary Source Book to Papua New
   Guinea National Museum and Art Gallery 163
4.1. Perspective 168
4.2. Kumeyaay Visual Storytelling Project team reviewing
   draft comic at the Sycuan Cultural Center, July 2013 209
4.3. Comic launch at the Barona Cultural Center,
   November 15, 2024 212
A.1. Sample project newsletter, page 1 226
A.2. Sample project newsletter, page 2 227
C.1. Sample project organizational chart 231
C.2. Project organizational chart from Kumeyaay Visual
   Storytelling Project 231
C.3. Example from Mesa Verde National Park Chapin Mesa
   Archeological Museum redesign project, 2020 231
D.1. Sample project infographic 233
G.1. Sample process outline 256

Preface

Dear reader,

    As I begin this book, I am writing to you from Boulder, Colorado—the traditional territories of the Ute, Cheyenne, and Arapaho peoples. Forty-eight contemporary tribal nations are historically tied to the lands of what we now call Colorado. As the curator of anthropology at the University of Colorado Museum of Natural History, I care for and steward items from these Native Nations that bear witness to their connection to this place and our museum endeavors to be welcoming to these, and all, Native Nations.

    I am a non-Native scholar who is first-generation Italian and originally from Chicago. My experiences, and my voice throughout this book, reflect this position. I am speaking from a place of learning, and sharing what I have learned, from Native community members. This book is me, a settler scholar, talking to other museum professionals and students, trying to put in one place some things that I hope will help us all drive the changes Indigenous communities have been demanding and many of us want to support. I also hope this book provides insight into and suggestions for the kinds of things

Indigenous community members can expect or request in working with museums and researchers.

Museums have played a role in colonialism and the subjugation of Native Nations and Indigenous people in the United States. There is a movement toward restorative justice and active support for Native Nations that is called different things by different people: decolonizing the museum, Indigenizing the museum, ethical museum practice. Whatever the moniker, we are all endeavoring to make museums accountable and responsive to the communities whose items we care for in museum collections.

This book arose from my own experience working at the intersection of museums, anthropology, and Native American communities over the last twenty-five years. It is intended to be a provocation and helpful guidance for those who are learning about museums for the first time or have been working in them for years and are looking for some insight into making them more welcoming and ethical places.

Collaboration is the subject and method of my anthropological research. It's central to what I teach, it's the foundation of my museum work, and it's at the heart of my leadership philosophy and practice. This approach came from my personal values and teachings from Native peoples. As Regna Darnell notes in her book about the Americanist tradition in anthropology, "For a long time Native Americans have been teaching anthropologists how to behave in a civilized fashion and respond to local communities' needs and concerns."[1]

What I share in this book is a series of teachings and lessons I have learned from working with Native communities—as part of community-based research projects, museum consultations, and exhibition making. My museum career began at the National Museum of the American Indian (NMAI), where I was a curatorial research assistant engaged in the process of community curating. My first assignment as a curatorial researcher at the NMAI in 1999 was to conduct research on tribal histories for one of the inaugural exhibitions called *Our Peoples*. With the other researchers and according to what we had learned in college, I started taking notes on a lot of historical resources and books. When we presented the sum of our work to our mentor and supervisor, Dr. Craig Howe (Lakota), he essentially told us: you're doing it wrong. He instructed us to seek Native voices in the archives, not secondary sources about Native peoples written by non-Native scholars who had a monopoly on telling Native American history for centuries. This museum was seeking a different perspective. So I went to the archives and found affidavits and letters and petitions, including a petition housed at the

Library of Congress that was signed by hundreds of Cherokees in opposition to the Treaty of New Echota. The petition demonstrated agency, diversity, resistance—it was a counter-narrative to the usual story, to the Western version of events.

Again while working for the NMAI, in 2001, I experienced another moment that shaped my practice in profound ways, even if I didn't realize it at the time (and not knowing I would end up with the job I have now). As a curatorial research assistant I was assigned to travel to the eastern Canadian Arctic on behalf of the museum to work with community members on developing content for their exhibit. While there, a committee of elders developing the Igloolik exhibit tasked me with interviewing Zach Kunuk about the importance of language. He had directed the Inuktitut language feature film *Atanarjuat: The Fast Runner*, which came out earlier in the year. All the kids in town were watching it on repeat. I made an appointment to meet with Zach. When I arrived at Isuma Productions, he invited me to sit down at a table with him and James Ungalak, an actor in the film. Before I could even explain why I came, they grilled me about my religious beliefs for almost an hour. I was not brought up in an institutionalized religion and had not articulated my beliefs out loud to anyone else in such a way. I answered all their questions honestly and then told them why I was interested in interviewing them: to discuss language. They seemed to relax after they assessed I was not being defensive, heard what the exhibit was about, and had a better idea of who I was and why I was there. They invited me to come back in a few days to do a recorded interview, and portions of it ended up in the exhibit. This experience taught me about expectations Indigenous peoples have about anthropologists and the importance of sharing who you are and being open. But more important was their demand that I be willing to be vulnerable to the interview, be willing to discuss my personal life or religious beliefs, as Native peoples are often expected to be. It was a profoundly unsettling experience that led to a wonderfully open conversation—and greatly informed my understanding of the interpersonal experience of decolonizing practice.

Another moment took place more recently, when I was working with the Mandan, Hidatsa and Arikara Nation (also known as the Three Affiliated Tribes) in 2016, though some form of this kind of exchange has happened to me in the field and in the museum many times—and for good reasons. A filmmaker and I were invited to be interviewed about our current collaborative video project with the community on a live tribal radio show called *KMHA The Voice*. About three-quarters of the way into an hour-long discussion, radio host Prairie Rose Seminole said: "Now both of you have studied anthropology, teach it. So coming into Indian Country, have you had any pushback? 'Cause we don't typically have good relationships with anthropologists . . . How are you kind of mending that historical, uh [pause] history, I guess [laughs]. [Everyone laughs.] I can't think of an appropriate polite word to say . . . How are you moving forward and building bridges and making connections that strengthen our story and our history?" Our laughs, whether nervous or because we understood Prairie's euphemism, were about the field of anthropology's history of extractive, objectifying research and representation regarding Indigenous peoples. In light of this history, we certainly may and should value collaboration for ethical and epistemological reasons, but I want to stress that relevance and reciprocity are righteous demands by Indigenous peoples. Strengthening their story and their history is part of the work they're asking us to do. This is the work I have been dedicated to over the last twenty-five years, both within and beyond museum walls.

After leaving the NMAI, I earned a PhD in cultural anthropology from Cornell University. My dissertation was the foundation for my first book, *Our Lives: Collaboration, Native Voice, and the Making of the National Museum of the American Indian* (2014). After graduating, I was a postdoctoral fellow for one year in the University of British Columbia's department of anthropology, which is associated with the University of British Columbia Museum of Anthropology—a public museum well-known for its collaborative methods in exhibits, repatriation, and partnerships with First Nations. I then became a curator and an anthropology professor at the University of Colorado, where I had the opportunity to develop a program in collaborative anthropology and to teach museum studies.

At the heart of all this is a commitment to reorienting the museum's purpose away from (only) preserving objects toward supporting cultural continuity and community well-being among Native communities today. I capture this idea in a phrase: posterity is now. I explain this in more detail in the introduction. You will notice that I include resources at the end of each section. Rather than provide an exhaustive reading list, I have selected mostly books but also some articles that I frequently use in my teaching and think would be good additions to your library. A note about language: I use the terms *Native* and *Indigenous* interchangeably, following the National Museum of the American Indian's example. Following the University of British Columbia Museum of Anthropology staff, I use the term *originating community* to indicate the community from which museum collections originated (sometimes referred to as source community elsewhere). I hope this book lowers the barrier to enacting more informed, ethical, and engaged museum and research practices by providing inspiration and concrete examples that are direct, specific, and accessible.

One final note. I know we can never perfectly enact our ideals. Please don't let perfect get in the way of a better path forward. It is understandable that you may not have the power within your institution or the means to follow all of the guidance and suggestions in this book and from Native communities. The point is to be aware of these issues and concerns, take these values into consideration, and be guided by the ideal and enact the possible wherever you are. Maybe you can't create a truly collaborative exhibit with an originating community, but you can avoid sharing ceremonial knowledge in the exhibit and include existing testimony or scholarship from that community. Can you get close to the ideal and be informed by it to do what's possible right now and work toward more comprehensive change in the near- and long-term future? Small steps are still steps in the right direction. If we all take steps forward in whatever way we can, I think we can shape a path toward building good relations and a promising future for museums and Native communities.

Jen Shannon
July 9, 2021

NOTE

1. Darnell, *Invisible Genealogies*, 29.

Acknowledgments

The ideas in this book are not necessarily all new or mine alone; they come from overlapping communities dedicated to similar work, including many professionals, scholars, and Native community members who have inspired or worked alongside me. In this book I represent my understanding of it all, bringing together what I have been learning, teaching, and practicing for the past twenty-five years. To some, these approaches will be new. For others, who have also been doing this kind of work for decades, they will seem familiar. I hope that drawing these ideas all together in one place, in accessible language and for broad and different audiences, will contribute to the change we all have been part of over the years.

There are far more people to thank than I can include here; it would be a book itself! Each of us moves in particular professional and learning circles, and those personal experiences and connections come to the fore in this book. Yes, there are many people out there doing good work! This is my own professional journey, and the examples and publications I point to are representative of the communities of practice I have participated in. So, I want to call out some individuals for their impact on my thinking for this manuscript beyond those noted in my dedication.

Thank you to Steve Lekson and Christina Cain in the University of Colorado (CU) Anthropology Department who have been wonderful colleagues; Jan Bernstein and her group of NAGPRA consultants; Woody Aguilar, Kristy Sholly, and Sheila Goff in our work together with Mesa Verde National Park; the Indigenous Collections Care working group organized by Laura Bryant and Marla Taylor, especially participants Jessie Ryker Crawford and Laura Elliff Cruz; Annette de Stecher, Gwyn Isaac, Chip Colwell, and Jennifer Kramer for ongoing conversations over the years about the discipline of anthropology; my NMAI colleagues for their trailblazing work in the museum field; Calvin Grinnell, Marilyn Hudson, Elijah Benson, Amber Gwyn, Justin Deegan, Tony Lone Fight, Logan Sutton, Jaime Arsenault, Jewyl Alderson, Ethan Banegas, Mike Connolly Miskwish, Stan Rodriguez, and Lorraine Orosco, whose good work and spirit of collaboration continue to inform and inspire me, as well as my fellow *NAGPRA Comics* producers Sonya Atalay and John Swogger, who are a wonderful team for working on the things that matter to us. A special thanks to John, who has been an insightful, inspiring, and collaborative colleague across multiple projects and for agreeing to make art for this book.

I want to thank all the students in my anthropology and museum studies classes, especially my amazing graduate advisees (so proud of all of you!) including PhD students Willi Lempert, Scarlett Engle, and Katie Donlan and master's students Claire Wilbert, Irina Fartushknikova, Kendall Tallmadge Tryhane, Kayla Kramer, Evan Hawkins, Jesse Dutton-Kenny, Kerrie Iyoob, Andrea Blaser, Emma Noffsinger Dixon, Bailey Duhé, Jane Richardson, Ashley Muggli, Alex Elliott, Melanie Matteliano, Emily Tarantini, and Katie Bruce.

Thank you to my writing accountability buddies Eve Hinkley, Tina Martinez, and Alison Boardman, who supported me from the start of this manuscript, and to the participants in the Ethnography in Progress program in the University of Colorado Anthropology Department, especially Kate Goldfarb and Arielle Milkman, who provided some early and detailed feedback that helped me believe this kind of book could *maybe* be a thing! I so appreciate the encouragement and confidence editor Robert Ramaswamy provided me in thinking that this kind of book could *indeed* be a thing and that we could work together to make it so. To the three peer reviewers, this is an essential and, by design, anonymous part of academic work; I thank you for your attention to detail and thoughtful and thought-provoking recommendations. A special thank you to the director of the press, Darrin Pratt, for taking up the baton with care to shepherd the manuscript across the finish line after Robert left in 2023.

The research represented in this book through projects, case studies, and anecdotes has been funded by grants and fellowships from the Whiting Foundation through a Public Engagement Fellowship, California Humanities for All, National NAGPRA, the CU Outreach Program, CU Undergraduate Opportunities Program, CU Center for Advanced Research and Teaching in the Social Sciences, CU Innovative Seed Grant Program, Association for Social Anthropology in Oceania, School for Advanced Research, Institute of Museum and Library Services, American Alliance of Museums, and the Smithsonian Institute in Museum Anthropology.

Finally, I express deep gratitude to my family, who I am so lucky to be close to and have great support from, including my uncles Keith and Mike, my cousins, and my friend Tiffany who's really a sister, and to my mom and my aunts Mary Ann and Lucy (yes, my aunties!) for our weekly Zoom visits, which was something good that came out of Covid. I am thankful to my dad for always believing in me and that he pulled through, and I am thankful for my cousin Jack—for the life he lived, the memories he left behind, and the love he shared with all of us. It's been a difficult several years for all of us, and I am so thankful we were in it together.

POSTERITY IS NOW

Introduction

Greetings, reader! I want to make my intentions in writing this book clear: based on what I have learned from my experiences at the intersection of Native peoples, museums, and anthropology, I want to guide and support changing museum and research practices through sharing what I have learned from working with Indigenous communities. As a non-Native museum professional, I believe it's important to take on this work of sharing what we have learned so that Indigenous people don't have to keep explaining or requesting the same things over and over—it's on those of us in positions of power to change, and change the field, to create more welcoming and relevant spaces for Indigenous peoples to visit, work in, and lead.

This book is focused on providing insight and suggestions for practicing collaborative research and museum anthropology informed by Indigenous peoples with whom I have worked and with the purpose of following their lead and supporting their self-determination and cultural continuity.[1] The varied content of the book comes from my own personal journey in this field and a desire to reach multiple audiences, which can be a challenge. As I wrote this text, I at times was speaking to or engaging with students and museum practitioners, anthropologists and researchers more generally, and Indigenous community members who are in these fields or engaging with people in these fields. For the former, I hope this book can provide food for thought and ways to practice; for the latter, I hope it suggests what you can demand of the people and institutions you engage with.

The values and practices presented in this book can be implemented at every level and in every department of the museum—from hiring practices to research projects to language used in catalog nomenclature. The methods we have learned in museum anthropology provide good examples for social science research more generally. Here, I am focusing on areas that relate to anthropology and museum collections originating from Indigenous peoples because that is my area of knowledge and experience. But I hope that—no matter what kind of institution you are in or what role you serve within it, what kind of studies you are dedicated to in school, or what you intend to pursue when you graduate—you can find some inspiration here to think and act according to the values at the heart of collaboration: honesty, respect, reciprocity, and shared authority. Of course, to be able to work collaboratively and enact these values, first we must establish trust. In my line of work, that has been a long and difficult process—for very good reasons.

1

Posterity Is Now

My personal vision for museums is that those with anthropology collections reorient their mission to supporting cultural continuity and community well-being rather than to storing and preserving objects. I believe the care and preservation of collections will remain central to museums' mission. These orientations are not mutually exclusive, but prioritizing originating communities today fundamentally transforms our purpose and practice in exciting ways for everyone who engages with museums. This notion of collections access and engagement as contributing to community well-being comes from the language of Native community members themselves; it's how they often describe our work together when they visit their cultural items in museums.

Preserving Objects	Supporting Cultural Continuity
maintaining the integrity of the object →	maintaining the integrity of cultural knowledge and practices, contributing to community health and well-being

The phrase "Posterity Is Now" is how I communicate this idea—it's a slogan, really![2] It was inspired by former Glenbow Museum director Robert Janes's turn of phrase when he explained that "the museum profession is fond of saying that 'museums keep things for posterity.'" Then, after returning ceremonial bundles back to the Blackfoot, he realized that "posterity had arrived" for the museum and for the Blackfoot community.[3] It's a powerful reorientation of what we take for granted: that posterity is this ever-receding horizon into the future and that it is the general public. But it doesn't have to be.

If we insist that posterity is now and that it includes Indigenous peoples, then museums have a role to play in the health and well-being of Indigenous communities. Posterity Is Now means that all those years of preserving objects can be viewed in part as aimed at Indigenous peoples today, as they engage with collection items to reawaken cultural knowledge and language or to feel connected to their people as they come into the presence of their ancestors or slide their hands into grooves worn by them. The museum enterprise, and its collections and their associated documentation, can support cultural continuity in many ways, including by inviting communities to engage with their ancestors' belongings, to interpret their experience in their own terms to the broader public, to get training to become cultural specialists and museum professionals, and to access, use, and sometimes return cultural items for contemporary ceremonial practices.

Teachings from Native Communities

I come to this reorientation for the purpose of museums by way of teachings from members of Native communities whose demands for supporting cultural continuity and Indigenous futures are righteous and strong. Responding to these demands contributes to what is often referred to as decolonizing the museum: the work of restorative justice and reciprocity with Indigenous peoples whose items we care for in museum institutions. In my view, decolonizing is a striving for, an ongoing process that can never be complete; it requires unflinching reflexivity and continuing acts of good faith.[4]

The American Alliance of Museums has concluded that museums are the most trusted source of information in the United States.[5] This is a big responsibility: how do we manage that, what do we do with it? I ask those questions from the point of view of someone who has studied, worked at, and taught about the intersection of Indigenous peoples and museums since 1999. Over the years, I have gathered teachings that help guide my practice. They are all informed by a fundamental truth stated by W. Richard West Jr. (Southern Cheyenne), former director of the Smithsonian's National Museum of the American Indian, while I was a staff member there: we love museums because they have our stuff; we hate museums because they have our stuff. Therein lies both the acknowledgment of a traumatic and troubled past and hope for working together in a place that is valued, even if in different ways, by both museum professionals and Indigenous community members. (These are not mutually exclusive categories, I would add, thus feeding that hope.)

That hope exists in the face of a difficult history between museums and Indigenous peoples, about which I will not go into detail here. But it is something each of us should educate ourselves about—especially if we work in institutions with collections that originate from Indigenous peoples—because museums have played a part in their oppression, perceived vanishing, and objectification. Scientific racism, colonial and extractive collecting practices, the disinterment of Indigenous people's ancestors for scientific study, the treatment of Indigenous individuals as specimens, representations that are "frozen in time," and the mere fact that Indigenous peoples' material culture and bones are housed in *natural* history museums are the context in which we work and attempt to build relations of trust. As museums embrace the turn to restorative justice and community engagement, I believe they should be guided by the peoples whose items they house in their collections.

At the heart of these teachings from Native peoples is a call to reframe how museum staff think about Native peoples, collaboration, and repatriation—a call to reimagine the museum and its purpose. We want to embrace a different value system, one that welcomes multiple ways of knowing, reconsiders what counts as sources of expert knowledge, and engages with Indigenous individuals as experts and partners. These teachings from Native community members are relevant to all museums, regardless of whether they have Indigenous collections.

This reorientation has been going on in scholarship and in the everyday practice of collections visits and consultations with Native peoples in the US for some time. Native peoples, anthropologists, and museum professionals have all influenced a transformation in museology in the United States to embrace this perspective. Change has been driven by Native peoples' activism, critical scholarship, and interactions with cultural and museum anthropologists during fieldwork; anthropologists' critiques of colonialism and representation; the Native American Graves Protection and Repatriation Act (NAGPRA, 1990), which mandates consultation between museums and US Tribes; and our embodied practice of working with Native American items in our care, shaped through consultations and instructions in proper care from an Indigenous perspective. Accordingly, our ways of seeing and relating to the items in our care have changed and, consequently, so has our understanding about the potential, purpose, and practice of museums with anthropology collections.

When working in this fraught field, first impressions really matter. How you begin a relationship with a community matters. Repatriation is the return of Native ancestors or human remains, funerary items, and ceremonial items from museums to their originating communities. The teaching I refer to as "repatriation is a foundation for research" points to the fact that when you begin a relationship in a good way—in some cases, by engaging in consultation and restorative justice through repatriation—partnerships can form and may go in unanticipated directions. My relationship with the Mandan, Hidatsa and Arikara Nation began when I invited them to come to the University of Colorado (CU) Museum of Natural History for a NAGPRA consultation. From the time we planned the consultation, our relationship evolved and we worked together on a number of projects—from a documentary to a collaborative film project to writing a book chapter together. Repatriation is a start, not an end, to productive relationships with communities.

When you collaborate, it also means you are not in control. That reality is captured for me in the phrase "failure is an option"—it has to be! That is what shared authority is all about: the community has the prerogative to end participation at any time. I am a big fan of space science history. For those who aren't, the usual phrase is "failure is *not* an option," which was popularized in the film *Apollo 13* and underlined the lethal consequences if the engineers' calculations about the endangered mission failed. But in collaborative work with communities, where the goal is to maintain an appropriate process or relationship, the opposite is true: failure *is* an option—this is a crucial component of the mission's success.

Finally, there is the notion that "Posterity Is Now," which I detailed above. It's my way of communicating that our efforts in museums should not only be about preserving and researching the collections we steward. Our efforts should prioritize actively supporting originating communities' cultural continuity, the maintenance of cultural practices, and the transmission of cultural knowledge. So, my approach to research and museum practice is grounded in restorative justice and reciprocity; it is committed to shared authority and seeks to contribute to community well-being. I invite you to reimagine the museum, alongside Native community members, as a place that addresses past injustices and endeavors to build new, more equal relations with Indigenous peoples.

3

Frameworks for Action and Accountability

There are frameworks for action and accountability that embrace the idea that Posterity Is Now and can guide our work in museums. We adhere to frameworks such as professional codes of ethics from organizations like the American Alliance of Museums and the Canadian Museums Association. But here I want to focus on Indigenous-centered frameworks to guide our practice in museums.

First and foremost, it's important to understand and acknowledge tribal sovereignty and self-determination. Native Americans in the US should not be conceived of as an ethnic group; their status is political and legal as citizens of Native Nations when they are enrolled tribal members. A phrase that represents this when referring to US tribal reservations is "the Constitution stops here." US federally recognized Tribes, and many other Indigenous nations depending on where they are in the world, have their own governments. In the US, depending on their size and legal and treaty rights, tribes may have their own constitutions, police forces, environmental protection agencies, tribal historic preservation offices, and supreme courts. It is important to also know that not all Tribes recognized as such are *federally* recognized; this means that federal American Indian law and its protections are not applied equally to all groups.

Museum professionals should be familiar with laws that affect our work and that we are accountable for in our institutions. A US example is NAGPRA, mentioned earlier. Internationally, the United Nations Declaration on the Rights of Indigenous Peoples (UNDRIP) was adopted by the UN in 2007, with 144 nations in favor and only 4 countries—all settler colonial nations—against: Canada, Australia, New Zealand, and the United States. Each of these countries later endorsed the declaration; Australia in 2009, the US and New Zealand in 2010, and Canada in 2016. Museums are uniquely positioned to enact a number of the rights outlined in the declaration, including ensuring that Indigenous peoples have the right to maintain, protect, and develop their tangible and intangible culture; the right to access, use, and control their ceremonial objects and repatriate their ancestors; and the right to dignity and appropriate representation in education and public information. States are charged with combating discrimination against Indigenous peoples and promoting tolerance; given their history, museums share that responsibility.[6]

There are also guidelines for more ethical practice that have been developed by Indigenous communities that can direct our actions, like the First Nations Principles of OCAP.[7] OCAP stands for ownership, control, access, and possession; the site and its training teach people about data sovereignty and data governance. It is a framework for ensuring that data collection is done in an ethical way that is accountable to originating communities. Other examples of how we might create frameworks for accountability to originating communities in our policies and practice include the Guidelines for Collaboration from the School for Advanced Research (SAR), the Protocols for Native American Archival Materials, the Indigenous Collections Care Guide, the Standards for Museums with Native American Collections (SMNAC), and the Smithsonian Institution's new policy regarding Shared Stewardship and Ethical Returns.[8]

A Culture of Learning

Engaging in the practices and perspectives proposed in this book works best when the whole museum or research institution, even those that do not work with collections or communities, are invested and committed to them.

In other words, leadership matters. Like community-based research, my approach to leadership begins with identifying core values. I mentioned these earlier, and they are likely familiar to anyone who works with Indigenous peoples: honesty, respect, reciprocity, and shared authority. It is the responsibility of institutional leaders to set the conditions for staff success, define aspirations through strategic planning, believe in the mission, and tell a compelling story so others believe in it too—to inspire people to engage with and support the institution. Throughout, leadership should consistently reflect on these questions: how can our practice reflect our values, and how can we communicate this to a broader public?

Values-Centered Leadership

The idea of Posterity Is Now, that the museum should reorient its mission to support cultural continuity and community well-being, is so much more achievable when that message is supported by museum leadership and even more so if it comes from the top. There are different leadership approaches, and some are more conducive than others to the values and principles Indigenous peoples want to see expressed by museums and universities. Leadership approaches like collective leadership and what Peter and Edgar Schein call "humble leadership" embody the values of collaboration and can set the conditions for staff to meaningfully engage in the practices recommended in this book.[9]

Collective leadership is a leadership philosophy that recognizes the value of diverse perspectives and contributions from team members and empowers them to work toward shared goals and to create change. This form of leadership can be practiced by managers of interns and volunteers, supervisors, unit heads, and directors. Anyone who supervises and leads a team can benefit from learning about this leadership approach. Staff can do wonderful work in their engagements with communities, but they can achieve so much more with the support of upper administration and a strong value-centered mission and philosophy from a museum's or institution's director.

Finding a leadership style that embodies your values is key. Practicing a leadership style that makes reorienting a museum toward supporting Indigenous communities' well-being more achievable is ideal—and it also increases the well-being of the individuals working in the museum.[10]

Embracing Diversity

The kinds of change proposed in this book insist on valuing diversity and may, for some museums and staff, feel risky or experimental. A commitment to diversity and inclusion is central to the values in this book, to the ethics of collaboration, and to great research and museum work. Innovation thrives with increased diversity and inclusion, creating opportunities to encounter and be inspired by new ideas and new ways of thinking. Diversity comes in many packages, including language, nationality, ethnicity, sexual orientation, religion, gender identity, socioeconomic status, age, physical and mental ability, political affiliation, and more. In this book, I am highlighting the diverse perspectives of Indigenous peoples. It should be recognized that the diverse experience Native community members offer is not just in relation to Western knowledge and practices or different according to tribal affiliation. Tribal communities are diverse across all of these measures internally as well.

Hiring and contracting are key components of bringing diversity and Indigenous individuals into museum and university workplaces. This means reviewing what counts as qualified experience in job ads, reviewing the language we use in describing the work and who should apply, and having a recruitment strategy for bringing in a larger and more diverse applicant pool. You may need to go beyond a museum staff's existing networks. For example, attend conferences like that of the Association of Tribal Archives, Libraries, and Museums or post job listings on the Association on American Indian Affairs website or in Native networks on Facebook. The point is not what you specifically do but that you have a plan that is intentionally created to recruit and achieve a more diverse workforce.

Developing a Culture of Learning

To ensure not just innovation but also a vibrant work environment, it is important as a leader to cultivate a culture of learning. This requires setting clear expectations and maintaining effective communication with staff and the broader public. It should be generally understood that good ideas can come from any rank (interns and students included, interns and students especially!) and that staff are encouraged to take risks. It is okay to fail, as long as we learn from it. And, if we make a mistake, we should explain what happened and how we aim to address it. These commitments together—risk taking, owning up to and learning from mistakes, and educating ourselves from diverse perspectives—are all a part of striving for excellence; the role of museum or institutional leadership is to ensure that staff have the preparation, feedback, and resources to achieve it.

Admitting mistakes is very important and connects to the core values at the heart of both this book and decolonizing practice. There will always be times when, despite our best efforts, we make a mistake. When we admit this publicly and how we intend to change or rectify the situation, we show that we are learning from our missteps, and we create a model for others to be more open and reflective. For example, during a meeting about redesigning museum exhibits for Mesa Verde National Park, I made the mistake of anticipating how another party would react to my suggestion by starting my remarks with "you may not like this but . . ." I know better. The right thing to do was state my concerns and then listen. This was not good communication or humble listening. It didn't represent the respect I have for our project partners, who did not actually have a problem with my suggestion. I apologized in writing and then forwarded that letter to my students so they could learn from the experience too: even their professor who has done this kind of work for years makes mistakes and sometimes in the moment forgets to practice what she preaches. So, as you read this book, please know that no one is perfect—especially not me!

It is important in this work to acknowledge and support the dignity and integrity of others. This requires effort, social awareness, and cultural sensitivity. We do our best in the moment, reflect on the experience if something goes wrong, and share how we will do better in the future. It is especially important to keep in mind that words are not enough: given the history of broken promises and extractive practices from these institutions, there is no benefit of the doubt if you are a university researcher or a museum institution working with Indigenous communities. Actions are what count: actions and follow-through.

5
Being a Model for Others

Part of embracing diversity and a culture of learning is to communicate your initiatives and discuss their successes and failures so others can learn from your experience. It is through partnering and knowledge sharing that we lift some of the burden on Native communities and tribal historic preservation officers (THPOs) of having to teach each individual museum staff member or researcher more appropriate ways of working.

In my own work and practice, I use three terms very deliberately: *consultation*, *collaboration*, and *partnership*. For me, consultation is when you ask for feedback on something already created, or it is a formal legal or political process (for example, a repatriation consultation or a national park reporting annually to tribes associated with that park). Collaboration implies reciprocity and an ongoing dialogue, shared authority and decision making in determining the goals, process, and outputs of a particular project. A partnership is the next level and goes beyond the life of a single project; there is a commitment to co-direction, co-management, and sharing of resources.[11]

I believe the way museum anthropologists engage with Indigenous communities can be a model for the broader fields of anthropology and museum studies and for research more generally. Museum anthropologists break the mold of the ivory tower curator who can't communicate with the public. We write for and with non-academics all the time and regularly produce anthropology for the public within the museum. Beyond the demands of originating communities, we work with exhibit developers and design specialists who are always saying "know your audience, no jargon!" And "I *know* you did two years of research, but still . . . give me 75 words." The emphasis is on "show, don't tell"—and we do that through thoughtful juxtaposition of images, text, and objects. It's those objects, those collections, that often bring us together—they are something Indigenous communities, museum anthropologists, and the public care about, even if for very different reasons and in very different ways.

Museum anthropologists are always in conversation with people beyond our field, whether originating communities, other museum and design professionals, or audience researchers. These consultations and collaborations among museum staff, Indigenous community members, and design professionals bring different ways of knowing and seeing together, sparking new ideas that might not come from an intra-disciplinary conversation alone.

In these ways, museum anthropologists are dedicated to public anthropology, the practice of sharing our research and what we learn beyond the museum and the academy. For those of us who do collaborative anthropology with Native peoples, this is an inherent part of our work. Being at the nexus of colonial relations, power imbalances, and historical trauma; having to figure out how to build relations of trust from a distrusted and suspect position (all for good reasons); and communicating with communities and the broader public—these are all woven into our research practice. Our work is by nature a risk. We seek to establish trust, but failure is always possible.

Museum anthropology in North America has led us in collaborative, experimental directions. In our work together, our community partners drive us to develop new ideas, to think outside our academic box. And their demands that we create something that is relevant to their communities and that reaches beyond the academy drive us to diverse and creative ways of sharing our research.

This book is a response to these demands. It is arranged in four main parts, each contributing in different ways to making museums and research more welcoming to Indigenous peoples in general and to those who partner with us as well. I introduce each section by identifying the audiences I am primarily talking to and why. I offer case studies and teaching experiences that influenced my practice, as well as questions and a representative sample of readings to guide your practice.

Teaching examples present ideas for practice and lessons learned that have broader applications beyond students, teachers, and the classroom. Being a teacher is another way to be a model for others. Learning by doing is a common concept in Indigenous communities and something I value greatly as well. It's why the courses I taught at the University of Colorado Boulder included some form of practice or hands-on experience whenever possible. Teaching has been a form of learning by doing for me personally in figuring out how best to communicate what I was learning from Native community members, providing me with the opportunity for iteration, for revising and reframing over time, with a thoughtful and critical audience. Teaching was an important part of how I reflected on and processed what I was doing in communities and in the museum, and it was what led me to conceive of and organize the ideas and structure of this book.

6
A Companion to Practice

This book is intended to be a companion to practice. This means two things: first, it is practical and aims to guide action, to influence how we do things (not just how we think about them); second, it is not meant to be a text that stands alone on how to do museum anthropology, collections stewardship, or research methods. It is meant to introduce ideas, questions, and suggestions as a companion to your work or to existing texts in these areas.

Part 1, Collaboration Is Theory in Motion, introduces the Indigenous and anthropological theories that are foundational to creating a welcoming space for Indigenous peoples and their ways of knowing and engaging with museums and collections. They include decolonizing methodologies and Indigenizing the museum, the relationship between language and power, multiple ways of knowing, and relationality. These theories help us better understand, and better accommodate the needs of, originating community members who may refer to collection items as kin or living beings, for example. Predominant theories change over time. This is as much a product of our current moment as it is an invitation to, at any time, consider the thoughts and beliefs and theories that underpin your practice and where they originate.

Part 2, Museum Anthropology, addresses areas of museum research and museum professional responsibility, including collections and community-based research, curation, interpretation, exhibition, repatriation law, and publication. Issues of language, authority, consent, and ownership are highlighted. This is about what curators and anthropologists do in the museum. Part 3 focuses specifically on engagement with collection items. For instance, part 2 may address the legal framework of repatriation, while part 3 discusses the experience of repatriation consultations in the museum.

Part 3, Collections Access and Care, addresses Native ways of relating to cultural items and prioritizing the maintenance of cultural knowledge rather than objects. This section suggests ways we can work to change museums from being hostile to more welcoming places for Indigenous peoples through the ways we steward and engage with their belongings. Cultural care, housing and conservation, repatriation consultation, digital assets and their management and dissemination, and collections records and policy are addressed in this section.

Part 4, Collaborative Research, shows how we can work toward ethical and responsive research practice and work beyond museum walls. This section also delves deeper into the practicalities of collaborative research design and practice. Models for community-based research are presented in detail, including how to communicate research publicly, how to design a budget for community work, and how to teach and mentor the next generation in these approaches.

The conclusion, "Reimagining Anthropology and the Museum," briefly recaps the vision of this reorientation in museums and summarizes some practical steps to getting there. The appendixes include exercises relating to specific book sections and a resource list of examples of museum policy documents and collaboration guidelines.

This book ranges from theory to practice and includes ideas of objects as kin as well as worksheets for how to design and budget collaborative projects. That is a result of my own personal journey and the nature of collaborative work. It can lead us in unanticipated directions and push us to adapt and acquire new skills if we let it, if we are open to shared authority and emergent outcomes. I hope this book provides some insight and examples to think with as you seek to participate in or change museum and research practice. Our knowledge and ways of doing things are always evolving over time, even more so when we work with communities. Thank you for joining me at this moment in what continues to be a work in progress!

INTRODUCTION NOTES

1. An early and influential book for many of us who do collaborative museology is the edited volume *Museums and Communities*, published in 2003. In her chapter, Trudy Nicks states in the section "Changing Perspectives on Objects and Museums," "As museums work with source communities, the focus on object preservation—as central purpose and guideline for practice—is being challenged by those who feel that the primary purpose of a museum should be presentation of indigenous cultures." She goes on to note the Aboriginal Australian idea of "keeping place," where the goal is to house items intended for use rather than for long-term preservation. Nicks, "Museums and Contact Work," 21.

2. Shannon, "Posterity Is Now," 5–13.

3. Janes, "The Blackfoot Repatriation," 255.

4. This section includes excerpts from Shannon, "Museum Mantras," 28–36. Republished with permission.

5. American Alliance of Museums, "Museum Facts and Data."

6. United Nations, "United Nations Declaration on the Rights of Indigenous Peoples."

7. The First Nations Information Governance Centre, "The First Nations Principles of OCAP®."

8. School for Advanced Research, "Guidelines for Collaboration"; First Archivists Circle, "Protocols for Native American Archival Materials"; School for Advanced Research, "Indigenous Collections Care Guide"; Smithsonian Institution, "Shared Stewardship and Ethical Returns"; School for Advanced Research, "Standards for Museums with Native American Collections."

9. Schein and Schein, *Humble Leadership*.

10. Jacobs et al., "The Influence of Transformational Leadership on Employee Well-Being."

11. For examples of defining different levels of engagement, see Bernstein and Ortman, "From Collaboration to Partnership at Pojoaque, New Mexico"; Colwell, "Collaborative Archaeologies and Descendant Communities."

FIGURE 1.1. Relationality. Artwork by John Swogger from *NAGPRA Comics* 1, 2017.

Part 1
Collaboration Is Theory in Motion

Collaboration is required to support cultural continuity in the museum—a commitment to bring different people and different knowledge systems into partnership. Oftentimes, collaboration is thought of or talked about as if it is mere method, but I think of it more as theory in motion. What I mean by that is it enacts particular theoretical frameworks. I include in this section some frameworks I see as most relevant at the moment. They are relevant to work in museums with items that originate from Native communities as well as to community-based research.

I do not present an exhaustive review of literature, with many citations and references. Instead, I selected a few examples with insights that shaped the approach to museums, anthropology, and collections that is represented in this book. So, please do not consider the authors cited in this section to be sole authorities or working alone—consider them part of a larger ongoing conversation. I am bringing some voices to your attention so you can listen in on the conversation and think about how understanding these ideas might help guide your practice as it has guided mine.

What you will learn in this section:
- Core values to guide work with Indigenous communities
- Examples of contemporary theory from Indigenous studies and Indigenous scholars
- Examples of ideas that can shape research methods, community-based research design, and exhibitions
- How to guide others through centering these values in their work.

7

Decolonizing/Indigenizing

First, I want to note that I use the terms decoloniz*ing* and Indigeniz*ing* specifically to emphasize that they are ongoing processes. As noted above, I do not believe that a mainstream museum is ever decoloniz*ed*; it is a striving for, an ideal that guides our decisions and practices that requires persistent reflection and action but is never complete.

To use the term *decolonize* is inherently to recognize that the US is a settler colonial state and to acknowledge the history and policies of genocide and ethnocide in America. Anthropology and museums were consequences of the colonization of Indigenous peoples—they were founded on the false assumption of an inevitable physical or cultural extinction of Native peoples. For some, that assumption inspired an attitude of "collect it all"—whether stories, language, songs, material culture, or bodies—before Native peoples died out or were assimilated. Disease, massacres, starvation—you can find those stories in other accounts, and I won't go into detail here. A phrase that helps me wrap my mind around that history appeared in a California Native woman's blog post that a student forwarded to me around ten years ago. She wrote that Indigenous people are living in a "post-apocalyptic present." This is a common conception in Native communities. They went through a near apocalypse in the nineteenth century when their communities, worldviews, and ways of living were targeted for destruction; now, on the other side, their communities are still here and are strengthening current and future generations. I believe museums and anthropology have a role to play in providing access to and returning knowledge and items that were collected in the past to support communities in the present and contribute to their continuing "recovery," as Calvin Grinnell (Mandan, Hidatsa and Arikara Nation) put it to me.

Decolonizing is a term used to critique and demand changes to institutions and practices that benefit from this apocalyptic history, that exploited marginalized peoples and their knowledge and rendered their experience, history, or knowledge invisible, devalued, or silenced. For many good reasons, there have been calls for and movements to decolonize anthropology and research in general, as well as museums, both from outside and within these institutions. Native activism and US laws have significantly contributed to changes in these fields. But change is uneven across institutions, and there is always more to do.

I hope this book shows that the field of anthropology is changing, that collaborative anthropology is significantly different from the stereotypes of the discipline that developed from its early practices. I have assigned to all my students Linda Tuhiwai Smith's *Decolonizing Methodologies: Research and Indigenous Peoples*, a poignant critique of research practice in general and how it is extractive and not beneficial to Indigenous communities; she also provides recommendations for how to do better. Smith's book was first published in 1999 and continues to be taught widely today.[1] I also assign excerpts from Vine Deloria Jr.'s *Custer Died for Your Sins*, published in 1969 and still relevant today, in which an infamous and very memorable chapter about "Anthros" offers a well-earned caricature of the anthropologist in America.[2] If you read between the lines of the principles and practices of research laid out in this book, you can imagine all the ways research, especially anthropological research, can go wrong and be harmful.

As for museums, for the public, the museum is a revered institution for truth telling. For others, whose ancestors and sacred items are held within its walls, it is a mausoleum. This seems an apt metaphor that helps those of us who work in and on behalf of museums to better understand an Indigenous point of view. But it is not a metaphor. In 2013, the estimated number of Native American bodies in all US university, museum, and laboratory collections was between 300,000 and 600,000.[3] Historically, dead and living Indigenous peoples were seen and treated as specimens by museums and anthropologists. Objections from Indigenous peoples and their allies weren't just about their ancestors in museums and inappropriate items on display but also about how Indigenous peoples were portrayed. Exhibits about Native Americans often made it seem like they were people of the past rather than peoples with a present and a future. They were treated as if only their past was to be valued.

I was asked recently about the difference between decolonizing and Indigenizing the museum. I responded with something I learned from Joseph "Woody" Aguilar (San Ildefonso Pueblo) during a talk he gave at the University of Colorado (CU) in 2020 about a museum project we were working on together at Mesa Verde National Park. I loved how he put it plainly and clearly: he said that to decolonize, you would have to raze the structure to the ground, remove it, and build again. To Indigenize is to go into what is already there and make changes that reflect an Indigenous sensibility and worldview. I would add that decolonizing is an ongoing practice that is the responsibility of those of us who work within the institution, to do the hard work to make the institution a welcoming space for Indigenous people to Indigenize it.

There is also a critical discussion among Indigenous scholars about the term *decolonization* in reference to museums. Joe Horse Capture (A'aniiih Nation), vice president of Native Collections and curator of Native American History and Culture at the Autry Museum of the American West in Los Angeles, has been outspoken in his dislike of the term in increasingly humorous but no less salient ways that have sparked interesting and thoughtful discussion. As he has put it over the years on Facebook, "Ok, the whole 'decolonize museums' narrative is getting old, need a new approach" (May 9, 2017); "Anyone wanna take a guess on how many times I'm going to hear the term 'decolonize Museums' at a conference next week? Ugh" (October 3, 2017); and, "the term 'decolonize' has been colonized" (January 28, 2018). His use of memes on Facebook to communicate this message to the larger world has also been great, too! Above a photograph of a statue of a lion looking maniacally angry, with raised sword over head, he quipped: "how I feel when someone uses the term 'decolonize' in reference to museum work" (January 28, 2020). Above a video clip of a surfer being totally demolished by a huge ocean wave, he wrote: "This is me trying to get the museum field to stop using the term 'decolonize' because it doesn't apply to museums" (April 9, 2021). He then shared a post from another Facebook user that stated "now let's talk about how 'decolonize' has been turned into a hot sauce you can put on everything" (January 17, 2022).

To those of us who have worked in this field for a long time, that last statement really nailed it. It is similar to the way I think about how the term *collaboration* is used so often that it has become meaningless without specifically defining what it means in a given circumstance or project. That is one of the reasons I dedicated an entire book to understanding exactly what was meant by collaboration in making the inaugural exhibits at the National Museum of the American Indian (NMAI). These exchanges also highlight that some of the most relevant and timely discussions are happening right now on social media and blogs—they are more inclusive of authors and audiences and can make ideas public faster than can peer-reviewed articles and books, which may take months or more likely years after their initial writing to be published.

I shared this online discussion to make sure that we use terms like *decolonizing* and *collaboration* intentionally and meaningfully, but I also want to stress that we should not let fretting over the terminology get in the way of good practice. We know that actions speak louder than words. Whatever you call the kind of work suggested in this book, it's important to be specific about what actions you are taking and what commitments you are making. Labeling is not enough, be open and explicit about your intentions. Joe Horse Capture's efforts have been seen by many to be decolonizing work.[4]

Collaboration, or working together with originating communities to determine our approach to stewardship and care regarding their tangible and intangible culture, is at the heart of decolonizing work in museums and anthropological research.

Language and Power

An important aspect of partnering with Native peoples and valuing their way of knowing is following their lead in the language we use. What we call something matters—it shapes how we think and behave, the expectations people have for their participation, and how we relate to one another. That includes what we name a group we work with, whether an advisory board, content development team, co-curator, informant, or participant. Do we call it an archaeological site or an ancestral site? Specimen or ancestor? Object, cultural item, belonging, or being?

Preferred language may change over time, but the process of coming to appropriate language stays the same: listening to and seeking input from Indigenous communities and reflecting on how we can do better. Sometimes we might get it wrong, and that's okay. The important thing is that we are striving to be respectful and reflecting on what we say and how best to say it.

Be open and honest about this process; publicly correcting our mistakes and trying to get it right matters.

Again, naming not only affects how community members understand where we're coming from but also indicates to them what we think of and expect from them. For example, what a difference it makes as to what an individual thinks is expected of them, and how they interpret what the museum thinks about their contributions, if they are called advisers versus curators. Or how much more welcoming is it for community members to hear someone say they care for items from their community rather than store them. I have noticed that using the terms *ancestors* or *ancestral site* (instead of archaeological site) really matters in communicating your perspective and how informed you are. It makes a difference.

Paying attention to the language we use in our work with communities and to the text we put on museum walls and in marketing materials is about conscientiously shaping our thinking and practice. Who is included and excluded from the language we use? Whose perspective is privileged? Whose relations are evident? Consider these examples:

"They" versus "We" on an exhibit label
~~Specimens, artifacts~~, objects, heritage, items, belongings, beings
Collections management, collections care, collections stewardship
Archaeological site, cultural resource, ancestral site
Advisory group, content development team, Native interpretation working group, co-curators
Native voice, Native interpretation.

Let's pause on that last one—especially because I wrote a whole book about "Native voice." Well, my language has changed over time, too. I now prefer Native interpretation because, to me, it represents action, the act of interpreting and providing interpretation in the exhibition process, as well as agency. Both Native voice and Native voices are nouns. For me, Native voice came to represent the possibility of simply putting quotes from Native people on the walls rather than engaging Native individuals in the content development and exhibit design processes.

A term I have used in the past that is widely recognized is *traditional care*. After talking with staff at the NMAI, I now prefer the term *cultural care*. Staff felt that traditional was not the right word because the care is practiced today in modern times, and because staff should not or cannot carry out care that is part of a Native or Indigenous community's long-standing traditions. Cultural care is something that is appropriate for staff to engage in given the circumstances and what knowledge is appropriate to share with them.

Another example is what we call collections in museums. In my lifetime, we have definitely moved away from the word *specimen* to describe material culture; in addition, artifact was replaced by object, then cultural item, and now we more often hear the term *cultural belongings*. Belongings is a term the University of British Columbia Museum of Anthropology uses for collection items, and it comes from the close relationship to the Musqueam First Nation, on whose land the museum resides. It is the community's preferred term. It may or may not be appropriate for other Native Nations. But consider the distance between the meanings and perspectives represented in the terms *specimen* and *belonging*. Shifting language shows that those who choose to make these changes have come a long way toward embracing other ways of knowing collections in museums.

Multiple Ways of Knowing

"Multiple ways of knowing" acknowledges that different cultural communities see and understand the world differently and insists that we value and keep an open mind regarding these differences. Learning about these knowledge systems helps us better understand engagements with Indigenous peoples in collections because that is often when these different ways of thinking and seeing the world become evident, especially in categorizing and interacting with cultural items.

While we often frame this in the museum world as Western versus Indigenous knowledge systems, that does not mean we assume that all non-Native people think one way and all Native people think another way. This section is about coming to recognize that these perspectives are different and culturally diverse, how valuing these differences makes for better museum and research practice, and how and why the museum is a place where these knowledge systems intersect.[5]

I will provide some brief examples here and will go into more detail in the Collections Access and Care section of this book (part 3). In short, when working with Native peoples in museum collections, we learn that for some people, being in the presence of bones of the dead or items that have been dug up from the earth that may be referred to as archaeological items can cause spiritual harm and require spiritual cleansing or ceremony. We also learn that some cultural items are known to be sentient. Some cultural items are referred to as kin, as relatives.

In a recent exhibition meeting, I reached for a shorthand way to communicate these ideas to people who were not familiar with Indigenous ways of knowing. I said "this is not a pipe," playing off the famous Rene Magritte painting that is an image of a pipe, and below it are words in French that say "this is not a pipe." That is because it is a *painting* of a pipe. I continued, "This is not a pipe (or just an object)—it's a prayer, an ancestor, a teacher, a relative."

Indigenous ways of knowing unsettle some very basic assumptions in Western thinking. Cultural items classified in Western ways of thinking as inanimate objects are anything but inanimate to those who created them, who seek to reconnect with, express respect for, and learn from them. They have agency, they feel and create connection. They teach and feel separation. In addition, for many museum professionals and the public, all information in museums is meant to be shared publicly. But that's not the case, according to the communities from which the items in collections originate. Some of those items or archives or photographs were never meant to be recorded or shared outside of their original cultural context.

This issue of not sharing publicly particular Indigenous items or knowledge recorded in the museum comes up again and again—from viewing the items in collections to viewing them in an online catalog to placing them in a public exhibit. When we take Native perspectives on collections seriously, when we center respect in our engagements, we have to change our assumptions—including the most basic ones that all collection items are inanimate objects and that all information is meant to be shared. Sometimes, even previously published information is not okay to share (again) in a publication or an exhibit.

Being open-minded and respectful of other ways of knowing, without appropriation, is key. I am not someone who has plants in the house, usually. But during Covid, when we were asked to stay home for months, I brought several plants into my home. What I loved about Robin Kimmerer's book *Braiding Sweetgrass: Indigenous Wisdom, Scientific Knowledge, and the Teachings of Plants* is that it inspired and encouraged me to look at the world around me and ask new questions.[6] I was just observing a plant, which frankly amazed me (a biologist by training and for a hot minute after college!) by how much it changed from day to day. So, my biologist brain was first asking: how much are the leaves changing, and how are they moving in relation to the sun? Later, I found myself asking, according to Kimmerer's invitation: what can this plant teach me? What a different way of seeing the plant—what a change in the relationship I had with it and to how it could act on me. I paused and took time to think about this. With that simple question, my relationship with and view of the plant changed. I don't mean to trivialize or oversimplify a more deeply profound teaching Kimmerer is providing. Instead, I am hoping to show how we can learn or be inspired to think differently. We have to be intentional about how we let in other ways of knowing without appropriating other people's beliefs. This was my way of being open to new questions and ways of seeing after reading her words.

More generally, there are examples of scientific research that embrace Native ways of knowing. Two examples come to mind that include people I have worked over the span of my career in museums. First is the Northern Science Award in 1998, which was given to Igloolik's Inullaarit Elders Society for its oral history project that contributes to studies of environmental change (featured in the Igloolik exhibit at the NMAI in 2004). Second, in 2023, a National Science Foundation proposal was funded that created a Center for Braiding Indigenous Knowledges and Science, run by my colleague Dr. Sonya Atalay (Anishinaabe-Ojibwe) at the University of Massachusetts Amherst, which includes global hubs of Indigenous scientists.

10

Relationality

A central tenet of many Indigenous ways of knowing is relationality. As I noted above, when working with Native communities in museum collections, they often relate to and talk about some items in ways that may be unfamiliar to those of us who have not grown up understanding the world in the same way. What a Western-trained person may see and label as inanimate objects, Native community members may name and relate to as other-than-human beings, as relatives, as ancestors. Not all items are related to in this way, and not all Native individuals see items in this way. Understanding this way of knowing has profoundly changed how I and others who work with Indigenous peoples see collections and our work in the museum.

Many Indigenous scholars have discussed the notion of relationality. For example, in *Research Is Ceremony*, Shawn Wilson (Opaskawayak Cree) helps those who did not grow up with this worldview to better understand this way of knowing the world.[7] Wilson talks about the relationality of "Indigenous ontology and epistemology," or the relationship between how we understand our being in relation in the world, and how we come to know what we know. These relations are with other people, the land, and all the beings on earth, human and other-than-human. If you think in terms of being in relation not just to humans but also to these other entities, it changes how you come to know the world around you and your place in it.

For example, in 2022, a tribal historic preservation officer (THPO) referred to repatriated birch bark scrolls as relatives and said they have responsibilities to the community. A drum that was returned was also called a relative, and its role after its return will be to support at-risk youth. In 2010 I invited NAGPRA officers Tim Begay and Tony Joe to consult with us at the University of Colorado Museum of Natural History (CU Museum) regarding the Navajo collections, which included medicine bundles—items often determined to be sacred under US repatriation law. Through consultation, the bundles were identified as sacred and so we began the process of repatriating the bundles, or *jish* as we were taught to refer to them, to the Navajo Nation. Since they would remain in our care as the legal process progressed, Mr. Joe and Mr. Begay gave us instructions for how to properly care for the jish, which they consider to be living beings with thoughts and feelings. Before they left, the cultural specialists blessed us to protect us during our future contact with these powerful items. The museum's registrar, Stephanie Gilmore, followed their instructions for two years until the jish returned home. She took them out once each season for sunshine and fresh air and talked to them, letting them know what she was doing before she did so. She might say, "Hello, I am going to take you outside today for some fresh air and sunshine. We will be going down the elevator." We refer to this as cultural care (see chapter 27).

I had instructed staff and students to respect and honor these requests when possible. Through the embodied practice of following through with these care instructions, they started to relate to and understand their work in new ways. They got a glimpse into how Native peoples might see the items in their care, too: not as inert objects but as non-human beings. And they began to better understand how different walking into a museum might feel to the Navajo (seeing sentient beings locked up, alone, and painfully divorced from contact with their people).

Relationality includes not only the idea that objects are kin relations of community members and that they are in contemporary and continuing relation with communities of origin, but also that these items bring museum staff into relation with communities. Relationality brings the community to mind as we work, and it brings community members to our workplaces in person. One outcome of this kind of work, as students and staff have noted, is a greater sense of purpose in the care of collections and a greater sense of accountability to something beyond the job: to originating communities and their future generations.

In the example in the next section, a national park is changing its interpretation of the park, the language it uses, and its presentation of archaeology to include Native ways of knowing the place and its past.

11

For Example

Mesa Verde National Park

The phrase that became the title for this section came to me while I was preparing a talk titled "Collaboration Is Theory in Motion: Redesigning the Chapin Mesa Archeological Museum at Mesa Verde National Park in Partnership with Twenty-Six Pueblos and Tribes" that I co-presented with Joseph "Woody" Aguilar (San Ildefonso Pueblo) in 2021.[8] I worked on the project from 2019 to 2021 (it is still ongoing).[9] The University of Colorado Graduate Program in Museum and Field Studies was invited to work with Mesa Verde National Park on its biodiversity initiative. The collaboration went so well that park staff asked if the museum studies program would partner with them to redesign the Chapin Mesa Archeological Museum. Indigenous theories such as relationality and the concept of multiple ways of knowing were intentionally part of our discussion and became the foundation for process, content, and design.

I distinctly remember the day the museum director invited me into his office to tell me about the proposed partnership. He asked me to "facilitate tribal participation." I can't remember if I actually said it out loud, but my initial response was "no!" As the talk title suggests, there are twenty-six Pueblos and Tribes associated with the park, so you can imagine my internal dialogue . . . wow, that is a big ask! That is going to take a lot of time and labor and resources! And then I thought about the potential impact—twenty-six communities and over half a million visitors a year—and felt grateful for the opportunity and got started. The first question I needed to figure out was: what is the best way to do this?

Typically, national parks work with the exhibition designers at the National Park Service's (NPS) Harpers Ferry Interpretive Design Center in West Virginia. This kind of collaboration was something new not just for CU but for the NPS as well. CU Museum director Pat Kociolek and the park's chief of interpretation and visitors services, Kristy Sholly, fully supported this longer, more expensive collaborative model, which was key to its success. They allocated funds for meetings, travel, honoraria, and student and contractor work through a combination of small and large grants and institutional funds. Leadership really matters—this became even more clear when a new superintendent, Kayci Cook Collins, was hired partway through the project and declared that the dioramas were going to be taken down. But I am getting ahead of myself.

I began in 2019 by preparing the park staff for what to expect when doing collaborative museology and devising a process for outreach to the tribes to invite them to determine an appropriate way for us all to work together. I introduced preferred language to park staff, such as ancestral sites and cultural items. In presentations to both the park and at a large tribal meeting, I started with two things: our shared values and identifying a goal for our work together. The goal for the project had nothing to do with the subject matter or location of the exhibition. It was simply that we all enjoy working together. If we could achieve the conditions for that, all else would follow in a good way (think about the presentation of different disciplines, the various tribes working together, a new partnership between federal government and state university, and so on). I witnessed a lot of moving parts and powerful moments in this project, which is still under way and by all accounts going well.

The shared values I identified for project partners included (1) connecting to and caring for this place, as both park staff and Native communities have meaningful relationships with the lands within the park and want to provide long-term care for it, though for different reasons and in different ways; (2) including Pueblos and Tribes in the interpretation of this place; and (3) facilitating and supporting student learning. Everyone also agreed that the archaeological story is important, but it should not be the only story and should not be considered a settled matter, as there is ongoing scientific debate about the interpretation of the site.

What excited me about this project was the opportunity to create something innovative, maybe even unexpected, in a museum exhibition. This was not about any single tribe, and the tribes had different connections to these lands. It was also a great example of what science is really like—questioning, unsettled, interpretive. There were questions under debate in archaeological interpretation of the site, and the park staff and participating archaeologists were willing to show this to the public. And the park staff wanted to privilege Native ways of knowing this place. The most exciting thing was that these different ways of knowing were not set against or beside each other—they were intended to be in dialogue. So, the process was set up to facilitate interaction among ways of knowing and to use that as a framework for and lesson of the exhibition. Multiple symposia and facilitated conversations supported this approach. We weren't sure what the outcome would be, which was also exciting for me.

One phrase came to mind as I listened to communities and the park staff talk about the meaning of Mesa Verde: one person's research site is another person's heritage. This museum project brought together people to interpret a place who view it very differently. It was a collaboration among three groups that have worked with each other in the past but never all together: the federal agency of the NPS, the twenty-six Pueblos and Tribes associated with the park, and university faculty and students. I always say, students are the secret sauce! Project partners valued and enjoyed working with the students and wanted to support them, which often prompted best behavior to set an example and teach the next generation.

Speaking of students, my PhD student Scarlett Engle participated in the collaboration as a participant observer and is writing her dissertation about it, which is good because as I was writing this section I kept thinking that there are too many details; it would take a book to cover them all! Knowing that her dissertation is forthcoming took the pressure off me from feeling the need to describe every detail here. I want to share some moments that stood out to me, including how we designed the process of the collaboration and some lessons along the way.

I want to emphasize that the interpretive team at Mesa Verde National Park (MVNP) sought the inclusion of Native community members and was already starting to change roadside signs and make efforts to incorporate their perspectives into the interpretation of the park and its lands. Both park staff and Native community members felt the redesign of the archaeology museum in the park was long overdue—most of the exhibits were more than thirty years old, some more than fifty. In addition, entry to the park was free for the twenty-six affiliated Pueblos and Tribes. We found out later that this fact was not widely known, so it was the first thing visible in our newsletter for the project (appendix A).

Mesa Verde National Park is located in southwest Colorado and is most known for and associated with cliff dwellings. Ancestral Pueblo people lived in this area for over 700 years, from 600 to 1300 CE. There is a persistent myth that this area was "abandoned." However, that term is offensive to the Native communities affiliated with the park. As Gary Roybal (San Ildefonso Pueblo) put it during our work together, "Mesa Verde people did not disappear or vanish. They moved south. Their descendants are still here."

We learned from tribal members that this is an ancestral place, that descendants of these people live in nearby regions, and that some of them return to these lands for prayer and ceremony or to visit with school groups or family. This place is a part of Native peoples' understanding about who they are, an important place in their communities in the past and today. It is a place to be respected, a place where ancestors are present, and it is the heritage of contemporary peoples. Park staff wanted to update these exhibits and include tribal perspectives such as these in the redesigned museum. They, and the Pueblos and Tribes, also wanted to use this project to repair relations and build a long-term relationship between them.

Multiple ways of knowing emerged as a theme from early conversations about how to interpret the park, and three working groups were created to work separately to develop content packets and then come together in dialogue. The Native Interpretation Working Group (it took quite a bit of deliberation to decide on that name) was made up of Native community members, including tribal historic preservation officers (THPOs), museum professionals, archaeologists, and cultural specialists. The Archaeology Working Group included archaeologists from the park, Crow Canyon Archaeology Center, the University of Colorado, and other universities—including the two Indigenous archaeologists who were in the Native Interpretation group. There was also a group convened by park staff regarding the history of the park. Through a series of small and large meetings both online and in person, as well as presentations and vetting sessions among the working groups and, later, with the contracted design firm, the teams developed, shared, workshopped, and approved content and design.

Respect was a major theme in everyone's work together. The park wanted to update the exhibits to show more respect for Native connections to and perspectives on the park, and Pueblo and Tribal members wanted to show park visitors how to behave respectfully in the park. I could tell that this opportunity meant a lot to the Native community members working on the exhibits during our first Native Interpretation Working Group meetings. There were long-standing disagreements among some of the communities, so they identified certain topics and agreed that they would be off the table so everyone could work together positively and ensure that the project would continue to move forward. This was a wonderful example to us and the students of how they respected each other and the process.

Shared authority was represented in the privileging of the Native Interpretation Working Group's preferences and guidance, in ensuring that all working groups were part of the development of content and review of the design. This demand was stated early on in the kickoff meeting when a series of tribal representatives stood up and spoke their minds. One individual said, thank you for caring for our ancestral site when we can't be here. Another expressed frustration when tribes are asked to collaborate and then the park does not follow their guidance. He said, if we say no, take no for an answer. While there were some tense moments during that initial kickoff meeting and some park staff felt attacked, my feeling was the opposite, and I told them so. I said, "Wow, this is great!" and explained that when tribal members stand up and provide guidance, this is a wonderful development because it means they are invested in the success of this project and its outcomes, and they are interested in participating in the collaboration.

The methods we employ when working with Indigenous communities are also applicable when we work with non-Indigenous organizations and institutions. Trust and relationship building need to occur in any project among all participants, no matter how alike you assume the institutions or individuals to be. This became clear when an unexpected, significant tension tested the Mesa Verde project early on—but it was not what we anticipated. It was not a tension with descendant communities or their reticence to work with the park. They were used to working with museums and felt the reinterpretation of the park was very important. Instead, the tension was between CU and park staff!

We took for granted that as predominantly non-Native state and federal organizations focused on education, we did not need to do the work to build trust. In fact, words we used often meant different things in each context, and there was concern by the park that its staff members were being cut out of the relationship-building process with community members. A lot of explaining was needed, including how and why we were taking time to work with the Pueblos and Tribes to design the collaboration and when we envisioned the park would step in. It was such an important meeting that CU staff traveled to the park to talk in person. We discussed tensions, established communication norms, and had a meal together. We ended up calling it the "marriage counseling meeting!" By all of us being transparent in our plans and concerns and developing some ground rules for communication, we were able to establish greater trust between our organizations, which greatly benefited the project and got us back on track toward our primary goal: enjoying working together.

As you will hear multiple times from me, I believe a great place to begin a collaboration or consultation is by asking community members how we should proceed. This project was no different. I invited members of the CU team, PhD student Scarlett Engle and consultant Sheila Goff, to conduct interviews by phone with THPOs from the twenty-six Pueblos and Tribes associated with the park. The following summer, Scarlett and master's student Mikayla Costales traveled to communities in person to meet with tribal leadership and cultural specialists to get recommendations for the structure of the collaborative process.

These meetings in the Mesa Verde region took place during the students' eight-week internship at the park and an additional two weeks of travel to Pueblos in New Mexico and Arizona. Going to community members rather than always asking them to come to the park was greatly appreciated and made a big, and good, impression. Scarlett and Mikayla provided a report to the park and community members summing up their findings, including the consensus to first host a large meeting with all descendant communities and then work with a select group of representatives who would contribute to decision making throughout the process. And that's exactly what happened.

The report was based on fifty phone and in-person interviews, including with thirty-four descendant community members.[10] The main advice collected included:

- Be explicit and be honest.
- Create a genuine sense of ownership.

- This will take time, give time to speak and listen.
- Compromise, don't say no.
- There needs to be reciprocity and equality.

Some early ideas about the exhibition included displaying instructions on how to behave respectfully in an ancestral place, weaving together Native community members' and archaeologists' interpretations, hiring Native interns at the museum, and inviting community review of collections. For the collaborative process with the park, tribal members suggested:

- Host a meeting with all Tribes at the park.
- Include a collections review; close the museum for an exhibit walk-through.
- Invite participants to select appropriate representatives to form a committee.
- Continue to build relationships and work with the committee.
- Regularly report back to the larger group in person, by phone, and through newsletters.

At the prescribed large tribal gathering in 2019, we gave a presentation about the project and outlined the roles and responsibilities of working group members. After we were finished and all questions had been answered, we left the room so the group could discuss the presentation. When we returned, they put forward a smaller working group to develop the content for the exhibit. Two Indigenous archaeologists on the list agreed to also serve in the Archaeology Working Group as part of a commitment to transparency, as was the newsletter I created and distributed to everyone involved. After I left the project, park staff continued the newsletter.

The Native Interpretation group met regularly on Zoom over many months to discuss content development. Sheila Goff was the project manager for tribal participation and the project liaison to the Pueblos and Tribes, documenting their content contributions and facilitating meetings. She also called people who could not attend meetings to ensure that their perspectives were included. A Native consulting firm was hired to facilitate meetings between the content development groups, each providing a content packet ahead of time. Now in design development, the primary main messages include "we are still here" and "there are multiple ways of understanding and being in relationship with this place."

There was a moment later in our work together, after many Zoom meetings and several gatherings, when the Native Interpretation group said "no" to something beloved by park staff and museum visitors: the 1930s dioramas created by the Civilian Conservation Corps. I thought, "Well, this will make or break the project. This will either solidify the relations of trust that have been building or confirm the original fears." The process of making this decision was slow and deliberative on behalf of the park. Park leadership worked internally to understand the reasons for and the consequences of making this change and prepared the staff to accept it. We provided park staff with explanations of why the dioramas were problematic and examples of where national parks elsewhere had removed dioramas from display. In the end, as noted above, the decision was made to remove them and create space for new forms of interpretation in the museum. I breathed a sigh of relief and began preparing a park staff member to take over my role in the project, completing the transition from the university to the park in coordinating and maintaining the collaboration and relationships with Native community members (Sheila Goff continued on in a support role).

On a side note, it is not always possible to bring people in from the start to design the collaborative process. I want to bring back a note from the preface: please don't let perfect get in the way of a better path forward. Just because you didn't start a project this way doesn't mean you can't make adjustments along the way. Before CU got involved in the partnership and the Native Interpretation group was formed, the park had already contracted a media company to create an orientation film at the Chapin Mesa museum. Ideally, local Indigenous film production companies or filmmakers would have been contacted for requests for proposals alongside the usual distribution, but the park staff didn't know to do that. We recommended that the existing production company contract with a local Native filmmaker. At first, the media firm suggested that it would use locals for site selection and camera work. But I insisted that it was important that a descendant community member be in the room where decisions were made, be part of the production team. In the end, the firm agreed to share authority and hired a Native filmmaker to be on the production team. He provided his own filmmaking expertise, assured Native community members that he would provide a check on the film development process, and was the film team's connection to community members when needed. The Native Interpretation group also reviewed and gave feedback on the film script.

Reciprocity was also something we wanted to build into the project. One example is a project Scarlett Engle carried out the second summer of the collaboration, in 2020. By then, community members knew her from her first

How Visitors Should Feel in the Space

Educated

"[Visitors should be] walking away being educated. Not everyone lived in tipis. They need the right education of the people that lived there and the people that are descended today."

— Tim Begay, Navajo Nation

Welcomed

"The first thing is to feel welcomed. It should be inviting that you want to go in. It should be engaging that they would want to learn or explore as they are learning about the place and about our ancestors. [The visitor] should feel enlightened, having learned."

— Gloria Lomahaftewa, Hopi Tribe

Amazed

"[I want visitors] to feel amazement. I guess in awe. A lot of cultures do not go that far back. I think that's what's intriguing to people. How it has been so preserved."

— Ben Chavarria, Santa Clara Pueblo

Awakened

"[I want visitors] being awakened. I curated the [Zuni map exhibit] (see Appendix 1), and one of the major purposes was that people would encounter a different knowledge system, a different way of knowing... Too often, people think Mesa Verde is cool or fun to experience, like a Disney Frontierland. I want visitors to feel awakened to the technologies and beliefs of the Mesa Verde people. They should know ancient Puebloan culture was thriving at the same time Egyptians were expanding their influence across Africa and Polynesians were exploring and populating vast areas of the Pacific."

— Jim Enote, Zuni Pueblo

Thankful

"If there is one word it would be a 'thank you'. The main thing I would like visitors to perceive is the contributions my ancestors have made and continue to make to the human experience and this nation. Visitors should leave Mesa Verde feeling thankful to the people of Mesa Verde."

— Jim Enote, Zuni Pueblo

FIGURE 1.2. Excerpt from the *Chapin Mesa Museum Exhibit Design Reference Guide* by Scarlett Engle, 2021

round of interviews and from her participation in the working group sessions and larger meetings.

I handed Scarlett Engle an extraordinary book I had been gifted in 2008, *Musqueam: A Living Culture*, which provides guidance on the design and representation of exhibits about the Musqueam First Nation in British Columbia.[11] I asked her to use this book as inspiration to create something similar with the Pueblos and Tribes associated with the park. We ended up calling it a "design reference guide" (figure 1.2). Scarlett conducted interviews with many tribal members and tribal museum professionals, asking questions about design, colors, appropriate language, fabrication materials, and more. We sent copies to the contracted design firm, the park, and the Pueblos and Tribes. (I also gave a copy to Leona Sparrow, designated liaison between the Musqueam First Nation and the University of British Columbia who worked on *A Living Culture*, to show how her Nation's work had inspired opportunities for other communities working with museums.)

Sharing authority with the Native Interpretation Working Group was not just the responsibility of the park or the archaeologists. We intentionally completed and shared this reference guide before the exhibit design firm began its work so its staff members would know that they, too, were accountable to the tribes in their design approach and that their aesthetics alone were not enough to guide the work. The designers were delighted to receive it. The reference guide was also something we could share back with the Pueblos and Tribes that they might find useful when working with other museums or designers. This project, and the booklet that resulted, served to build relationships and increase the personal interaction of project partners, insisted that tribal perspectives on interpretation and exhibition were prioritized, and provided an example of sharing and follow-through.

The redesign of the Chapin Mesa Archeological Museum—which is now called the Chapin Mesa Museum by the park staff—has been a catalyst for learning new perspectives and developing new relations, for creating innovative exhibits and culturally informed design. The project has been an opportunity for all of us to work toward building a broader, stronger relationship among ancestral place, Pueblos and Tribes, and Mesa Verde National Park staff. As Scarlett and Mikayla's report noted, "While relationship building was imperative to the process [of exhibit development], it was mentioned multiple times to commit to continuing the relationships past the point of completing the project." So far, so good—the new orientation film is already up and running in the museum, and we all look forward to seeing the new exhibits in the coming years!

12
Questions to Guide Practice and Additional Resources

Some questions to consider:
- How are your theories and practice related?
- Whose theories are you reading and citing?
- What are the terms you use, for example, when referring to collections, items, communities, or working groups?
- What language do you hear when community members talk about their belongings or why they are working with museums?

- Are you considering other ways of understanding this item, subject, label, exhibition?
- Have you considered how your project's design may influence relationships and outcomes?

Indigenous approaches to Research and Knowledge:

- *Decolonizing Methodologies: Research and Indigenous Peoples* (Smith 2021 [1999])
- *Research Is Ceremony: Indigenous Research Methods* (Wilson 2008)
- *Indigenous Research: Theories, Practices, and Relationships* (McGregor, Restoule, and Johnston 2018)
- *The Continuous Path: Pueblo Movement and the Archaeology of Becoming* (Duwe and Preucel 2019)

PART 1 NOTES

1. Smith, *Decolonizing Methodologies*.
2. Deloria, *Custer Died for Your Sins*.
3. McKeown, *In the Smaller Scope of Conscience*.
4. Horse Capture, "Native People Have a Story to Tell—Their Own."
5. I am talking in generalities here, but you can find community-specific methodologies and theories—for example, Māori: Smith, *Decolonizing Methodologies*; Mvskoke: Harjo, *Spiral to the Stars*; and Anishinaabe: Simpson, *Dancing on Our Turtle's Back*.
6. Kimmerer, *Braiding Sweetgrass*.
7. Wilson, *Research Is Ceremony*.
8. University College London, "Conference: Heritage, Participation, Performativity, Care." Pueblos and Tribes is the preferred language by which to refer to Native communities associated with the park.
9. National Park Service, "Museum Renovations—Mesa Verde National Park." Woody inspired my phrasing. At a talk he gave, I noted that he said "Indigenization is collaboration in motion," and it got my wheels turning.
10. Costales and Engle, "Collaborating with Descendant Communities to Re-Imagine Chapin Mesa Archeological Museum."
11. Musqueam Indian Band, *Musqueam: A Living Culture*.

FIGURE 2.1. Repatriation. Artwork by John Swogger from *NAGPRA Comics 2*, 2021.

Part 2
Museum Anthropology

The main message of parts 2 and 3 of this book is to orient museums that have anthropology collections toward the purpose of supporting cultural continuity, not just preserving objects. The question these sections intends to answer is: what does this mean for mission, policy, and practice?

This section is dedicated to Native and non-Native museum professionals as well as museum studies and anthropology students. The aim is that we become more informed and prepared to continue to shape the museum anthropology field to be more inclusive of and beneficial to the communities whose items are housed in museums—and that we highlight the field's collaborative practice as a potential model for ethical research methods and community engagement more broadly.

Museum anthropology is a diverse field that includes studying museums anthropologically, curating anthropology collections, and creating exhibits based on those collections—and so much more! It can also be a model for anthropology research in general because it has been a subfield of anthropology with a robust tradition of collaboration with originating communities, especially in North America. Because North American anthropologists write in a language their research participants also speak and those participants live nearby, there has been a stronger demand for accountability to communities and a turn to collaborative research by anthropologists in this region. In addition, originating communities' access to anthropology collections has been mandated by repatriation law in the United States.

Museums are powerful institutions, well-known for reflecting and shaping public understandings. They remain the most trusted source of information after friends and family. Although museums were responsible for creating and reinforcing stereotypes about Indigenous peoples, they can be repurposed to support dignity and appropriate representation of Indigenous peoples in education and public exhibitions, combat discrimination against Indigenous peoples, and promote tolerance for difference. Museum anthropologists can play a central role in these commitments by turning a critical eye to museum practice and building relationships with originating communities.

What you will learn in this section:
- What museum anthropology is
- What kind of work anthropologists do in museums
- Examples of contemporary practices in the field
- How we might ethically and responsibility operate at the fraught intersection of museums, anthropology, and Native peoples
- How to teach museum anthropology informed by Native perspectives.

13

Anthropology of Museums

I unexpectedly fell into doing the anthropology of museums as a graduate student after I had worked as a research assistant at the National Museum of the American Indian (NMAI). I was thinking through my experience working at this new museum, about its process and claims to be different. I still had questions, and I also thought the museum was a historical event that needed to be documented and understood. While I didn't start with the idea of making a museum the focus of my dissertation, it became the focus of my PhD research, and I ended up writing an ethnography of collaborative exhibition making.

By the time I became a professor at the University of Colorado, I had conducted anthropology of and in museums. While I separate these approaches here into two sections, it is common for museum anthropologists to do both.

Museum anthropology is a subset of anthropology, which has four fields: cultural anthropology, archaeology, linguistics, and biological anthropology. I will discuss anthropology of and in museums from the perspective of a cultural anthropologist. Museum anthropology is different from museum studies, which is an interdisciplinary field that brings together preparation for entering museum-related professions and studying the role of museums in society. Museum studies courses may include museum education, collections management, museum ethics, exhibit development, marketing, audience evaluation, and more. These roles are often part of museum studies graduate courses aimed at preparing students for a career in museums. Readings in these classes may include museum anthropology articles, but they are not anthropology classes.

Museum anthropology includes working as an anthropologist *in* the museum, usually in the role of museum curator and based on a degree in biological, archaeological, or cultural anthropology (see next section). The anthropology *of* museums is something cultural anthropologists do. The invitation is to take what we learn from the discipline of cultural anthropology—for example, critiquing power, investigating colonial legacies, documenting everyday practices, interrogating cultural representations—and apply it to thinking critically about museums, their role in society, and the everyday work that goes on within them. We apply this not just to anthropology museums but to any museum.

Whether their focus is anthropology, science, history, or art, museums are powerful institutions worthy of in-depth study and analysis. Museums are the most trusted public institutions,[1] and they provide the knowledge that guides understanding for generations of Americans, especially in their youth. It's important to study and understand these institutions of power and the representations produced by them—how they are formed and what informs them, how we produce knowledge, how the resulting narratives change over time. Once we understand these issues, we can feel empowered to make change. Anthropology in general prompts us to question received categories, to question the feeling that how we live or what we think is somehow natural and inevitable versus a result of human action and social practice. Looking into the changing ways we remake exhibitions and the changing narratives about Native peoples in museums over time certainly drives this home.

As Michael Ames put it in his call to do anthropology of museums, "The objective, then, is not simply to criticize museums but also to attempt to locate them (and the critiques) within their social, political, and economic contexts."[2] Dr. Ames was a former director of the University of British Columbia (UBC) Museum of Anthropology and the first person I read who called for anthropologists to turn their attention to museums as objects of study. I want to highlight him here for a minute—his book *Cannibal Tours and Glass Boxes*, published in 1992, is what led me to believe that my idea to do an ethnography of a museum was possible, even called for.[3]

Ames's book helped me think about an anthropologist's role in studying museums and what we uniquely have to offer compared to other forms of analysis. *Silencing the Past: Power and the Production of History* by Michel-Rolph Trouillot, published in 1995, was another influential book I read early on.[4] The book is about the silencing of the Haitian revolution over time, and it asks us to investigate who tells history and what is at stake. It connected with my thinking about the power and role of museums in affecting millions of people's ideas about a topic—especially at an institution like the Smithsonian Institution and specifically regarding Native Americans—and the potential role of the NMAI to un-silence the history of Native peoples in America. I was also inspired by Edward Linenthal's *Preserving Memory: The Struggle to Create America's Holocaust Museum* from 2001, which showed how a narrative we think we already know—the Holocaust—was contested and debated in the making of this national museum.[5] Who is included in the story, and how should it be told? All of this is food for thought in thinking through an ethnography focused on the National Museum of the American Indian. But none of these books were ethnographies, the quintessential outcome of cultural anthropology.

There are many anthropological approaches to studying museums, including Foucauldian analysis and cultural critique. Ethnography is a specific approach; it is both a method and the written outcome of research. It includes living in a place for an extended period of time to better understand a community's everyday practices, perspectives, and worldview. To understand the world from their point of view. Over the decades, what counts as a field site or a community has changed. In its early days, ethnography was aimed at studying cultures as closed systems, with people who are foreign to one's home community. In the United States, early ethnography sought to salvage or save Native Americans' knowledge and material culture because it was assumed they would die off or even become extinct. In fact, this practice is part of the reason Native communities are wary of anthropologists and anthropology as a field, and it's part of the reason their cultural belongings are in museums. Today, field sites can be at home or abroad, one place or many. Anthropologists now work with communities rather than study them. For museum ethnographers, the museum and its staff, or a single exhibition team, can be both the community they learn from and the field site. The focus is on everyday museum work, often through the frameworks of knowledge making, representation, and power.

History, art, and science museums from all over the globe are now featured in museum ethnographies, which have increased in number in recent years. When I started my PhD research there were just a few, so it has been encouraging to see more examples in this genre. An early example of studying museums cross-culturally is Christina Krep's 1994 dissertation, which is a critique of colonialism and the state's push for the populace to become "museum-minded" in Indonesia based on fieldwork at a regional museum.[6] Examples of ethnography of science museums include Sharon Macdonald's *Behind the Scenes at the Science Museum* from 2002. She provides insight into the staff's daily decisions and exhibition outcomes at the Science Museum in London. More recently, Diana Marsh's *Extinct Monsters to Deep Time: Conflict, Compromise, and the Making of Smithsonian's Fossil Halls* from 2019 is about the development of an exhibition on dinosaurs at the Smithsonian Institution's National Museum of Natural History.[7]

Two influential museum ethnographies about tribal museums based on fieldwork in the 1990s came out in the 2000s: Patricia Pierce Erikson's *Voices of a Thousand People: The Makah Cultural and Research Center* (2002) and Gwyneira Isaac's *Mediating Knowledges: Origins of a Zuni Tribal Museum* (2007).[8] Both of these anthropologists volunteered in some capacity in the tribal museum as visiting researchers or advisers. Isaac writes about the interface between a public museum institution and systems of knowledge control in the Zuni community—as a visiting researcher she was subject to these protocols. Isaac, like Erikson, provided her research to participants to archive, review, and critique. Erikson writes about how the Makah community created their own tribal museum through a partnership with non-Native researchers and Indigenized this form of institution. She lived in Neah Bay for twelve months, where she often faced local critiques of anthropological practice in the form of the question "why should I tell you anything," stories about helicoptering (drop in, research, leave), and critiques of ethnography as plagiarism. Erikson urges us to imagine research participants as part of our audience. Some of her chapters are coauthored with community members to tell the story.

I published my own museum ethnography in 2014 that was based on my PhD dissertation and titled, *Our Lives: Collaboration, Native Voice, and the Making of the National Museum of the American Indian*. I chose the Our Lives exhibition as my field site and spent time with museum staff and Native community members who created the exhibits together through a process called community curating.[9] I conducted two years of fieldwork from 2004 through 2006, living for six months or more in three of the nine communities involved in the making of the exhibition: the museum professionals at the NMAI, including Native and non-Native staff; the American Indian community of Chicago, a multi-tribal community residing throughout a large city; and the Kalinago community (or Island Caribs), who manage their own territory on the island of Dominica in the West Indies. I had been a curatorial research assistant at the NMAI from 1999 to 2002 and a contractor in 2003, so I had also participated in community curating from the museum's point of view.

Fieldwork for me was a combination of being in a large museum and in Native communities and cultural centers. This was my approach to viewing the various sites of collaborative exhibition production as well as the lived experience of its producers. I volunteered in the museum in which I conducted ethnography, was made keenly aware of the troubled relationship between Native American communities and the discipline of anthropology, and shared transcripts and photos with the participants in my research. In this work I highlight that the museum is not only an institution of cultural production but also a bureaucratic workplace.

I was initially motivated by a number of questions, such as: what did the NMAI curators and community co-curators think about the exhibition-making process? Did they like the final product? Did they think it reflected their voices and intent? How and why were these particular people selected to do this particular kind of work with the museum? And what were the motivations and consequences for people who engaged in this kind of work, during and after the exhibitions were created? Ultimately, it was an ethnography of collaboration itself, of museum staff striving toward decolonizing museums—to make a "museum different" that serves Native people rather than exploits them—and the politics of expertise. While the outcomes on the museum floor and in the museum's relationships with originating communities were not perfect, they did lead communities to claim the museum as their own, which was an important first step for this new museum next to the United States Capitol on the National Mall.

14
Anthropology in Museums

In this section I want to begin with my path to becoming a museum anthropologist, discuss the role of an anthropologist in the museum, and then focus on how working with originating communities has influenced the way we work in the museum and why. When we center relationships and originating communities in museum anthropology, we often find our work extending beyond museum walls into the field, which I discuss in detail in part 4. In this section I focus on the role of the anthropology curator, but anthropological training is also a great foundation for working in education, exhibitions, and other professional roles at the museum.

I was always amazed at the students who applied to work with me in the University of Colorado museum studies program. So early in life, they knew exactly what they wanted: not only did they want a career in museums but specifically a position as a collection manager! My path to museums was not so planned or straightforward. I was open-minded, followed unexpected opportunities, and ended up working in museums, getting a PhD, and being a professor—things that were never what I had specifically aimed for and that were a surprising outcome, but they did reflect my values and I am so grateful that this is where my path led.

When I was an undergraduate, I chose to be a biology major, to pursue marine biology. And while I did earn a biology degree, I picked up a second major along the way: anthropology. I pursued anthropology mainly because it fit with my own worldview, which included valuing other cultural ways of being in the world, wanting to learn from other perspectives, and not taking for granted that the circumstances I was born into or the cultural practices I learned are the only right ways of doing things. I realize that my path is related to my subject position and privilege, and not everyone has opportunities reveal themselves in the same way; accordingly, cultivating mentors is important, and I highly recommend that you seek them out no matter what your stage in life or career. And don't think it's a burden to ask someone to mentor you. I am sure that many professionals and professors feel the same way I do: advising students and emerging professionals is an honor, an important responsibility, and one of my favorite parts of my job.

I was working in a marine biology lab for about six months after I graduated from college when I decided that I missed people. Between that experience and reflecting on an applied independent study I did with an Aboriginal Australian community while I was in college, I decided to apply to graduate school to study cultural anthropology. After a year working in a lab and then as an administrative assistant to save money for school, I earned a master's degree in social science with a focus on cultural anthropology. My undergraduate thesis was on Alaska Native and Aboriginal Australian land rights and land claims, and my master's thesis was on an American Indian legal case in Alaska—in other words, not about material culture or museums. But as I was graduating, a new museum in Washington, DC, was under construction, and it needed research assistants to develop the inaugural exhibitions. I was hired as a curatorial research assistant at the NMAI about five years before it opened to the public on the National Mall. After curatorial research for the exhibits was complete, I was advised by my supervisor at the museum that if I wanted to be a curator, I needed to get a PhD—so I did.

In the past, anthropology curators were stewards of collections and were considered the experts on the collections in their care; their knowledge and voice were paramount in the documentation and interpretation of Native peoples' cultural items. Anthropology in museums has changed significantly in the last several decades due to Native activism, the changing field and focus of cultural anthropology, and laws such as the Native American Graves Protection and Repatriation Act (1990). I believe museum anthropologists' close association with Native peoples has spurred the subfield to be more collaborative. Collaboration and ethical practice are now expected and valued in the field of cultural anthropology.

The anthropologist's position in the museum is often labeled "curator of ethnology." It's an old term, meaning the comparative study of cultures. I renamed my position when I was hired at the University of Colorado (CU) to be "curator of cultural anthropology." (I might suggest something more creative now and generally encourage people to rethink the titles received in these kinds of positions.) Curatorial responsibilities vary greatly among different museums, depending on whether they are large or small, urban or rural, freestanding or associated with a university. I have worked in a national museum and a campus museum, where my roles were vastly different, but the core of the anthropological work remains the same and is focused primarily on collections. What was wonderful about my role at CU is that I was both a curator in a campus museum and an associate professor in the Department of

Anthropology. I loved being in a teaching museum. My office was in the same building where the general public and families visited exhibits, school groups attended tours, students assisted in our work on the collections, and I got to teach classes.

Practicing anthropology in museums, in the role of curator, includes conducting research and publishing about collection items and their history of ownership ("provenance"), working on exhibits as a content specialist, correcting or adding to collections' catalog records, collecting or removing items from collections ("accessioning and deaccessioning"), engaging with originating communities for all of these activities as well as repatriation and more. In my case, working at a university museum also included teaching undergraduate and graduate courses on museum studies and anthropology. I will address these various responsibilities in the sections that follow.

Curators often supervise collections managers, who attend to the day-to-day care of collections while curators are associated more with the research on and expansion of collections. Typically, in large museums, a curator is a subject matter specialist with a PhD, and the collections manager may have a master's degree in museum studies, specializing in collections management. In a small museum, one person may do both jobs and be an educator as well. Depending on the size of the museum, the backgrounds of the curator and collections manager vary widely. The responsibilities for repatriation may also belong to the curator, collections manager, or, in larger museums, a repatriation specialist. Anthropology curators may provide insights to ensure, based on their research and work with originating communities, that interpretations of collections or topics are culturally appropriate, accurate, and respectful.

Whether you are Native or Non-native, as a museum professional you may be seen as representing the troubling history of museums and their exploitation of Native American communities and their ancestors. A major assumption of nineteenth- and early twentieth-century collecting was that Native communities, or at least their traditional knowledge and material culture, would not be around in the future. Even if a museum has a good reputation for redressing the injustice of this history, the collection that founded the museum was most likely built in that vein.

Given the history of museums and anthropology, museum anthropologists need to be ready for and accommodating of skepticism from Native community members. Expect to be, and welcome being, challenged or unsettled. You may be confronted with anger, sadness, or frustration because items from their ancestors or community are away from them—and in the museum you work in. They may ask, why can't we have them all back? This can be a form of unsettling the power imbalance between community members and museums. It is important to listen without being defensive. It doesn't feel good to be on the receiving end of anger or pain, but it is a positive thing for your relationship in the long run if you listen without interrupting and with respect, keeping this history in mind.

I often think about it this way: when we first meet, we are representative figures, whether of the museum or a tribal community. It's not about you, it's not personal. It's about acknowledging this history. If we listen with an open mind, show respect, and are honest and not defensive, the conversation can move on to be one between individuals who have common goals, including a desire to do what's best for items in the museum (even if ideas of what's best differ). One of the most common mistakes in these encounters is not bringing an open mind, and honest concerns, to the table (you will see this same theme in other sections as well). We need to check to be certain that we are not behaving in a way that operates on our assumptions of what the other party thinks or wants. Never start with "no." Instead, be open about your concerns and listen to what the other party has to say. This approach often results in creativity and consensus rather than intractability.

The Guidelines for Collaboration is a great resource that offers succinct advice to keep in mind when embarking on this kind of work.[10] The guidelines were developed over a three-year period of collaboration among Native and non-Native museum professionals, cultural leaders, and artists. There were multiple vetting sessions (I was at one) and conference presentations for feedback. The guidelines are short and direct, and the critical considerations are helpful to anyone who will be working at the intersection of museums and Native peoples. Here is a selection from the guidelines that I shared with my students:

> **Listen, Learn, and Don't Take It Personally:** As a museum staff member, you may be approached by a community member who has grievances about museums they need to express, even if they have nothing to do with you or your museum. Remember that past museum practices and policies have impacted Native peoples negatively, and while times are changing, deeply felt emotions remain for some. Do not take expressed grievances personally—this is an opportunity for you to learn more about the context for such feelings of hurt or anger. Often the best approach is simply to listen and not feel pressured to reply or resolve the situation.

Knowledge Appropriation: Native knowledge has often been inaccurately or inappropriately used or shared to further a museum's or an individual's research, publication, or other projects. To build trust with communities, it is important to discuss and agree how collected information will be used, shared, and archived.

Restrictions: In Native communities, access to knowledge is not a universal right. For many communities, cultural, religious, or ceremonial knowledge is restricted to certain individuals. There may be recognized individuals who have the authority to restrict access to certain collections. Be aware that restrictions can change.

Flexibility: Working with a community requires an ability to "go with the flow." You may not get a timely response to an email or phone inquiry, or a visit may be canceled unexpectedly due to a community's unforeseen cultural observances. You may also get unexpected visits from community members. Be prepared for these occurrences and be accommodating or politely explain your time constraints. Agendas for planned visits, while necessary, also need to be flexible.

Keeping in Touch: Discuss the best way to stay in touch with the community contact or group, and check in on a regular basis to maintain the relationship. If you are unable to meet face to face with community members, consider alternatives to maintaining communication and forwarding the project's goals.

Collections: Museums and communities view items in collections differently. Community members may see collections as having a life or a spirit and not as inanimate objects. Listen to and make note of how community members refer to collections. They may use language that avoids words such as object, artifact, and specimen. Incorporating their terms in your work with them demonstrates you are listening and respecting their cultural perspective.[11]

Today, museum anthropologists are not just stewards of collections, they are also increasingly stewards of important relationships between communities and their cultural items and ancestors, between communities and institutions of power. Managing these responsibilities and maintaining relationships in good standing can be challenging and delicate. And those relationships rely on the behavior and actions not just of the museum anthropologist but of the institution as a whole, the exhibits it displays, and the ways it does or does not make its collections accessible. Often, a museum anthropologist becomes an advocate and a guide within the museum for how to be in better relationship with and accountable to originating communities. One way to do this: have everyone in a museum read the Guidelines for Collaboration, not just collections managers or curators but also the director, visitor services staff, and others, and then facilitate an all-staff meeting to talk about the guidelines together.

One concern when you are a curator working in collaboration with Native communities on behalf of a larger institution is keeping promises and following through when your authority within the museum is limited. If there are areas where you know a decision is out of your hands, such as changing a design feature, postponing an opening, or increasing the budget to accommodate another collections visit, be transparent and let community members know that you will strongly advocate for these changes but cannot promise that they will happen.

As anthropologists in the museum, we can also ensure that materials that result from museum-community partnerships are shared in accessible formats and according to community interests. Include ways to send information and the results of museum-based projects out into communities through media that is different from exhibits or programs, that meets communities where they are. For example, our collaborative research has been featured in tribal newspapers and radio, DVDs that were distributed around the community, websites, classroom teaching kits, and even a comic book. For the oral history documentary we made with members of the Mandan, Hidatsa and Arikara Nation, there were two versions: one for the general public and one for the community that included fifteen extra minutes focused on the CU museum, its collection, and the 2014 repatriation of sacred items to the tribe. The idea was to let community members know, in a medium they requested and are familiar with, what the museum holds and that we welcome them to visit.

15
Collecting Practice and Policy

Native community members have consistently critiqued museums for their past collecting practices (which led to repatriation law) and for valuing, collecting, and displaying only the oldest examples of their cultural expression. They encourage museums to also collect contemporary arts—whether part of a continuing tradition like a cedar bark basket, or a work inspired by tradition, like a basket woven from 35 millimeter film; perhaps a replica using traditional techniques and materials, or a traditional technique with a modern design, or a two-dimensional painting or mixed-media piece.[12]

Some Native people, both in the past and today, appreciate and value having their ancestors' or relatives' cultural items in a museum, where they act as ambassadors to their future generations and the general public. Others believe none of the early collection items should be in museums. There is far more agreement that desecrated graves, the bones and funerary items of Native ancestors, should never have been collected and should not be in museums. United States repatriation laws affirm this (see the next section).

Collections old and new are important sources for learning and research, whether you are a curator, a Native community member, or both. However, the collections in museums don't always fit easily into the kinds of stories we want to tell. Collecting practices from the eighteenth and nineteenth centuries led to the majority of collections in major museums in the United States. We now rely on these collections that were amassed under different value systems and ideas about museum audiences to make modern exhibitions. This mismatch can create opportunities for creativity in developing exhibitions or lead to loaning, commissioning, or collecting new items.

When I introduced early collecting practices in my classes, I began with Michael O'Hanlon's introduction to *Hunting the Gatherers: Ethnographic Collectors, Agents, and Agency in Melanesia, 1870s–1930s*, published in 2001, and Ira Jacknis's *The Storage Box of Tradition: Kwakiutl Art, Anthropologists, and Museums, 1881–1981*, published in 2002.[13] Both men were anthropologists who worked in museums. Jacknis was a research anthropologist at the Phoebe Hearst Museum, writing about the Pacific Northwest coast. O'Hanlon was a professor of museum anthropology and director of the Pitt Rivers Museum at the University of Oxford whose work focused on Melanesia. Each was writing about the "long nineteenth century" of museums and the collecting practices of the time.

Jacknis presents an almost farcical image of fierce competition among museums and frenzied collecting of Kwakwa̱ka'wakw material culture among collectors, and O'Hanlon highlights the agency of Indigenous people in the collecting encounter. They both acknowledge that collectors relied on Indigenous people in different ways. The aim in bringing these two accounts together was to ask questions about the origins, collections, and values of early museum collectors that often made the foundation of the museums we work in. What we learn from these and other sources is that early collecting was centered on objects that were identified as the least influenced by European contact or were significantly old. Sometimes collectors painted or otherwise changed the object to make it look older! Keep in mind that most collectors were men, which affected what they collected because of their own interests or because they primarily met with male representatives of a community. Sometimes they bought or were gifted objects, other times they cajoled or stole objects. Most collectors did not care if there was associated documentation about the items, but others would not collect an item unless there was extensive information on it.

Jacknis and O'Hanlon show how Native community members participated in early collecting. They could be intermediaries helping to connect collectors to community artists or collect on their behalf. They could limit what was available to collect. They also increased the number of items for sale over time and increasingly made them more decorative and less functional, or they made smaller models that were easier for collectors to bring home. These were savvy moves made to adapt to demand and a changing economy. However, collectors also took advantage of difficult economic times when community members sold items to survive, and they benefited from discriminatory laws like those that banned Native ceremonies and allowed for the confiscation of ceremonial items.

In the field and in museums, there is both active and passive collecting. The former occurs when an individual drives the selection process, such as seeking out a particular artist to purchase pottery from or purchasing items to fill a gap in collections—for instance, if a museum has a Southwest pottery collection but nothing from Santa Clara Pueblo. Passive collecting occurs when an individual selects from what is offered—for example, accepting a donation to a museum. In the past, typically, an individual was sent out into the field, but sometimes an expedition was chartered. Today, most museums are passively collecting, through donations or bequests. That is why defining a scope of collection and collecting policy is so important. It is very easy to accept donations, but then museum staff must care for them in perpetuity—meaning forever, which requires space, labor, and a lot of resources. So, being selective can help the long-term health and well-being of the collection. Also, when developing a scope of collections or collecting policy, consider how it might influence the museum's relationship or engagement with originating communities. Consider how you might develop your scope of collections in collaboration with communities whose items are in the museum's collections or whose lands the museum resides on.

A scope of collections outlines what you will prioritize; it can be regional or describe the kinds of items you collect. This can guide decisions about what you decline or agree to add (accession) into the collection from a donation, for example. If your scope of collections is the Plains and the Southwest, you can politely decline the offer of a mask from Mexico. The scope may also help identify items to be removed or deaccessioned from the collection, which can perhaps create room to better house remaining collections or create room for new ones. Duplicates or damaged items can also be considered for deaccession. It is important to review codes of ethics and for deaccessions to be transferred to another museum or cultural center, destroyed, or sold. In the last case, the funds go to the direct care of collections.[14] When deaccessioning, consider offering the item to the originating community's museum or cultural center first or to a non-Native museum near the community of origin.

For decades, the University of Colorado Museum of Natural History (CU Museum) had a birch bark canoe hanging from a ceiling in the collections space. The canoe was collected by an anthropologist and donated to the museum in 1925. Due to a renovation project, we had to take it down and would have no space to house it when the changes were complete. In addition, it was from New York, outside our scope of collections. We contacted the St. Regis Mohawk Tribe, which was labeled the maker of the canoe in the catalog description, to see if they wanted it to be returned. We sent images, a condition report, catalog information, and details we were able to find about the collector. The Tribe agreed to take the canoe, which took some time to arrange for and fund. In the meantime, to provide a place for the canoe to rest, we created a new changing exhibit in the university museum titled *What in the World*, where it was displayed until it could be shipped home.

A collecting plan is also helpful in making intentional accessions to the museum. It requires reviewing the collection and identifying where there is room to grow, often to fill gaps but also to consider increasing items from communities whose lands the museum resides on or contemporary Native art or fashion. Depending on the size and type of museum, consider writing into the collecting policy that originating communities be consulted about new accessions to determine whether they are appropriate for the museum to obtain.

Leadership matters. Models for collaborative museum practice can come from unlikely places, including a high school prep academy in Andover, Massachusetts! Under the directorship of Ryan Wheeler, the Phillips Academy Robert S. Peabody Institute of Archaeology agreed to enter into a memorandum of understanding (MOU) with the White Earth Band of the Minnesota Chippewa Tribe at the suggestion of Tribal Historic Preservation Officer (THPO) Jaime Arsenault. The MOU includes that the Tribe will assist in cultural identifications of collection items and that the museum will include the Tribe in decision making regarding digitization of White Earth Nation items, consult with the Tribe regarding future purchases or donations, and seek the THPO's approval for any requests to research or publish material about the items related to their community.[15]

16
Repatriation Law

It is the responsibility of the curator to collect items and sometimes to return them. In the US, the curator or collections manager in charge of anthropology collections is usually the person who enacts the laws associated with repatriation. Even if there is a dedicated and separate position in the museum, such as a NAGPRA liaison or coordinator, they rely on the collections manager and curator to inventory and research collections, provide findings, prepare for NAGPRA consultations, and respond to claims. If you are in a museum, it is important to know who makes the ultimate decision to deaccession items in the collection. At the University of Colorado Museum of Natural History (CU Museum), it is the university's regents; in other museums, it may be a board of trustees. Having a policy in place that identifies how the law is applied in a specific museum can help make the process and time line more transparent if a request for consultation or a claim is made.

In my experience, when tribes are equal partners and repatriation consultation is done in good faith, everyone benefits and feels a part of something larger than themselves and that they are engaging in meaningful work. In teaching about repatriation in museum studies and anthropology classes, I appreciated that the next generation of museum professionals takes for granted that repatriation is a positive and necessary museum practice.

At the CU Museum, I was proactive in repatriation consultations. I contacted Tribes knowing the museum had items they had requested for repatriation from other museums, and I responded to community requests. I did not participate in the repatriation of Native ancestors or human remains because that was the responsibility of the archaeology curator. As the cultural anthropology curator, I focused on the return of sacred objects and objects of cultural patrimony. My colleagues Dr. Steve Lekson and Christina Cain did extensive work to return Native ancestors from the museum. Their efforts to prioritize compliance with the law made my work possible because the process of returning ancestors was under way when I arrived and was later completed, providing me with a foundation of being on the right side of the law when I engaged with communities for collaborative research or repatriation.

The main thing I emphasize when teaching is that repatriation is a transfer of ownership.[16] It is also a law that seeks justice and dignity and respect for Native peoples, their ancestors, and their cultural beliefs and practices. Two main laws in the United States refer specifically to the museum repatriation process: the Native American Graves Protection and Repatriation Act (NAGPRA, 1990) and the National Museum of the American Indian Act (NMAI Act, 1989).[17] The NMAI Act applies to all Smithsonian Institution museums that have Native American collections. NAGPRA applies to all other institutions, including other federal agencies, that have Native American collections and have received federal funding in the United States. This includes any university, institution, or museum that has ever received federal grants, for example.

The NMAI was founded from George Gustav Heye's massive collection and museum in New York. The NMAI Act created the National Museum of the American Indian to bring this collection to the Smithsonian, and it required an inventory of all Native ancestors and funerary items in the collection so they would be returned to their communities of origin. In 1996 the act was amended to include the additional categories for return identified in NAGPRA. Both laws now apply to

- Human remains
- Associated and unassociated funerary items
- Sacred objects
- Objects of cultural patrimony.

Under the NAGPRA law, the term *cultural items* specifically refers to funerary items, sacred objects, and objects of cultural patrimony "according to the Native American traditional knowledge of a lineal descendant, Indian Tribe, or Native Hawaiian organization." That is why consultation is crucial for implementation of the law. It is important to note that in everyday museum language, the phrase *cultural items* can refer to collections objects in general that are not archaeological.

Briefly, NAGPRA enables Tribes to request the return of the bones and burial items of their ancestors that were taken without consent. It enables the return of sacred or ceremonial objects so they can be put back into cultural practice today (which in some cases may include being retired or returned to the earth as part of their life cycle) and the return of objects of cultural patrimony that no single individual had the right to sell or give away (think of the United States Constitution: no US citizen can sell it or give it away because it belongs to everyone). The law provides museums with the legal means to deaccession items for return, and it has instructions for what to do when burials are newly discovered—for example, while building a road. There are procedures for consultation, for notifying other Tribes that a museum intends to affiliate and repatriate ancestors or cultural items, and so on. Be sure you know the law, its categories, and its requirements.

It is important to know the NAGPRA law's regulations as well. The United States Congress left the implementation process of returning Native ancestors that were not affiliated with a federally recognized Tribe to be determined after the law was enacted. The NAGPRA regulations published in 2010, which inspired us to create *NAGPRA Comics*, were referred to as the "10.11 regs" because that was the section of the law in which they were located.[18] The section addressed "the process for the disposition of culturally unidentifiable human remains" (I address the problem with the term *unidentifiable* later in this section). Unlike the rest of the law, the associated funerary items with culturally unaffiliated individuals, or those whose originating community was not determined, were not required to be returned ("a museum or Federal agency may voluntary transfer control of funerary objects that are associated with culturally unidentifiable human remains" [emphasis added]). In other words, whether all of the contents of a burial were required to be returned depended on cultural affiliation. *NAGPRA Comics* co-producer Dr. Sonya Atalay (Anishinaabe-Ojibwe), myself, and many others felt this was contradictory to the spirit of the law, which returned culturally affiliated ancestors and the items buried with them. There were also concerns that museums would "game the system," choosing not to culturally affiliate Native ancestors so they could keep the associated funerary items.

This is no longer an issue because in 2024, the regulations changed. Leadership matters: in 2021 Deb Haaland (Pueblo of Laguna) became the head of the agency that oversees NAGPRA, the United States Department of the Interior.[19] On December 6, 2023, the department distributed a press release titled "Interior Department Announces Final Rule for Implementation of the Native American Graves Protection and Repatriation Act," announcing that new regulations were forthcoming that, as Secretary Haaland said, would "strengthen the authority and role of Indigenous communities in the repatriation process . . . Finalizing these changes is an important part of laying the groundwork for the healing of our people." Similarly, Assistant Secretary for Indian Affairs Bryan Newland (Bay Mills Indian Community, Ojibwe) explained, "NAGPRA is an important law that helps us heal from some of the more painful times in our past by empowering Tribes to protect what is sacred to them. These changes to the Department's NAGPRA regulations are long overdue and will strengthen our ability to enforce the law and help Tribes in the return of ancestors and sacred cultural objects."[20]

The 2024 regulations were intended to expedite the process of repatriation of Native ancestors. The 10.11 section was deleted and the subsequent section numbers were moved up. The phrase *culturally unidentifiable human remains* was removed from the law, and new phrasing, Duty of Care, was introduced. Geography is now also a mechanism for determining who the ancestor should be affiliated with for return home, along with their funerary items. According to these new regulations, museums have until 2029 to consult and update inventories of Native ancestors and their associated funerary items to prepare for repatriation.

The language of the "Duty of Care" clause is similar to the United Nations Declaration on the Rights of Indigenous Peoples (UNDRIP), whereby museums and federal agencies must obtain "free, prior and informed consent" from lineal descendants and originating communities before allowing any exhibition of, access to, or research on human remains or cultural items. Following the announcement of the 2024 NAGPRA regulations, a number of news articles highlighted the covering or closure of entire galleries at major museums like the Field Museum of Chicago and the American Museum of Natural History in New York City.[21] Perhaps they were interpreting "cultural items" in its broadest sense, or perhaps they were erring on the side of caution because, until you consult, you may not know what falls under the legal classification of cultural items. The prompting of museums to revisit and revise decades-old exhibitions has been a positive outcome of these regulations.

NAGPRA law has spurred major shifts and changes in museums and communities and, most recently, in broader public sentiment as well. Twenty-five years ago, the general public did not know what repatriation is. Today, after events like an iconic scene in the blockbuster *Black Panther* movie (2018) and sustained news coverage, the public and students entering universities know what repatriation is and are taking museums to task. In anticipation of the change in regulations and the evolution of the law, *ProPublica* and the *Washington Post* conducted investigative reporting projects in 2023 and 2024 that highlighted institutions that had not fully complied with the NMAI Act and NAGPRA law.[22]

In 2022, a new law was passed to protect cultural items as defined in NAGPRA by making it a federal crime to export them internationally without certification. The law also facilitates the voluntary repatriation of Native American human remains and cultural items that are overseas back to Tribes and Native Hawaiian organizations in the United States. It is called the STOP ACT, or the Safeguard Tribal Objects of Patrimony Act of 2021; additional regulations are forthcoming.[23]

Knowing the law is one step, creating museum policy is another. A description of how your institution will apply the law can be included in a collections management policy or be a separate repatriation policy. Policy helps define how the law is enacted specifically at your museum. It may include who at the museum reviews and determines cultural affiliation, what is the standard of proof, and whether your institution will apply the law in a broader sense, such as repatriating to international Indigenous peoples or to state-recognized tribes, for example.

In April 2022 the Smithsonian Institution adopted a Shared Stewardship and Ethical Returns Policy, under the leadership of Secretary of the Smithsonian Dr. Lonnie Bunch III—who is African American and the founding director of the National Museum of African American History and Culture—and undersecretary for museums and culture and former director of the National Museum of the American Indian Kevin Gover (Pawnee Tribe of Oklahoma). The policy applies to all Smithsonian museums, enabling not just Native

Americans but any lineal descendant or community of origin whose ancestors or belongings are in a Smithsonian museum to request that they be returned home due to ethical considerations. Dr. Bunch is the first secretary of the Smithsonian who had been a museum director. He required that all Smithsonian museums draft procedures by the end of 2022 for how they would implement this policy and include the procedures on their public websites. They were up by January 2023—a remarkably quick turnaround for such a large institution and such a complex topic. Again, leadership matters!

A note about the language of repatriation laws. It's important to know and use the legal terms in the context of claims and official work under the law—for example, human remains, funerary object. But legal and scientific language can be off-putting and even offensive when discussing issues of repatriation. As noted in the Language and Power section above, using language that signals "welcome" to those who are engaging in collections consultation goes a long way, especially in the understandably fraught and difficult context of repatriation. While the legal term a museum used in the past to indicate that staff members had not determined cultural affiliation for a Native ancestor was "culturally unidentifiable," as if it can never be known, this was offensive to communities, especially if they were claiming affiliation. We chose to say "culturally unidentified" instead. While it is no longer a phrase in the law, we want to be sure the language doesn't continue in our everyday museum conversations. I have come to use the term *Native ancestors* in reference to human remains, thanks to Dr. Sue Rowley many years ago during my time at the University of British Columbia Museum of Anthropology. *Human remains, ancestral remains*, and *individuals* are also respectful terms. The term *specimen* should never be used.

Repatriation work can be difficult and also uplifting, as we commit to acknowledge the past and do better in the future. In her talks and trainings, Jan Bernstein has taught many of us engaged in repatriation that repatriation is about human, religious, and civil rights. It also contributes to cultural continuity with the return of items to reawaken ceremonial practices and enables ancestors to complete their journey or finally be at rest, as was intended when they were first interred. But this is no simple process, where you just send the individuals home and all is right again. Many individuals in collections have little information associated with them, sometimes not even where they were disinterred. Some communities, due to their beliefs, will not accept unknown ancestors back onto their lands. The Ute Mountain Ute, in contrast, have agreed to return to the earth not only their own ancestors but also culturally unaffiliated ancestors and those from other tribes who cannot rebury them on their homelands for these or other reasons.[24] I also learned about a community that took two years to develop an appropriate reburial ceremony. They had conducted burial ceremonies, but there was never a need in the past to rebury an individual. It took time, contemplation, and community effort to determine the best path for bringing ancestors home.

Students ask me why community members parted with treasured items—inferring that if they were sold by a community member in the past, the museum has them rightfully. I explain that, first, there are many examples of museums having engaged in theft or wrongful collecting in the past. Second, we often hear that items were sold "under duress" as one of the reasons why repatriation is necessary. Duress is "a situation where one person makes unlawful threats or otherwise engages in coercive behavior that causes another person to commit acts that they would otherwise not commit."[25] Acts of assimilation and ethnocide, such as boarding schools and the outlawing of Native religions, were a form of duress where US policies and institutions forced Native people to relinquish their cultural practices and language. Religious freedom for Native Americans was not guaranteed under the law until 1978 when the American Indian Religious Freedom Act was passed.

In discussing a potential issue of *NAGPRA Comics* with Jaime Arsenault, then THPO for White Earth Nation, and staff at the Berkshire and Peabody Andover Museums, we focused on a specific example of what "under duress" means. During the early 1900s, numerous sacred items were taken out of the community and placed in museums while they were being swindled out of their homes, lands, and allotments. It became so bad that families lacked shelter or adequate food. Illness such as tuberculosis spread, children were forcibly removed to boarding schools, and many families were left struggling to meet basic needs while grieving these losses. The United States government provided these families with unheated canvas tents to live in, and an Indian commissioner was sent to investigate.[26] The museums repatriated items to White Earth Nation and changed their policies and practices after working with the THPO.[27]

The context for repatriation is not just ethnocide or coerced assimilation but in some cases genocide. In the nineteenth century, while hobbyists and anthropologists were collecting items from tribal communities that they assumed would vanish in the future, there were bounties to kill Indians in Northern California. The results were devastating not just to communities but also to the intergenerational transfer of knowledge.

Repatriation Law | 63

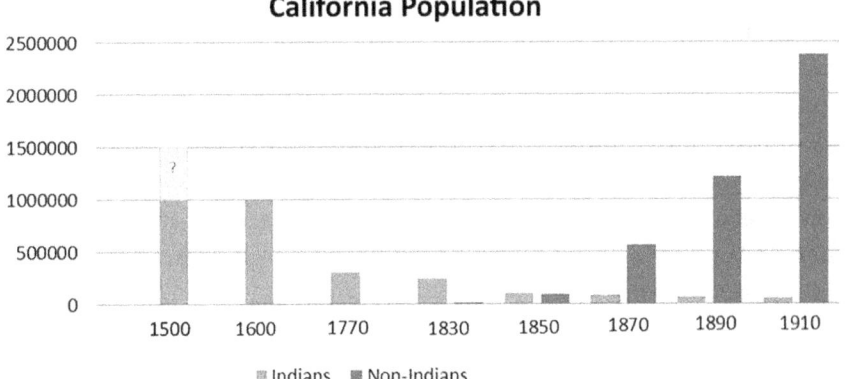

FIGURE 2.2. California population over time. Laguna Resource Services, Inc., "Kumeyaay Heritage and Conservation (HC) Project," 19.

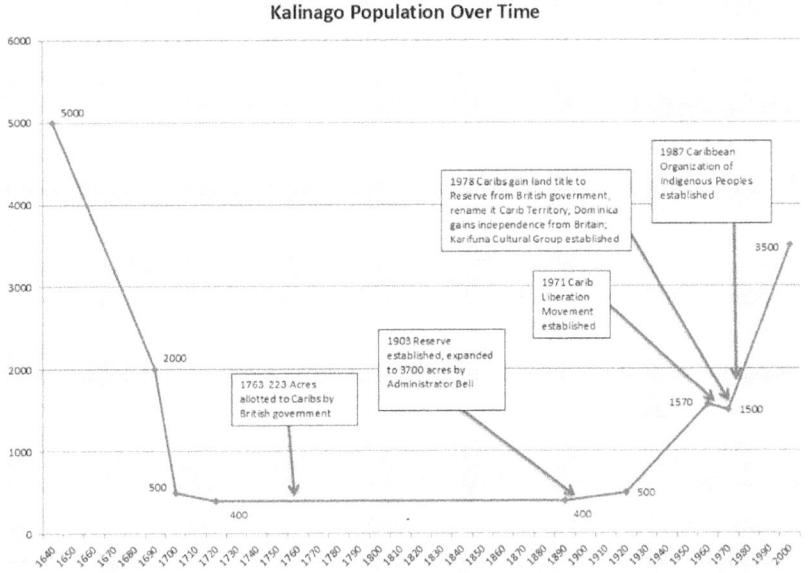

FIGURE 2.3. Kalinago (Island Carib) population over time. Numbers accounted for in the nearest decade. From Shannon, "The Professionalization of Indigeneity in the Carib Territory of Dominica," 30.

Consider these U-shaped graphs that are representative of the loss and resurgence of populations in many Indigenous communities in the Americas (figures 2.2 and 2.3). Imagine the loss of community knowledge, especially when different kinds of knowledge are kept by different groups of people.

Cultural care practices, discussed later, show that knowledge may only be accessible and maintained in some cases by either men or women or by individuals in a particular ceremonial society or clan. Not only does repatriation bring ancestors home to continue their journey and be returned to rest, but it also brings home cultural items that carry knowledge and enable or reawaken cultural practices. The notion that knowledge or language is sleeping and can be reawakened comes from Native communities and is a term currently preferred over revitalization. The term might change again in the future, but right now it is the one I use.

We can also think in terms of "the spirit of the law." For example, NAGPRA only applies to institutions in the US that receive federal funding and to federally recognized Tribes. However, there are ways that museums can address these limitations—for example, by returning culturally unaffiliated ancestors or items to a federally recognized Tribe, which may transfer them to a non-federally recognized Tribe of origin. Museum policies can help fill in the gaps, too. For example, we made it our policy at the CU Museum to treat international repatriation requests the same way we did domestic ones; in other words, we applied the same definitions and processes as NAGPRA.

We can teach private collectors about the spirit of the law, too. When an individual wanted to donate an item that was a known sacred item, I contacted the THPO for the originating community who said they would happily receive it from the donor. Unfortunately, while the donor seemed eager at first and took down the THPO's address, in the end she said her son wanted the item, so she never sent it. More recently, a woman named Barbara, in her seventies, showed me some items her father had taken from a scaffold burial. She was a little girl sitting in the car when she saw him do this. She remembered where they had stopped the car, so she knew the exact location from which the items had been taken. More than fifty years later she still felt remorseful about this and wanted to know what to do. I contacted the THPO from this region, who reviewed the items, identified the community of origin, and invited Barabara to mail the items back to their home. We wrapped the items in red cloth and packaged them, and she sent them to the THPO office. She included a letter expressing that she was happy that the items were returning home.

Museum staff and anthropologists are often the point of contact for people who are not familiar with Native communities. People can be intimidated by the idea of cold-calling communities to work with them or to return something to them. It took us one week from the time we identified Barbara's situation to returning the items to their home. I believe and hope there are others like her out there who just need a connection and a little help in knowing what to do and who to call.

Finally, I often tell museum professionals and Native communities that if a museum says it lacks the capacity to comply with NAGPRA—whether due to funding or staff capacity—that is no excuse. National NAGPRA grants are available to provide resources to do the work. The CU Museum alone has been awarded hundreds of thousands of dollars to support collections documentation, consultation, and physical return and reburial. We have received grants that provided funding to hire a temporary registrar to inventory the collection and update records in preparation for consultation (consultation grant), to develop a website for ease of access to records and to prepare for consultation, and to crate and ship or pay for someone to come and retrieve items or individuals to bring home (repatriation grant). Seek out institutions that have great reputations in the field of repatriation, and learn from them and the grants they have received—CU Museum staff and I regularly share successful grant narratives with Native and non-Native museum institutions. There are plenty of successful grants on which to model your own, so don't be shy about asking for examples from colleagues or museum professionals doing similar work. Supporting each other's success is an important part of moving the field forward.

The next section discusses collections research, which can be conducted for many reasons, including supporting and evaluating repatriation claims.

17
Collections Research

You can do research on anthropology collections as a curator within your own museum or as a visiting researcher. A "visiting researcher" does not have to be a university student or professor. Originating community members who want physical access to collections may need to make a research request to visit the museum so they can spend time reviewing collections. You may be classified as a visiting researcher, depending on the museum and its procedures.

One of the main things originating communities want to know when visiting collections is how the collections came to be in the museum. Doing research on that question in preparation for a community visit can be a welcoming gesture as well as offering transparency. This is called "provenance research," or research about the history of an item and its "chain of custody," or who had it over time and when. We often think of collection items as having biographies, thanks to Igor Kopytoff.[28] Provenance research is essentially writing as much of an item's or a collection's biography as possible from the information available. Where did it originate, who made it, how was it collected or inherited, how did the museum acquire it, and what has been its experience since being in the museum—exhibition, consultation, conservation, subject of researcher visits? This kind of detective work can be fascinating and sometimes frustrating when little information is available.

Even when information is available, it's important not to assume that all museum records are accurate given the who, when, and why of collecting. Originating communities, researchers, and museum staff should not rely on museums or museum records alone as authoritative knowledge. The records can be incorrect, or they can reflect colonial perspectives or voice. For instance, typical reference lists used for naming Native American items in museum catalogs can misidentify items and their use or be offensive, such as calling something a fetish. We often need to go beyond the museum's records to other archives or do comparative collections analysis to piece the story together.

Research on collections has evolved over time. In the past, a museum curator or scholar often conducted intensive literature searches and materials studies to understand the history, use, materials, techniques, or cultural affiliation of cultural items. Their expertise and determination trumped all. Today, it is far more common to include working with originating community members as part of the research and attribution process (attribution is the identification of the community of origin or the item's creator). In addition, in the past you had to go to the museum to see if any of the collection items were pertinent to your work. Now, you can often do preliminary searches online or request reports of the collections of interest to review ahead of time. Sometimes the report and images are all a researcher needs; other times a visit is necessary.

Purposes for collections research may include preparing for community visits to collections, conducting research for exhibitions, updating catalog records, doing proactive repatriation or responding to claims, responding to inquiries from researchers, preparing for class (if a university museum), doing collaborative research projects with originating communities, or publishing books or articles about the collection items or the people and place from which they originated.

If known, research on artists or collectors, their biographies and archival papers, can be a good start in learning more about a collection. Another form of collections research is "close looking," or paying close attention to the materials, construction, and use-wear on an item. For example, Dr. Candace Greene effectively shows why close looking is important in collections research, and she cautions against moving away from the object too quickly to look for documents and text. Through close looking, she reveals the different kind of plant fibers that adorn Plains garments in the same manner as porcupine quills and the role of women's knowledge in the use of these materials.[29]

Another avenue for collections research is associated documentation, which can include letters to the museum, receipts, field notes, photographs, and more. Whether you are a researcher or a community member, always ask about associated documentation. In addition, multiple museums can have collections from the same collector or the same community. Tell communities where those related collections and archives are and, if possible, reach out to the staff at those museums to see if they have documentation you could access for further insight.

As noted above, one thing to keep in mind, and to let visiting community members know, is that the museum records are not necessarily accurate. When she was teaching at the Summer Institute in Museum Anthropology at the National Museum of Natural History, Dr. Greene used to repeat the phrase: says who? This was her way of reminding students to always question attribution, or the catalog record's information about where an item came from and who made it. Historically, the catalog did not indicate who decided the community of origin or why. It was often a curator who did so, but there was no indication as to whether that was something the curator knew based on purchasing an item from a Lakota artist or because the design style looked Lakota. Today, museums such as the NMAI address this issue through their collections information system or database. Attribution in the record includes who made the determination and when, as well as a scale of degree of confidence as to whether the attribution is accurate.

If you are hosting researchers to collections, be sure to tell them what the law and your policies say about accessing collections, particularly regarding culturally sensitive items and those classified as cultural items under NAGPRA. NAGPRA regulations released in 2024 state that free, prior, and informed consent is required by originating communities for exhibition of, access to, or research on human remains, sacred or funerary objects, and objects of cultural patrimony (see the Repatriation Law section above for more on NAGPRA and the NMAI Act).[30] Through a museum or an organization's policy, these requirements can be extended to non-federally recognized tribes, private collections, communities outside the United States, and others (see chapter 35, "Collections Management Policy and Shared Stewardship").

When conducting research on museum collections, it is ideal to contact the originating community about your intentions. In some circumstances, as noted above in the Peabody Museum example, a museum may not allow research to be conducted without consent from the originating community in general, regardless of whether it is on NAGPRA cultural items. Consider who might benefit from the outcome of your work—share what you learn with the originating community if you have not personally engaged the community in the process. I like to think about "giving first"; if I am going to engage with a collection, I share the report provided by the museum or put together a digital or printed resource of all collections information I have collected and send it to the originating community. If you publish something about a collection, send a copy to community members you have been working with. If you did not work with community members, consider sending your publication to a cultural center or THPO office of the community of origin. (If you are hosting community members in collections as part of your research process, see chapter 25, "Community Visits to Collections." For specifics about designing collaborative research projects for when hosting a collections visit leads you to work with an originating community outside the museum, see chapter 41. For the quintessential method of engaging with communities in the curatorial process, community curating, see the next section.)

18
Exhibition Development

In larger museums, two main areas in which anthropology curators have influence in exhibit development are the subject matter of the exhibit and the content development process. In a smaller museum, they may also do exhibit design, mounts, and all the steps to completing an exhibit. One of the biggest changes in museum anthropology work over the decades has been the sharing of authority with originating communities and an increasing presence of Native peoples in the museum—as content specialists and as staff. There are many ways to engage with originating communities in the museum. Below, I focus on content development for exhibitions because that is a primary way museum anthropologists and curators work with communities.

When I teach about exhibition development with originating communities, when I teach about anything having to do with collaboration and communities, I always make the point that these are examples to think with and not what I am saying you should do. They are examples meant to spark ideas, to critique or be inspired by in your own work. Later, I provide some ideas for how the museum as a whole can also engage with communities beyond exhibition development.

Exhibit Content

Depending on the museum, the curator may propose exhibition topics or be tapped to provide research, object selection, or content for a particular subject matter in an exhibit. What we have learned from Native communities when working on exhibits is that we should break away from traditional molds and traditional subjects of museum exhibits and include them in the exhibit process when their items or histories are going to be on display.

We want to avoid falling into the trap of appearing to only value Indigenous peoples' pasts, especially because that is what early collections most easily represent, which reinforces the general public's impressions about Native peoples. We can attend to the present and future as well through creative interpretation of these items or incorporating more recent works. This could occur through mingling historical and contemporary arts, as in the Indigenous Arts of North America galleries at the Denver Art Museum, or doing an exhibition dedicated to Indigenous futures, such as *Indigenous Futurisms: Transcending Past/Present/Future* at the Institute of American Indian Arts in 2020 or the Autry's *Future Imaginaries: Indigenous Art, Fashion, Technology*, which opened in 2024.

I want to share a few more examples to provide food for thought. Also, I tend to love when exhibitions reveal relations and process (no surprise there!). Museum professionals learn from one another's work, and one of my favorite examples that inspired me is the University of British Columbia Museum of

Anthropology's display of a Kwakwa̱ka'wakw mask in the Multiversity Galleries. The mask was wrapped in cloth and hidden from view. Mikael Willie (Dzawada̱'enux̱w First Nation) explains on the label:

> In our Kwak'wala language there is a word—*k'wik'wała̱dlakw*—which means "things that are hidden." Traditionally, our wolf headdresses, whistles, and other objects with *'nawalakw*, or supernatural power, were put away when not being shown in ceremony. For some of our people, to have these things on display for the public is very disturbing. That's why we were invited here to the Museum to discuss this issue. Our elders had mixed feelings: some said that we should educate the people of the world by showing the masks; others said that we need to put them away properly and respectfully. I thought that one thing we might be able to do is wrap some of the masks on display. This is so that the public can understand that not everyone is meant to see these things. *Gilaskas'la* (thank you)!

If we simply remove from view something that is inappropriate for display, the public never knows that a conversation ever happened between community and museum or that some things are not meant to be shared. In one small display, we learn that the museum consulted with First Nations people, prioritized their expertise, and erred on the side of caution. It also shows that there is a diversity of opinions on the matter within the community.

We were explicit about the opposite case in a 2013 exhibit at the CU Museum. We hosted a traveling exhibit, *To Feel the Earth: Moccasins in the Southwest*, which was curated by Dr. Cynthia Chavez Lamar (San Felipe Pueblo, Hopi, Tewa and Diné). What attracted me to the exhibit was that it was created with moccasin makers and included their perspectives, statements, and questions to museum visitors.

I invited graduate student Kendall Tallmadge (now Tryhane) (Ho-Chunk Nation) to select moccasins from the CU collection and write labels for them to complement the banner exhibit. An extended label for one pair of moccasins offered us the opportunity to show that we don't always know for certain the origins of collection items:

> These moccasins are most likely from the Pueblo of Acoma. They have been viewed by the Pueblos of Santa Ana, Cochiti, San Ildelfonso, Taos, Sandia, Zuni, Santa Clara, Nambe, Laguna, Acoma, Jemez, Zia, Tesuque, and the Hopi, as part of consultations associated with the Native

American Graves Protection and Repatriation Act (NAGPRA). This Federal law directs museums to consult with tribes to determine sacred objects and objects of outstanding cultural significance that can then be repatriated—or returned—to the tribe. During these consultations tribes are invited to view all objects in our collection associated with their tribe, such as these moccasins—which were determined not to be NAGPRA items.

We were also able to highlight our extensive consultation efforts and how they informed our selection. Otherwise, this kind of work would be invisible to the public.

An exhibit we curated at the CU Museum in 2011 was about a project called iShare, funded by a grant from the American Alliance of Museums that included the Navajo Nation Museum, the National Museum of Taiwan, and the Paiwan Cultural Center. The focus of the exhibition was on the collaborative process, how we worked together, and some of the gifts we exchanged that represented our partnership. The opening panel stated: "Our goals were to strengthen relationships between communities and museums whose objects they house and to provide those communities greater access to materials in museum collections."

The exhibit included an introduction to the partners, what we were creating together, hosting and gift exchange, Navajo and Paiwan foods that were a big part of our cross-cultural experiences, and what we learned about each other. It also explained how we used technology to share our knowledge, how we built our partnership through a series of trips, and the collaboration itself. We wanted to be open about our experience and be a model for others to learn from, so we noted in a text panel that "there are many rewards—and challenges—that come with embarking on a collaborative project. We highlight the rewards of the project throughout this exhibit. Some of the challenges included working in four languages, addressing concerns about intellectual property rights, managing online data, and keeping the momentum going at different stages of the process."

These exhibits at the university museum were small in size and accomplished by a small team, but they shared with the public the museum's interest in and commitment to working with Indigenous communities. For larger-scale exhibits, there are far more robust processes for developing content, as the earlier example at Mesa Verde National Park and the next section demonstrate.

Content Development Process

There are many ways to involve community members in exhibition development (see, for example, appendix F, with selections from a "Guide to Thinking about Collaboration for Exhibit Planning"). Below, I give some examples, but they are not meant to be prescriptive. They invite you to think critically about your decisions on how to structure a project and associated relationships. Not every project merits collaboration or partnership; not every community has the capacity or wants to invest the time. The point is to know about different options, think through what's best for a given relationship or project, and be intentional and clear about how and why you are doing the work.

The curatorial approach the NMAI adopted for its inaugural exhibitions was called "community curating" or "community co-curating." Imagine three exhibition teams working with twenty-four representative groups from Indigenous communities in North, Central, and South America to determine the content of the new museum's first exhibits. I learned about and practiced community curating during my first museum professional experience as a curatorial research assistant at the NMAI. In that role, I was responsible for conducting research and doing fieldwork in support of the development of the inaugural exhibitions. I have always thought of that experience as my first PhD—for three years I learned so much about museum practice and had mentors who guided my learning. At the time I did not realize how different my experience was from those who worked in other museums because this was my first museum job.

I go into a lot of detail about this process through a case study approach to the making of one of the inaugural exhibitions in the book *Our Lives: Collaboration, Native Voice, and the Making of the National Museum of the American Indian*.[31] Here, I just describe the basics of community curating as an example of one method of collaborating with communities in exhibition development. Basically, community curating or community co-curating is sharing authority and developing content with a representative group from a community. And it includes compensation to the co-curators. The number of curators who comprise the group is up to the community, but it is often between four and eight people. Native co-curators held meetings with and without NMAI staff to direct the content, thematic structure, and object selection for their exhibits. Museum staff regularly visited Native communities to talk with co-curators, get a sense of place, and better represent their interests in the exhibition development process.

Community curating should not be confused with an advisory group, which can be quite large but is not involved in the details of exhibition development. An advisory group provides advice about direction and may review and give feedback on materials, but community curators take on some of the responsibilities usually associated with a curator, such as making decisions about content, providing subject matter expertise, and writing or contributing to and approving labels. In this model, the curator acts in part as a facilitator who convenes and guides the process, documents the content developed by the group, and puts it into the formats needed, such as an exhibit script.

A guest curator is a model in which the individual is essentially taking on all the roles of the curator in place of or in collaboration with a museum's curator. A combination model that has garnered critical acclaim recently—both for its approach to collaborative curation and for the content of the exhibition—is the School for Advanced Research's (SAR) *Grounded in Clay: The Spirit of Pueblo Pottery* exhibition.[32] SAR worked with more than sixty "collaborators" on the project who could simply select an item from SAR's Indian Arts Research Center collection and write the label or opt to do more. In other words, beyond contributing to the catalog and the exhibit through a written label, participants were able to determine their level of participation.

Each participant received a travel stipend that could be applied toward visiting the exhibition in one of the cities in which it was displayed, and they could also request a certain amount of funds to propose projects that would allow them to give back to their home communities. At the start, participants were provided with a copy of everyone's entries for the items they selected and were asked to identify the big takeaways and major themes across all entries to inform the exhibition's initial design. Since this was a traveling exhibit, each institution was required to give two presentations of the exhibition design to the participants for their feedback. The director of SAR's Indian Arts Research Center, Elysia Poon, described how additional outcomes emerged:

> Everything was loosely structured . . . even project components were often developed as we progressed (by the end, we had a documentary, short film clips, activity book, curriculum, a ton of programming, and more). What was amazing was that because the projects themselves were coming from the community, funders seemed to be willing to go along with us on this serendipitous journey and we were always able to meet our fundraising needs. Basically, being able to glom on to that serendipity and to have

trust in an intentionally informal process (within reason, because yes, we had a set date for opening!) worked really well for us and allowed us to develop trust and for people to feel engaged in the project.[33]

An important part of operating at the intersection of exhibition and community is to manage expectations and be transparent about the process. For example, you may want to discuss: what is our time line? Why and how do we want the community to participate? Who will make decisions, and how? Does everyone have a good idea of what is expected, from whom, by when?

Community updates can be a part of any effort, regardless of what kind of content development model you choose. You can share project plans and progress through tribal steering committees or advisers, tribal news and radio stations, and Facebook. Based on years of experience and research, here are some notes to keep in mind. Every community and every situation is different, so you and your staff or fellow community members can decide whether these suggestions apply to your experience:

- Collaboration will likely make a project take longer and be more expensive, but the results often include much greater community interest and sense of investment in the exhibit produced.
- The process is just as or even more important than the product if you want the community to be invested in and feel ownership over the outcomes of your project. A content development process that honors and values trust, transparency, and open-mindedness and treats its contributors with respect will produce something beyond an exhibit people are happy with: it will provide productive and positive relationship building in the community. If these values and respect break down during the process, then the relationship between the museum and the community can be placed in jeopardy.
- If you invite community members to participate (and give their time, share their knowledge), it is important to honor their contributions. You do not want to invite people to participate and then discount their contributions or say they have decision-making power and then ignore their suggestions. Explain how their contributions will inform the process and content development, especially if there is not enough room to include them all in the final exhibit text.
- Be sure to arrange a special opening for the people who helped develop the content, before the official opening. Perhaps you can have a meal together. It is very important that community contributors have time to visit with the work they helped create before the public enters the

space. Sometimes, people may want to do a blessing or have quiet time in the exhibit space. This is a way to thank and honor them for their contributions and is also a very meaningful moment for the staff and teams who have worked with them on the exhibits.

The curator is often the person in exhibit development who has an existing relationship with the originating community or communities whose items or knowledge are to become part of an exhibit. This places the curator in the position of advocating for a community in their workplace or sometimes mediating between a community and a large bureaucratic institution. It can be discouraging if a curator's commitments and community relationship are not prioritized in larger museum decision making. Whether curator or community member, be strategic about choosing which hills you are willing to die on, as they say! It can be a challenging space to manage, so it is important to not over-promise, to be honest, and to keep everyone informed as the process and project evolve.

19
Interpretation and Display

How anthropology research and collections are interpreted is another area where we have learned a lot from Native community members. Curators are often taught or expected to work with originating communities regarding content and label text, but exhibit mounts and color schemes and fabrication materials are other avenues for collaboration as well. In this section interpretation refers to label writing and visual strategies, and display refers to how things are arranged and articulated in space.

As the old saying goes, you never get a second chance to make a first impression. (I believe in second chances, but still! This is an important reminder.) Exhibits and their interpretation are the audience's first encounter with the museum, including Native visitors who may be part of the general public or passing through on the way to a collections visit or repatriation consultation. Exhibitions—their visuals, collections on display, content, and tone—affect whether Native community members feel welcome in the museum. The museum is already a difficult space for many Native individuals to walk into;

if you get this wrong, such as by having Native ancestors on display, it can derail a project and jeopardize your relationship.

While developing an interpretive strategy and labels, consider: who is the intended audience? What do you want visitors to feel? What do you want people to keep in mind after they leave as a result of the experience? Some additional considerations when working with Native cultural items, photographs, and archives include: what is and is not appropriate to share with the public? What language should we use to model for the audience how best to talk about Native experiences and cultural items, according to the communities themselves? Are we avoiding playing into existing stereotypes? Even better, are we actively working against them? Are we replacing ignorance with appropriate knowledge in a way that is responsible and respectful to communities and visitors?

In label writing, active voice is key, especially when talking about Native history and colonialism. Passive voice tends to leave a perpetrator out of sight. It is the difference between "they were massacred" and "the colonists massacred them." Also consider whose voice is represented in the label. Who are the "we" and the "they" represented in the language of the text? Is there an authoritative and anonymous museum voice, or is it multi-vocal? How will credit be attributed to Indigenous community members who worked on the content or labels? Will there be signed labels, so to speak, or a credit panel where the authors of each section are identified?

Educational interactives represent another interpretative strategy that can highlight Native perspectives. One of my all-time favorites is the Catlin Cubes at the Denver Art Museum (figure 2.4).[34] On the wall next to a painting of a Mandan ceremony by George Catlin was a display with eighteen cubes tucked into cubbyholes around the question "Why is this considered one of the most controversial paintings in the museum?" The painting was of a Mandan sacred ceremony. Each cube had a question on one side and the phrase "it depends on who you ask," with different people's answers on the other sides of the cube. It was a physical and an intuitive way to communicate perspective and include Native community members' points of view.

Questions included: why is this painting important? How do American Indians feel about Catlin today? What were Catlin's motivations? Does this painting exploit a sacred scene? Was Catlin a racist? Is this painting factually accurate? Did Catlin sensationalize? Is this a good painting? Was Catlin a sympathetic or prejudiced observer? On the cube with the question "why is this painting important," Calvin Grinnell, cultural preservation resource

FIGURE 2.4. Catlin Cubes, Denver Art Museum. Interpretive text and photograph. © Denver Art Museum.

specialist for the Mandan, Hidatsa and Arikara Nation, answered in 2006: "I would say that in the study of our people, we owe a lot to people like Catlin ... we complement that information with our oral tradition." On "does this painting exploit a sacred scene," the answers on each side of the cube included one by Lyle Gwin (Mandan/Hidatsa) in 2003, who said "whether it's fortunate or unfortunate," future generations will need Catlin's paintings because no one is telling these stories and they weren't written down; former NMAI director Rick West Jr. (Southern Cheyenne) in 2002 called him a "crass huckster trading on other people's lives and lifeways," and Catlin himself wrote in 1841 (also on the cube), "upon [my sketching] they looked with decided distrust and apprehension, as a sort of theft or sacrilege."

These kinds of interactives or interpretive displays do not always have to be made in-house. There are times when exhibits have been up for a long time and there is no capacity or intention to overhaul them at the moment. One strategy you might consider is inviting originating community members or Native artists to do interventions—create alternative labels, mark up existing labels, install a pop-up counter exhibit, or propose other ways to reframe an exhibition or reorient the space to a different perspective and narrative.[35] If that is not possible, consider hosting a public program with a panel discussion of responses to the exhibition or inviting a group of Native artists, scholars, or originating community members to do something like an "Excellent Judges" review of the exhibition to provide leadership with insight for future initiatives.[36]

Design is another area to consider. In 2008 I was invited to give a talk at Musqueam 101 in Vancouver, British Columbia, a seminar by the University of British Columbia that is hosted at Musqueam First Nation. I talked about the development of the inaugural exhibitions at the National Museum of the American Indian, specifically the community curating process for developing exhibit content. Afterward, the community gifted me a book, *Musqueam: A Living Culture*, published in 2006.[37] The book is remarkable. It has remained one of my favorite books of all time because it invited me to expand my ideas about what is possible in collaborative exhibition development and interpretation, and it gave me new questions to ask when working with Native communities on creative projects. This book is a guide for anyone working with Musqueam First Nation on museum exhibits or other kinds of display. It includes what materials, colors, and language to use, and what not to use, when representing Musqueam. It includes, in clear language, "dos" and "don'ts" and glossy full-color pages to give a sense of the design feel. I *loved* it!

I was inspired by it. But it wasn't until more than ten years later that I finally figured out how to apply that inspiration, which I shared in my discussion of the Mesa Verde National Park redesign in chapter 11.

Even mounts in the exhibit can be culturally informed or reflect preferences of the originating community. For example, the Denver Art Museum hung a Navajo chief's blanket as if it were being worn around the shoulders rather than displaying it flat, like art on a wall. At History Colorado, Ute tribal members directed that a feather bonnet be placed in a museum exhibit. A special mount had to be constructed so the cap and long feather train could stand upright, as if being worn.[38] This is all to say, if you are working with communities, don't restrict their input or your questions to content alone.

As to the "feel" of an exhibition, the words I most often use are *vibrant* and *contemporary*. When I first arrived at the CU Museum, the anthropology hall was painted in browns and "muddy mauve," as I used to call it. After I talked about this with the exhibit designer, without any specific colors discussed, the hall was repainted in bright greens and blues. It was refreshing and energizing. That idea of actively working against stereotypes is not just about text and content; it can happen in design, too—the colors you choose, the fonts and visuals. Especially when working with designers who have not engaged directly with Indigenous communities, unconscious bias can sometimes come forward unintentionally. I remember when we worked with a design team in Taiwan for the iShare website and they sent us the prototype, which was all in sepia tones—the horror! We simply asked them to provide something more lively, more contemporary, and they returned with a steel-blue gray and sans serif font. Designers sometimes need adjectives to work with, so think ahead as to what those might be to best represent the desired outcomes of your collaboration.

Another thing to consider is how you might extend reciprocity to the communities who contribute to an exhibition. For example, can you take the exhibit or content that has been developed and make it more accessible to the community, perhaps through an online exhibit or a digital publication? Is there an opportunity to create a traveling exhibit, a simple banner exhibit, or a pop-up exhibit in the community—perhaps at a cultural center, tribal college, elder center, or high school? How else might you utilize the materials developed in your collaboration beyond the museum's walls?

Finally, a provocation to museums and communities alike: if a Native community is partnering with a museum to create an exhibition, I find it is easy to guess what it will look like and what it will include. I think this is because of a failure of our education system. That sounds like a big leap, but here's what I mean: Native communities and individuals still feel the need to establish in these spaces that "we are still here." That was the message in 1999 when I worked on the inaugural exhibitions for the NMAI, and it is also the main message the Pueblos and Tribes wanted to communicate in a project I was involved in at Mesa Verde National Park twenty years later (see chapter 11, "For Example"). In general, Americans do not know Native history; it is not part of the story of America that they learn growing up. So, when provided with a venue to speak to the public, Native communities start with "we are here, and this is who we are." Imagine if it could be taken for granted that the public knows these national and local stories of Native presence and perseverance and they could move on to other stories. NMAI's Native Knowledge 360 is attempting to fill the gap in school curricula, but until the school texts and educational system are more inclusive, we still have a lot of work to do in museums to get those stories out there.

20
Community Engagement across the Museum

Community engagement is not just about repatriation, exhibition development, and curatorial practice. It can happen in many ways at the museum—when you host programs with Native scholars or performers or comedians, when you lend space to artists to create or sell their work, when you share your space with the community for their own events at no cost, when you host Native interns in different departments, and more. Community engagement can also happen outside the museum, including creating a pop-up exhibit in a tribal college, hosting a workshop about how to clean and repair baskets at a cultural center, providing a virtual presentation to a reservation classroom, or bringing collection items to a high school so teachers can connect youth to their heritage through lesson plans and close looking exercises.

If you are a museum anthropologist with training in cross-cultural communication and valuing other ways of knowing, with experience in repatriation consultation or community-based research, invite museum staff to consider doing these kinds of engagements and offer yourself as a resource to those who may want to include collaboration with Indigenous communities as part of their work. If you are a Native community member, consider asking a museum to think creatively with you about opportunities that can take place in your community rather than in the museum.

Often, museum staff may not know where to start—they may be concerned about doing something inappropriate, not knowing where they can find resources or who to contact to develop this kind of program. They may not feel comfortable reaching out to communities to begin a conversation. Below are some additional ideas about how museums can broaden their engagement with communities. Invite community partners and museum colleagues and staff to come up with more ideas!

First and foremost, develop recruitment strategies to increase the number of applicants and the hiring of Native individuals. If you don't have funds to hire someone, consider applying for grants for temporary hires and fundraising for endowed positions. Place tribal members in positions to influence decision making in the museum: for example, inviting them to be members of the institution's board, creating a Native advisory board, or appointing a tribal liaison. You can contract Native cultural specialists to be guest curators, lead educational activities, give scholarly talks, or lead workshops. You can also commission artwork for exhibitions or provide space for Native artists to come in and sell their works in the museum.

Consider the museum store, if you have one, as another place to showcase your values and center relations with communities. For example, include contemporary Native art, books authored by Indigenous people, and items made by community members whose heritage is represented in the museum. Do an audit of what is sold in the store to ensure the products are ethically sourced and culturally appropriate. I remember walking into the store of a museum that had asked me to help improve its community relations, and front and center was a book that lauded itself for providing Native symbols and art that did not break copyright laws. Review everything from exhibits, to the website, to docent training, to the store to ensure that that your value-centered practice at the museum and your relationships with communities are not inadvertently undermined.

21

Acknowledgment and Compensation

Whether in exhibits, catalog record updates, research projects, public programs, or other activities, you need to consider appropriate acknowledgment of community partners and appropriate compensation for their time. The work they do with a museum is often not their day job—it is important to compensate them for the time they allocate to your project or program as you would any consultant or specialist. For too long, museums relied on volunteered time and knowledge from communities while museum professionals doing the same work were paid. It's important to discuss this up front so it's factored into any collaborative work as much as possible.[39]

Part of getting this right is planning ahead to have the resources you need to do this work (see chapter 42, "Grant Writing for Collaborative Projects"). It can be uncomfortable to discuss compensation, but it is now standard practice for museums and institutions that are engaging with Native individuals or community representatives as experts, content contributors, or reviewers. Honoraria are expected by those who contribute to institutional programs or projects. National Park Service and other institutions have standard rates. Compensation is less the norm for research projects outside of museums but should be included when possible.

If you are a small museum, student exhibit, or other unfunded effort, do not assume that you cannot do this kind of work. If you are unable to secure enough funding to provide the kind of compensation described above, once you know what you have available, be upfront and honest. Don't assume that community members will not participate without monetary compensation—but also do not assume that they will. Talk to them honestly about your resources and capacity and ask if they want to participate. Invite them to identify appropriate ways to honor their time and commitment. Perhaps together you will come up with something that feels right in ensuring mutual benefit. Consider other ways to reciprocate: propose and invite ideas from community partners to show gratitude and respect for people's time commitments such as bringing them food, offering to conduct comprehensive searches on their heritage in museums and archives, offering museum space for free for community use, or volunteering time to support activities and events in the community. They may agree to carry forward with you. They may also, understandably, say no.

Acknowledgment includes naming contributors in your work, whether in publications or exhibitions. The days of the pseudonym or anonymized community are over, unless requested or agreed to by community partners for their safety or other reasons. The point is, there have to be explicit and agreed-upon reasons. In the past, anthropologists would write entire manuscripts and claim them as their own work without acknowledging that they were based on the knowledge of Native individuals and sometimes even edited or written by them. Depending on the collaboration or contribution, there is a spectrum of ways to credit people. Works can be coauthored, authored "with" someone; contributors can be identified in acknowledgments or quoted in the text. The same goes for museum exhibits. Contributors can be quoted on the wall, named in credit panels, or listed as authors of particular text labels. Each label in the NMAI's inaugural exhibits was authored, whether by a curator or community members. Their names were below specific label sections. This was done in part to acknowledge their contributions and also to recognize that who is speaking matters. Authored labels by originating communities, then and especially now, can bring value and legitimacy to an exhibition that features their cultural belongings, histories, or experiences.

22
Teaching Museum Anthropology

Some classes I have taught that have drawn on museum anthropology include Introduction to Museum Anthropology (a split graduate/undergraduate course focused on the subfield), Introduction to Museum Studies (a graduate course in which students choose a museum ethnography to read as part of a museum professions assignment), Exploration of a Non-Western Culture–Native North America (an undergraduate introductory course that included a week-long unit on museums, a case study about NMAI, and a class about repatriation), and Collections Research in Cultural Anthropology (described in detail in For Example, below).

When I taught Introduction to Museum Anthropology to undergraduates, I invited students to consider that exhibits are created by people, that there are decisions and compromises on the way to the finished display, and that those decisions and compromises result from personal perspectives, deadlines, funding issues, and more. We ask who wrote the labels, and for whom? We deconstruct the exhibit as seeming like something that was always supposed to be that way and the labels as the disembodied authoritative museum voice. Through that process, we see how people and their circumstances and beliefs affect what comes to be seen as authoritative knowledge. Different peoples, or different times, might have resulted in a different exhibit. Then, we take that process of deconstruction and look at change over time through the concrete example of museum exhibits, which makes it easier to realize that the "way things are" today is not natural. Next, we expand this process to how we understand textbooks, news, and all the narratives we consume. Once we realize that the status quo is not just the way things are, that it is a result of actions by people over time, it is easier to identify colonial assumptions and narratives in the past and feel empowered to make change.

The kinds of changes advocated for in this book are happening right now in some museums; for others, they will come with a new generation of museum professionals. I am confident about this because of what I have seen in my classrooms and in discussions with students across the country. Students take repatriation for granted as something museums should do. They appreciate the greater purpose of supporting contemporary communities through their professional work in museums, and they are committed to increasing diversity, equity, and inclusion in museums. This book's orientation is not a hard sell for emerging museum professionals, in my experience at least.

Bringing more Native community members into the field can still be a challenge, given the history of anthropology and museums. Creating a welcoming space in the classroom is essential, which includes paying attention to the language, content, and sources we use.[40] In the museum studies program at the University of Colorado Boulder, we worked hard to create a reputation through practice, publication, and networking so Native individuals who want to work in museums considered our program welcoming of their perspectives and aspirations. It took ten years to establish the program and gain standing that was trusted. These things take time. Factors outside our control may arise in other areas of the institution that jeopardize this reputation, so educating colleagues and leadership on how to maintain this trust was essential.

Whether you are teaching museum anthropology or museum studies students, mentoring anthropology graduate students who engage with Native communities, or supervising interns in a museum or a Native cultural center—these are the individuals who will be driving changes in our field for years to come. They are committed Native and non-Native individuals who we have the privilege to work with and who will shape what museums can be and can become. Below is a more detailed description of one course that sought to reflect and contribute to the changes we are seeing in the field.

23
For Example

Collections Research Course in Cultural Anthropology

I am a big fan of sharing how we do what we do and why—in exhibits and other public formats like blogs and public talks and in ways that the public and community members can access. I love teaching students how to do the same, whether they are in museum studies or in anthropology (see also chapter 46, "Teaching Collaborative and Public Anthropology"). I taught a practicum in collections research in cultural anthropology that was cross-listed between both programs. Similar to how the Introduction to Museum Anthropology course provided a way for students to more concretely understand that all knowledge is constructed, this course provided students with a more concrete way to understand colonialism and duress, ingenuity and resilience, and other lifeways and worldviews through learning from and engaging with cultural items in the museum—sometimes relating to their own communities of origin but more often made by other peoples.

I developed the course based on my experience as one of the first faculty fellows in the Smithsonian National Museum of Natural History's Summer Institute in Museum Anthropology (SIMA) in the summer of 2015. Until then, SIMA had focused on training graduate students to view anthropology collections as a site for theoretically engaged research. The faculty fellowship focuses on "teaching the teachers" to help disseminate the SIMA model for teaching collections research. Part of SIMA's commitment to dissemination also includes providing a lesson repository where faculty fellows' course materials are publicly available.[41]

At the conclusion of the SIMA program, I was asked to give a presentation about what I learned through this new fellowship. The title of my presentation was "SIMA as a Teaching Model for Engaging University Collections." My talk began with "Confessions of a Non-Object Centered Curator." My work to date had involved curating exhibits with Native communities, conducting repatriation consultations, and connecting communities to collections in various other ways such as online interactive websites and collections visits. The focus of my work had not been the objects themselves but rather providing access to them and facilitating relationships between communities and collections.

So, while objects were central to my relations with communities and I had worked with objects in exhibition development, they were not the focus of my research inquiry. After a repatriation consultation with Mandan, Hidatsa and Arikara (MHA) Nation community members, I asked if there was anything more they wanted to learn or have us research about the MHA items housed in our museum in Colorado. They asked us to conduct an oral history video project about the collection donor. This was an exciting opportunity, and we began a video documentary project—but it also moved us away from researching the collection itself. On one of my visits to the community, I brought a big binder filled with photos of all the MHA items housed in our museum. As we were flipping through the pages, a community member asked about an item, and I didn't know what it was or what it was used for. I felt unprepared, and irresponsible, and the situation highlighted a particular oversight in my training and practice. I noticed this oversight in other areas of my work as well. For instance, I taught a course Research Methods in Cultural Anthropology about ethnographic methods to graduate students in the anthropology department. I had incorporated a unit on archives, but there was no unit on collections research.

The SIMA teaching model places objects first in the research process, and each curriculum unit is accompanied by "object lessons" in which instructors use items from the vast anthropology collections at the National Museum of Natural History. Dr. Candace Greene encouraged students to "sit with the object," to really spend time with it. We often have a look at a collection item and then, as was my predilection before being a SIMA faculty fellow, jump straight to the documentation and archives, seeking context and text—something we are more comfortable with reviewing, interpreting, understanding. But we learned from Dr. Greene and other instructors what an extraordinary amount there is to read from the object itself: from its materials to its use-wear, its design and shape, its smell, and the traces of the hand of its maker. We became skeptical of associated documentation and learned how to critique the reliability of the information at hand. We learned how to situate this item within broader historical and social contexts and in broader questions of theory in anthropology—such as gendered practice, relations of power, economic changes over time, and others.

I brought the SIMA teaching model back to our anthropology and museum studies programs through the establishment of the cross-listed course ANTH 4470/5470, MUSM 5912 Practicum: Collections Research in Cultural Anthropology. I wanted our students at the University of Colorado to experience what I witnessed among the students at SIMA: an amazing transformation as they honed their questions, research design, and theoretical approach to the materials over the course of the semester.

The Anthropology Section of the University of Colorado Museum of Natural History includes more than 1.5 million collection items and nearly 50,000 associated images. The collections are primarily archaeological, but the section also houses around 7,000 cultural items from all over the world, with emphasis on the US Plains and Southwest. The archaeology collections had been extensively studied over time and used in practicum classes. The ethnographic collections had been placed in displays throughout the years, but they were not a focus of curatorial research except for the Navajo textiles (I was the first cultural anthropology curator hired in the museum, in 2009). The collection, and our institution, seemed a perfect place to implement the SIMA teaching model. It was also a great opportunity for me to engage in collections-based pedagogy and research.

Semester-long SIMA-like courses can engage students in university museum collections that are often used by outside researchers but less so by students. Through teaching SIMA-like classes, we can encourage university faculty to move beyond viewing the university museum as simply a source of borrowed objects for class, and we can show students that a museum has more potential for learning than just earning extra credit for visiting an exhibit. By engaging the anthropology collections as a site for research, students can learn skills in primary research, help increase the documentation of collections, highlight the value and relevance of the museum to the wider campus and its administration, and be accountable to communities beyond the academy.

I adapted the intense four-week SIMA program into sixteen weeks; the largest class was thirteen students. I added a unit about connecting collections to communities and the opportunity for students to exhibit their work in the university's museum. This course was open to both undergraduates and graduates, and it broadened research engagement with the anthropology collections. It also brought greater attention to student work, the university museum, and anthropology collections through public events and exhibits.

Over the course of the semester, students were asked to take on roles beyond that of student—researcher, curator, exhibit developer, public speaker. To do this, we needed to establish a sense of community and shared values in the course; set clear expectations by providing examples of research articles and learning to do something as a group before being asked to do it on one's own; demonstrate mutual respect and support to facilitate honest and productive critical feedback; and encourage individual autonomy and sense of discovery.

Through independent projects, the course introduced students to collections research. Through a group project, it introduced them to exhibit content development. There were no prerequisites for the course, and it was open to students in any major or field. Students utilized the anthropology collections in the CU Museum to gain skills in primary and secondary research, collections and object research, and narrative story development for an exhibition. This class could not have functioned without the museum studies graduate assistants, who acted as both students and collections managers, facilitating student access to collections spaces. A goal of the course was to have students think critically about the collection and interpretation of anthropological items in the museum. While two-thirds of the ethnographic collections are from North America, over half the students chose to research collections from beyond this region. As a by-product of students selecting the collections they studied, the museum learned about and better documented cultural items in the museum that were beyond the typical scope of collecting and research, and there are now improved records and knowledge of these items.

The assignments and reading materials closely followed the SIMA graduate program, including a major research project about an item or group of items in the collection. The assignments were designed to build on each other and prepare students for each step in their research process.[42] There was one major addition: for this course, students also produced a group-curated public exhibit in the museum's anthropology hall. This meant that the students had to adapt how they communicated their research project and findings to three different audiences and in different media: (1) the discipline of museum anthropology: they wrote a paper using the guidelines of the journal *Museum Anthropology*; (2) a general audience: they gave a five- to ten-minute public talk in the museum that was advertised to museum members and the university (the time depended on the number of students in the class); and (3) museumgoers of all ages: they produced an exhibit in the anthropology hall incorporating examples from each student's research project.

For the exhibit, I provided the structure, and the students decided on the theme and collaboratively wrote the introductory and concluding panels. This is how we managed to complete an exhibit within a semester's time. It was a "work in progress" exhibit until the public talks at the end of the semester, when the final object labels and concluding text panel were installed. This approach achieved several things: it reduced exhibit design staff involvement and labor, it kept the students thinking about communicating what they were learning to the public, and it took the audience behind the scenes of exhibit making as the exhibit changed from week to week. Students placed representative items in the exhibit cases, with no text labels, and wrote an introductory panel for the exhibit. Clipboards with basic object information hung in the exhibit, and students filled out notes on the clipboards to share what they were learning each week as they engaged in collections research. At the end of the semester, they made final selections of items for display, created a concluding panel for the exhibit, created brief identifying labels for each item,[43] and composed seventy-five-word text panels that represented each student's project. The clipboards remained below the text panels to reveal the research process and highlight that curators make choices to distill what they learn into such short labels.

For the course to succeed, students needed access to collections and collection records. They also needed space to work with collection items during and outside of class. The museum hosts a museum studies graduate program, including training future anthropology collection managers and exhibit developers. Students in the program acted as researchers and as collections managers or exhibit developers in this course, preparing and pulling collection items for students and managing and editing the collaborative writing of exhibition labels. This gave these future museum professionals résumé-building experience. It also increased the quality of the course, as one undergraduate noted in a course evaluation: "I really appreciated the structure of the course and like how collaborative the course is overall between students and across undergrad and grad students. I've never experienced such a successful meshing of the different groups before and it was great to not only learn from the professor, or the texts for my project, but from everyone in class. It really became a community rather than a class."

Assignments included a series of short online quizzes and "process papers," which helped guide students through the research process and ensure that I had opportunities to give direct feedback on their ideas and written work. Students were required to submit ten of sixteen short quizzes, which included prompts like "brainstorming your collections interests," allowing me to match their interests to potential collections; "any concerns about the work plan," checking in and answering questions; "what objects will you photograph," preparing them for assignments that were coming due; "identify a thesis in your research for content development," inviting them to talk to me directly about how they wanted to frame the interpretation of the collection item(s) they were researching; "what are the challenges you are facing at this point in your project"; and "what is the narrative you have planned to present your work to the public?" The three process papers included a work plan outlining the scope of their independent research project, a research design document that included the research problem and how the students would go about answering it, and a final research paper outline. Students included a short half-page "afterthoughts" essay for each of these assignments and their final paper. I read these reflections about their concerns, challenges, and lessons learned before evaluating their assignments. Along the way, students experienced the excitement of discovery, the flow of hands-on work and attention to detail, and the satisfaction of contributing something that has impact and meaning beyond the classroom.

One thing I loved about the course is that it created an opportunity for students to do primary research. I had the experience—more than once—of a student bounding into the classroom, excited, telling me and the students present how they found the most amazing book! Or they talked to a scholar who filled in so many gaps! Or they got an email back from the originating community about display protocols. It was exciting when they found a piece of information that unlocked an item's origin, use, purpose. It's an absolute joy to see the thrill of seeking and finding knowledge. We talked about collections research as though it is detective work—finding clues and following them, being skeptical and seeking corroborating evidence, piecing together a best-fit story based on what we learn. Evidence comes from the object itself, the associated documentation, books and articles (and clues to follow in their bibliographies), and talking to experts, which can be scholars or originating community members, when appropriate.

We not only expanded what counts as research for students (look beyond text), but we also expanded the way they conceptualize and think about research. One of the assignments we read is about the research process itself, and it was a surprise to see how much the students appreciated the article and its message. We reviewed Carol Kuhlthau and coauthors' study that identified how students refer to many tasks as the same thing: "research."[44] When I asked if this article was helpful, students insisted that it be included in any future iterations of the class. The authors show that by breaking down the "research" process into initiation, selection, exploration, formulation, and collection, students feel a greater sense of progress. After "research" is complete, the final step is presentation. The other point the article makes is not to let the ease of access to certain kinds of information drive the research questions or process. We often don't discuss research at this process level in university classrooms, but it served the course and students well in my experience. I checked in each week, and students could point to their current task in the research cycle.

In addition, students had to connect their research questions to anthropological concepts. As a result, they produced research papers about, for example, Indigenous agency in collecting encounters in the Pacific, the construction and meaning of basket hats and the artwork of contemporary Native artists in California, gender and livelihoods in Peru, and the relationship between Indigenous ingenuity and market forces in the Southwest.

But what made the course unique for students was its hands-on activities and workshop-like quality. We met for three hours once a week, which enabled us to incorporate activities with collections during class. Like the quizzes and process papers, we did things together in class before I asked students to do them on their own for their individual research projects. We dedicated class time to learning object handling, close looking, reviewing and evaluating associated documentation, and object photography. I will describe a few of the activities we did in class.

One exercise that had a big impact was when I invited students to bring objects from home to class. I adapted this activity from Dr. Sue Rowley's presentation in a conference panel about pedagogy at the Council for Museum Anthropology conference in 2017.[45] Students were asked to bring in a "personal object." During class, each student passed the object to the person to their right and asked that person to describe it. After everyone had a chance to speak, we passed the item back to its owner and asked them to describe it. Then we reflected on the difference between the two sets of descriptions and how those different perspectives might affect, or be excluded from, collections research and museum exhibits. Most often the change is from identification or physical description to context and meaning for the owner. We debriefed about this discussion's application to thinking about how an originating community versus a museum curator might interpret an item.

We did a number of close looking exercises in class to prepare students for researching their own object selections. The first was an ingenious activity devised by Dr. Candace Greene. We read Sir Arthur Conan Doyle's *Sign of Four* (published in 1890), which includes Sherlock Holmes's deductions about a pocket watch.[46] Then in class we passed around and looked closely at the details of a colleague's pocket watch, essentially doing the same thing Holmes did in Doyle's essay. Like I said, detective work! Students discussed observation versus deduction. As the watch was passed around, each student announced an observation and I wrote it on the board. As we went, students looked up clues online about the make and model of the watch and when it might have been made, attempting to deduce what kind of person may have used this watch and even who specifically it might have belonged to. In the end, considering my connections and the blue marks and scuffs on the watch that were likely from the pocket of a pair of jeans, they eventually (with some hints) got to archaeologist Dr. Steve Lekson. It was really fun. After they did a lot of sleuthing online, I often had to remind them that the collector was sitting in front of them; what questions did they have? We did this same exercise again with a carving from Iqaluit in Nunavut, Canada, that had the artist's signature on the bottom.

During another class, each student selected an item from the anthropology collection to describe and draw. They were given forty-five minutes to an hour to spend with the item. At first they mumbled and seemed skeptical about the amount of time dedicated to this task—but after an hour of drawing and annotating their drawings, they talked about what more they noticed and how relaxing it was to do this in the midst of what felt like the otherwise hectic pace of school and life. We later did an exercise in which we took an item we had done close looking with and turned to the various museum records to see what more we could learn. I provided a relevant article from *American Indian Art Magazine*, along with a stack of issues of the magazine, for students to peruse during a break to see what collections research articles might look like (the magazine has great color photos and an online searchable index). In another example, we viewed a hide scraper from the collection. Attention to its grooves and patina can suggest how the person who used the scraper held it due to its wear patterns and whether they were left- or right-handed. By placing our hands in the grooves of the scraper and then reviewing photos online, we learned that the way the scraper is held is not how the students originally imagined.

We also engaged with collections during class to talk about issues of interpretation, naming, and contextualizing objects. Students viewed an item on the table, such as a pot, and discussed, is this art or artifact? Why? A sash: art or artifact? Why? What if we place the sash in the context of a wedding outfit or among a set of sashes from around the world? This led students to discuss issues of labels, intellectual frames, and assumptions. What different kinds of questions might we have with these different juxtapositions and frames?

Another powerful object exercise comes from my colleague and senior museum educator Jim Hakala. He uses different objects for this activity. One time he passed around a coin and asked each student, as they held and handled it, to provide a one-word observation. They said "shiny, metal, circular." He then told a personal story about the coin and passed it around a second time. He asked the students to again state a one-word observation; this time they said "difficult, kindness, sad." Jim emphasized the difference between a top hat and Abraham Lincoln's top hat, and how we come to understand items differently when they are interpreted through stories. He explained that we can think about interpretation as tangible (first observations), intangible (second observations), and finally the aim: universal, something people can connect to, such as universal themes of generosity, compassion. When someone walks away, what do you want them to remember? What Jim was asking students to do, in part, was imagine an audience for their research and think about how their interpretation might impact others.

As noted above, students were required to adapt how they communicate their research to three different audiences: the discipline of museum anthropology, a general audience, and museumgoers of all ages. We discussed how the language and genre of communication is different for a journal article, a public talk, and a museum exhibit. And students developed their presentation and public speaking skills, including how to devise a main message for a talk or an exhibit label. When the audience for their efforts was broader than just their professor, they felt a greater sense of responsibility in their coursework. In short, it became more than an assignment or a requirement to fulfill. This greater sense of purpose led to great projects that often surprised the students themselves with what they accomplished. As a teacher, this is wonderful to witness.

The exhibit was a mechanism through which students grappled with the challenges of representation, language, interpretation, selection of items for display, word count, and agreeing on a theme. They had to decide what was important to communicate and articulate why they made that decision. The exhibit was also a manifestation of their semester-long work and what they learned together over time—in a format that their peers, family (for graduating students), and the wider community would see. To prepare for creating the exhibit, we read articles like Pauline Turner Strong's "Exclusive Labels," which inspired us to interrogate who are the "we" and "them" inferred in label text;[47] students reviewed online exhibits related to their region or subject matter and discussed and critiqued them together in class; and we read a practical guideline on how to create an exhibit from the Smithsonian Institution's Traveling Exhibit Service titled "Show Off Your Story: How to Create an Exhibition." We discussed what the main message is in museum exhibits and did in-class workshops to create the exhibit's introduction label early in the semester and the concluding panel, when students could reflect on all they had learned.

We also workshopped their object labels, asking, what are your goals for the label? What effect do you want it to have on visitors? What do you want them to feel? What mood should be set through text and design? Students wrote a quick draft, then brought it to class to read out loud and get group feedback. We set aside one class for a consultation with our museum's exhibit developer/designer; each student got one-on-one time to review their selected collection item(s) and draft label with the designer and to receive feedback. Each student also, in rotation, had one-on-one time with me to brainstorm or troubleshoot their project. When students were not with either of us, they were working on their own.

By creating an exhibit together and workshopping their research projects throughout the semester, the students learned not just about their own area of focus but about all the research being conducted in the class. The experience was comparative, and it highlighted the fact that different people ask different questions and that different items with varying amounts of documentation offer different opportunities for research. This was reflected in the concluding panels for each exhibit the students curated. In the exhibit they titled *Questions in Culture*, the 2017 students explained "you are seeing museum studies in practice" and invited visitors to "return weekly as we share new insights on our clipboards about the history, use, and meaning of the objects on display." In their concluding panel, titled "Discussions in Culture," the students noted: "When studying culture—especially a culture not your own—answers often lead to more questions. To care for, display, and interpret museum objects, we must consider their complex histories and the perspectives of originating communities." They concluded: "A common theme in all of our research has been ethics. Who collects objects? Are they collected by anthropologists, artists, travelers, or soldiers? How are they collected? Are they traded in times of economic uncertainty . . . in wartime . . . stolen or looted? Now that we have these objects, what do we do with them? Should we even keep them? There are no easy answers to these questions, but we are advocating for the thoughtful representation of cultural material."[48]

In their introductory panel to the exhibit they titled *The Secret Life of Objects*, the 2019 students asked: "How can objects of material culture help us understand the world around us and those who inhabit it?" They invited visitors to "follow along with us as we make exciting discoveries about our objects each week throughout the Fall 2019 semester—what can you discover about the lives they had and the ones they are still living alongside us?" In their concluding panel, co-written at the semester's end, they stated: "This semester, we learned that while we saw the lives of these objects as secrets to be revealed, they were already known by their originating communities . . . As we hope you can see in this exhibit, we discovered that working together to explore collections from different parts of the world helped us all to better understand and appreciate cultural and global diversity."[49] In some cases they appreciated and demonstrated respect for cultural diversity by not displaying the objects they studied for the exhibit (more on that below).

The exhibit and the public presentations certainly created a sense that the students' work was intended for more than a class. This was an important aspect of the course for students. Even those students who had a fear of public speaking agreed to do the presentation and felt a great sense of accomplishment in the end. Part of the willingness to challenge themselves in this way came from a sense of preparation, practice, and support prior to the public talks. The students learned about how to give a presentation inspired by TED talks. During one class near the end of the semester, they practiced their presentations in one of the university museum's exhibition halls, with microphones and a projector to rehearse the public event. Students filled out a feedback form for the speaker immediately after the talk, and then we invited questions. Each student received feedback forms from all the other students in written and verbal form as well as comments from me as they developed their final presentation. The day of the public event, students gave their revised talks in the classroom as one more practice. During the evening event, students were grouped into themed panels, with question-and-answer sessions at the end of each panel. The public events were well attended and the audience included their peers, family members, professors and museum staff, museum members, and the general public. I videorecorded the talks and provided copies to the students after the conclusion of the course as a thank you and a record of their outstanding work.

In addition to the public talks, the students knew their research would live on in the museum records as associated documentation of the collections—informing future researchers, originating community members, and exhibit developers. Their papers were placed in object files, and aspects of their prose were copied and pasted into our database records. Some of their object photos were attached to the database records as well.

Some students' work went beyond updating records and contributed to exhibitions in our museum. For example, Jesse Dutton Kenny's research was expanded through a graduate assistant position, during which she turned her class project into a three-rotation public exhibit about California baskets at the museum titled *Weaving the World into a Basket*. Undergraduate student Isabella Vinsonhaler's interest in Oceanic collections for her class project alerted us to extensive documentation and field notes in our files about a collector and his relationship to people who lived on Bougainville Island in the late 1940s; this led to an online exhibit (see chapter 38, "For Example").

Other students learned the importance of Native perspectives on collections and how to honor those perspectives in research and exhibitions. One project led us to contact the originating community because the student deduced through close looking that although the item was identified as a replica in the documentation, it seemed to have been used. She contacted the Tribe and learned that it is a ceremonial object and should not be on display. We were happy that the Tribe was now aware of an item it may want to request for repatriation. In her part of the exhibit, the student put a sign in the item's place that indicated it was not appropriate for public display. A similar sign was utilized by a graduate student who wanted to learn about and contribute to the repatriation process. Her research produced a report about an item that was potentially an Apache mask, and we knew the Apache had requested that such items be returned from museums. Her work provided the information necessary to contact the Apache and invite them for a repatriation consultation. Her report, intended to support categories of findings under the law, was provided to a tribal historic preservation officer during a repatriation consultation in May 2019.

A student's inquiry about replica Haudenosaunee masks in our collections led to her exhibiting a similar restricted sign in the exhibit as well as a label that included protocols from the Haudenosaunee about not displaying these types of items. We learned that for this community, replicas are as restricted as original carvings; consequently, we alerted a community member to the fact that we have these kinds of items in our museum. Another student's class project led to her museum studies master's project digitizing Hopi Katsina and Zuni Koko figures in our collection so we could send information about the items to Hopi and Zuni THPOs. We wanted to make the Pueblos aware that these items are at the museum so they can provide collections care guidance and determine which items are appropriate for display and which are not. This project also helped the museum to be more prepared should the Pueblos be interested in doing a repatriation consultation, whenever the time is right for them. Until then, none of these items will be displayed in the museum. These decisions were made to follow the CU Museum Anthropology Section's values and policy. Today, this approach is essential under the 2024 NAGPRA regulations, which prohibit the display of funerary objects, sacred objects, and objects of cultural patrimony without the consent of the affiliated tribe.

While the above were graduate student projects, undergraduate projects led to further work in museum anthropology as well. Aaron LaMaskin studied an item from Japan, then went on to write an honors thesis about a collaboration between Native communities and the Museum of Indian Arts and Culture in Santa Fe, earning the university's Arts and Sciences Student of the Year Award. Madison King's research about a collection of items from the Arctic donated to our museum by an ecologist and his wife—and her discovery of an associated photographic archive in the university library's special collections—turned into a subsequent semester-long independent study with me to research the entire collection, create a report with images, and contact potential originating communities. She later got in touch with Smithsonian curator Dr. Stephen Loring and an archivist in Nunavut who facilitated sending the report to the originating community. Maddie was awarded research funds from the museum program to travel to and access the Hudson Bay archives (canceled due to the pandemic), and she published an essay on the topic in the *Arctic Studies Newsletter*.[50] (A lovely side note: twenty years earlier I was a young research assistant, and Dr. Loring invited me to publish an essay about my fieldwork in Nunavut in the same newsletter!)

A course like this can be maintained in any university that has a collection, a willing instructor, and students who are interested in doing primary research. The research, exhibits, and public presentations the students produced in this course publicly demonstrated the diversity of our collections and allowed me to curate a broader range of items in our museum. Most important, it allowed the students to follow their passion and develop independent research skills. It also increased their understanding of the history and contemporary lives of peoples whose items are in museum collections through a semester-long mentoring process.[51]

To follow the idea of a culture of learning, I want to note that this course was designed with the best intentions and an emphasis on Indigenous perspectives and ethical curatorial practice. The last time I taught it was in 2019. If I were teaching this course today, I would approach it differently, with the 2024 NAGPRA regulations Duty of Care guiding our learning, collections selection, and research process. One example is the mask a graduate student researched and did not display because we believed it may be a cultural item under NAGPRA. Our intention was to gather and provide as much information to the community as possible about the items in our care. A change I would make regarding this and other examples described above is to ask permission from the THPO first before allowing a student to conduct research.

The takeaways from this course that go beyond the classroom include being skeptical of museum records and attribution, asking originating communities for permission to research cultural items, taking time to learn from the items themselves through close looking, connecting items to their communities of origin, and gaining a greater understanding of the history of collecting and museum practice. Pursue this not just in general but very specifically: seek to understand a specific item's biography and journey in the context of the people, lands, regional colonization, and other factors. Ground the broader stories of colonialism, duress, erasure, persistence, ingenuity, cultural knowledge, connection, and beauty in a specific item and a specific community's experience. And plan ahead. The class I described responded to students' interests in the moment, but if I were to teach it again, I would identify collections for potential research in advance and reach out to originating communities to seek approval to include the items in the class, as well as their interest in research or participation, well before the course begins.

24
Questions to Guide Practice and Additional Resources

Some questions to consider when working as a museum anthropologist:
- What are you researching, why, and for whom?
- How might you engage communities in your work?
- How can your research on collections serve communities as well?
- How are you enacting and presenting anthropology—do you talk about "studying" people, or do you envision working together with people on a common goal, project, concern, and so on?
- If an originating community member or a Native individual entered your exhibit or museum, how might they feel about the content, text and language, items on display, mood and design?
- How can you seek mentors and build a professional network with shared values in this field? And, when the time is right, how can you be a mentor to others?
- Is there a plan for compensation when engaging with community members on museum projects?
- Is it appropriate to publicly share cultural information or images of collection items in an exhibit, publication, or website?
- How do the NAGPRA regulations and Duty of Care apply to or guide your research, curation, or teaching?

Museums and Anthropology:
- *Cannibal Tours and Glass Boxes: The Anthropology of Museums* (Ames 1992)
- *Native North American Art* (Berlo and Phillips 1998)
- *Voices of a Thousand People: The Makah Cultural and Research Center* (Erikson 2002)
- *Museums and Source Communities: A Routledge Reader* (Peers and Brown 2003)
- *Mediating Knowledges: Origins of a Zuni Tribal Museum* (Isaac 2007)
- *Decolonizing Museums: Representing Native America in National and Tribal Museums* (Lonetree 2012)
- *Museum as Process: Translating Local and Global Knowledges* (Silverman 2014)

- *Visiting with the Ancestors: Blackfoot Shirts in Museum Spaces* (Peers and Brown 2016)
- *Museums and Anthropology in the Age of Engagement* (Kreps 2020)
- "Decolonizing Museums: Perspectives from Indigenous Museum Professionals" (Echavarri 2021)
- "Pausing, Reflection, and Action: Decolonizing Museum Practices" (Macdonald 2022)
- *Museum Anthropology* journal, a publication of the Council for Museum Anthropology, a section of the American Anthropological Association

Repatriation:

United States
- *Grave Injustice: The American Indian Repatriation Movement and NAGPRA* (Fine-Dare 2002)
- *In the Smaller Scope of Conscience: The Struggle for National Repatriation Legislation, 1986–1990* (McKeown 2012)
- *Accomplishing NAGPRA: Perspectives on the Intent, Impact, and Future of the Native American Graves Protection and Repatriation Act* (Chari and Lavallee 2013)
- *Plundered Skulls and Stolen Spirits: Inside the Fight to Reclaim Native America's Culture* (Colwell 2017)
- "NAGPRA at 30: The Effects of Repatriation" (Nash and Colwell 2020)
- "Repatriation as Pedagogy" (Anderson and Atalay 2023)

Canada
- *We Are Coming Home: Repatriation and the Restoration of Blackfoot Cultural Confidence* (Conaty 2015)
- *Indigenous Repatriation Handbook* (Collison, Bell, and Neel 2019)
- *More than Giving Back: Repatriation Toolkit, a Toolkit in Support of Moved to Action: Activating UNDRIP in Canadian Museums* (Canadian Museums Association 2022)
- *Moved to Action: Activating UNDRIP in Canadian Museums* by the Canadian Museum Association (Danyluk and MacKenzie 2022)
- *UNDRIP and Indigenous Heritage* (Bell and Erikson 2022)
- *Repatriation in Canada: A Guide for Communities* (Bourgeois 2024)

Europe
- *Restitution and Repatriation: A Practical Guide for Museums in England* (Arts Council England 2023)
- "Routes to Return: Working Towards International Repatriation" (Shakespeare 2023)

PART 2 NOTES

1. American Alliance of Museums, "Museums and Trust 2021"; King and Griffiths, "InterConnections."

2. Ames, *Cannibal Tours and Glass Boxes*, 5. See also Ames, *Museums, the Public, and Anthropology*. A chapter title asks and answers its own question: "What Could a Social Anthropologist Do in a Museum of Anthropology? The Anthropology of Museums and Anthropology." Ames also states that museums must be accountable especially to those from whom they collect.

3. It was not just Dr. Ames's book that was inspiring. In 2001, at the request of Musqueam First Nation and university leadership, he was one of three individuals who started the Musqueam 101 seminar at Musqueam First Nation, on whose lands the University of British Columbia (UBC) resides. After Ames, and since 2004, UBC Museum of Anthropology curators Sue Rowley (now director) and Jennifer Kramer, along with Leona Sparrow, continued the seminar. Musqueam 101 is meant to bring together the university and First Nation communities, and each seminar includes a community meal and a guest speaker who presents a subject determined relevant by the Musqueam. I experienced this course when I was invited to be a guest speaker as a postdoc at UBC.

4. Trouillot, *Silencing the Past*.

5. Linenthal, *Preserving Memory*.

6. Kreps, "On Becoming 'Museum-Minded.' "

7. Marsh, *Extinct Monsters to Deep Time*; Macdonald, *Behind the Scenes at the Science Museum*.

8. Erikson, Wachendorf, and Ward, *Voices of a Thousand People*; Isaac, *Mediating Knowledges*.

9. Shannon, *Our Lives*.

10. School for Advanced Research, "Guidelines for Collaboration."

11. School for Advanced Research, "Guidelines for Collaboration," 3–9.

12. At the CU Museum, I commissioned a Navajo first-phase chief's blanket to fill a gap in the textile collection, and we purchased a Navajo textile that featured the twin towers of 9/11.

13. O'Hanlon and Welsch, *Hunting the Gatherers*; Jacknis, *The Storage Box of Tradition*.

14. American Alliance of Museums, "Direct Care of Collections."

15. Wheeler, Arsenault, and Taylor, "Beyond NAGPRA/Not NAGPRA," 8–17.

16. Here I focus on US law because that has been my experience. I include resources for Canadian repatriation at the end of the section. Currently, Canada does not have a NAGPRA-like law but is guided by UNDRIP and the 1992 *Task Force Report on Museums and First Peoples*, which was sponsored jointly by the Assembly of First Nations and the Canadian Museums Association. Repatriation is done on a case-by-case basis under these frameworks.

17. The National NAGPRA website is an excellent source of information and resources, including grants. National Park Service, "Native American Graves Protection and Repatriation Act."

18. Atalay and Shannon, "Completing the Journey."

19. In 2021 Haaland started the Federal Indian Boarding School Initiative, requesting an investigative report from the assistant secretary, and she hired Charles Sands III (Confederated Tribes of the Umatilla Indian Reservation) to head the National Park Service, which has been increasingly open to co-management of federal lands with US tribes.

20. United States Department of the Interior, "Press Release."

21. Jacobs and Small, "Leading Museums Remove Native Displays amid New Federal Rules."

22. *ProPublica*, "The Repatriation Project"; Tran, Healy, and Dungca, "Search the Smithsonian's Records on Human Remains."

23. For more information about the law, which was introduced in 2016, and its inspiration, see Fonseca, "Law Protects Export of Sacred Native American Items from US."

24. Mimiaga, "Burials, Sacred Objects Returned to Tribes."

25. Cornell Law School Legal Information Institute, "Duress."

26. Personal communication, Jaime Arsenault, August 30, 2024. See also Moorehead, *The American Indian in the United States*; Shannon, "Drawing Together."

27. Wheeler, Arsenault, and Taylor, "Beyond NAGPRA/Not NAGPRA."

28. Kopytoff, "The Cultural Biography of Things."

29. Greene, "Plant Fibers in Plains Embroidery."

30. "Obtain free, prior, and informed consent from lineal descendants, Indian Tribes, or Native Hawaiian organizations prior to allowing any exhibition of, access to, or research on human remains or cultural items. Research includes, but is not limited to, any study, analysis, examination, or other means of acquiring or preserving information about human remains or cultural items. Research of any kind on human remains or cultural items is not required by the Act or these regulations" (NAGPRA 10.1(d) Duty of Care).

31. Shannon, *Our Lives*.

32. Brown, "Relationships Carved from Clay Bring New Partners to Museums."

33. Personal communication, Elysia Poon, December 16, 2022.

34. Denver Art Museum, "New Angles on Interpretation in the DAM's New Hamilton Building."

35. For a classic example, see Strong, "Exclusive Labels."

36. For what this kind of review entails, see chapter 37, "Teaching Museum Studies and Professional Development"; Serrell, "Judging Exhibitions."

37. Musqueam Indian Band, *Musqueam: A Living Culture*.

38. Goff et al., "Collaborating beyond Collections."

39. A rare and useful article about compensation for community members who work with communities is McMullen, "The Currency of Consultation and Collaboration."

40. For an example of Māori and Pākehā (non-Indigenous) co-instructors' approach to teaching museum studies together, see McCarthy and Tamarapa, "Teaching a Master's Course on Museums and Māori."

41. All of my course materials and examples of exhibit labels are available at the Smithsonian Summer Institute in Museum Anthropology lesson repository at https://repository.si.edu/handle/10088/105938. Other faculty members have posted their syllabi there as well.

42. The class assignments are to complete ten of sixteen weekly quizzes (20%), an annotated bibliography for the midterm (10%), a digitized collection sample of collection items for student research and exhibit developer consultation (10%), and three "process papers" with reflection essays (30%, 3–6 pages each). The final project (30%) includes a research paper following *Museum Anthropology* journal guidelines, an exhibit label, and a five- to ten-minute public talk.

43. These kinds of labels are frequently referred to as "tombstone labels," but we can choose to change that language going forward. Thanks to the anonymous reviewer who recommended that we stop using this term—a great suggestion!

44. I assign this version to the students: Kuhlthau, "Information Search Process." For a more robust study, see Kuhlthau, Heinström, and Todd, "The 'Information Search Process' Revisited."

45. "Engaging Students and Activating Collections," by Susan Rowley (curator, Museum of Anthropology, University of British Columbia), Museum Anthropology Futures, Council for Museum Anthropology, Saturday, May 27, 2017.

46. Doyle, "Chapter 1."

47. Strong, "Exclusive Labels."

48. *Questions in Culture* (2017) was co-curated by museum and field studies graduate students Claire Steffen, Veronica Rascona, Andrea Blaser, Emma Noffsinger, and Jane Richardson and anthropology seniors Caroline Goussetis and Elise Tomasian.

49. *Secret Life of Objects* (2019) was co-curated by undergraduate students Maddie King, Aaron LaMaskin, Jacks Pastuer, Jack Piephoff, Alexis Thiel, Gina Sandoval-Gibson, Brianna Shriner, Brian Weinberger, and Jade Zimmerman and graduate students Alex Elliott, Patrick Cruz, Ashley Muggli, and Emily Tarantini.

50. King, "The John Marr Collections from Nunavik."

51. Many thanks to Dr. Candace Greene for adding the faculty fellow program to the SIMA experience. This university course would not have been possible without her example, teachings, and vision for supporting and ensuring a promising future of museum anthropology.

FIGURE 3.1. Collections stewardship. Artwork by John Swogger, 2025.

Part 3
Collections Access and Care

This part is dedicated to tribal historic preservation officers (THPOs), elders, cultural specialists, and Native museum professionals. I hope this brings people to your door who are more informed, prepared to start off on the right foot, and ready to build a relationship that leads to meaningful work together in museums. For those, Native or non-Native, who work in museums or steward collections in some other kind of institution or at home, throughout this section I invite you to consider your actions with this in mind: if someone from the originating community came to visit, how would they feel about the way their cultural items are being cared for, organized, documented, accessed, and shared? The biggest takeaway is to not take for granted existing museum practice, purpose, or organization. Be intentional about these things, reconsider and make decisions, don't just follow precedent. You may decide not to make or call for change, but at least it will not be because it was always done this way. Make it a conscious choice for specific reasons. You will be asked why at some point. The field is changing, and it is exciting and rewarding—for all involved—to be a part of this change.

This section focuses on the access to and care of anthropology, history, and other collections relating to Indigenous peoples, but the ideas are good to think about in any kind of collection, including those in biology! And they can be considered in reference to a museum or private holdings. We want to consider: who is related to these items, what is our responsibility to them and the items we steward, and how can we best serve future generations through our work? Taking into consideration Native ways of knowing, we learn that caring for collections may entail housing relatives, living beings, treasured family heirlooms, items that bring forth ancestors, and more. In this section, I look specifically to the practices of creating a welcoming space for communities to visit collections and to honoring Native ways of knowing in how we care for, document, repair, and return cultural items.

Originating communities and museum staff have a common interest (I like to begin by identifying shared values)—we care a lot about the items that are housed in museums. What counts as appropriate care may differ depending on one's upbringing, role, and point of view. But I think it is a good place to start: we all care about the items, even if for different reasons and in different ways. This section examines some of those differences and how to respect and honor them. One of the underlying assumptions in this section is that when originating communities touch and engage with cultural items in collections, it is good for community members and good for the items.

What you will learn in this section:

- How to create a more welcoming space for originating community visits to collections
- How to welcome and incorporate culturally informed methods of collections care and stewardship (also known as collections management), collections repair, and conservation
- Different paths for museum items and digital records to return home to originating communities
- How to create the conditions for a welcoming repatriation consultation experience
- Concerns to keep in mind regarding ownership of data and dissemination of cultural information associated with collection items
- How to share information with communities.

25
Community Visits to Collections

There is a scene in the video documentary *Everything Was Carved* that I show in my museum studies classes.[1] It is a joyful scene. It opens with hands clapping over a table with grouped rows of wooden sticks laid out on it; the camera pulls back, and we see people standing, gathered around the table and singing along to a steady rhythm from a handheld drum. A group of Haida community members are laughing and smiling and playing a gambling game. A man places a coin on the table as a woman takes the sticks in her hands and waves them in the air to the rhythm, then places them behind her back. She brings her hands forward toward the man once again with palms down, and the man guesses which hand the sticks are in. He guesses wrong and moves the coin closer to her. They go again, and he guesses right despite the dancers trying to distract him. People are swaying, heads thrown back with open-throat laughter, and the music continues. The thing is—she is wearing purple nitrile gloves, and they are in a museum collections room. As the camera pans back, we see a host of museum staff along the edges of the room observing, smiling—the joy is contagious. When it is the man's turn to hold the gambling sticks, he is not wearing gloves (figure 3.2).

FIGURE 3.2. Video still, *Everything Was Carved*.

When I saw the delight expressed in this scene, I wanted my students and future museum professionals to witness it, too. I am so grateful that Pitt Rivers documented this moment, as well as the past harms the Haida identified in interviews. Earlier in the video the Haida make clear that they came with an interest in repatriation and that the items in the museum were sold under duress. The fact that the Haida were able to visit their belongings in collections, engage with them on their own terms, and handle and reawaken them created positive relationships and increased understanding between the community and the museum. We can say what is possible, but to see it with our own eyes makes it more achievable. This is what being a model for others is about—sharing what we do and what we learn from it so others can be informed and inspired.

In the past, museums were created and organized with the assumption that Native peoples would not be the audience, interpreters, researchers, or caretakers of the collections. Visitors to collections are no longer mainly researchers in search of data for a peer-reviewed paper but are also and increasingly community members in search of connections to ancestors and cultural knowledge. If we know that is a purpose for the collections, then how we organize, document, and share knowledge about collections should change. So should the spaces in which we house collections.

More recently built museums include architecture that is expressly intended to welcome originating communities and their ways of knowing. For example, the National Museum of the American Indian has an indoor ceremonial room with changing rooms just outside the door. The University of British Columbia Museum of Anthropology has a community lounge with access that doesn't require guests to go through security as well as a welcome plaza so communities are greeted with appropriate protocol by the host nation, Musqueam First Nation. Both museums ensure that community spaces are near elevators to accommodate elders and those in wheelchairs.

As noted in part 1, from the perspective of many Native Americans, museums can be painful places to visit, in part because their peoples have been represented in *natural* history rather than *American* history museums and also because, for more than 100 years, museum displays contributed to the stereotypes of Native peoples as vanishing or frozen in the past. To Native community members museums are mausoleums, literally—hundreds of thousands of Native ancestors in drawers and on shelves. Museums sometimes appear as gatekeepers, standing between Native researchers and their own cultural heritage. What non-Native people see as "inanimate objects" or art are viewed and understood differently by Native community members. Native people may see museums as prisons because what a museum catalog might call "fetishes," a Native person may consider sacred items, living beings who are locked up in cabinets and isolated from their people. So, community visits to collections can be very emotional for community members, as well as for staff who witness their feelings—which are sometimes positive, like seeing an old friend, being embraced by a relative, or feeling the groove worn by an ancestor's hand and feeling a connection. At other times they may feel devastated or angry or sad at being separated from these items or beings for so long, or they may feel the pain and loss of how the items ended up in the museum in the first place. People may want to talk about what they are feeling, or they may need the visit to pause so they can have some time alone.

In the video *Everything Was Carved*, I also appreciated how the museum prepared the staff for the Haida visit and their engagement with collections—being ready for and allowing the handling of collections. At a screening of the documentary at the Denver Museum of Nature and Science, Vince Collison (Haida) said they had coached community members as well prior to them visiting the museum, which is generally conceived of as a hostile place. This commitment to prepare by both sides of the partnership is part of what made joy possible in that context.

I have interviewed a number of Native tribal historic preservation officers, artists, and cultural specialists who regularly visit museum collections. What came to the fore from their shared experiences and recommendations for community visits to collections was that staff should be prepared, welcoming, and humble. In fact, that feeling of welcome begins before community members enter the building.

What you do before community members visit your museum can really affect their experience while they are in the museum. As noted earlier, the Guidelines for Collaboration provide some helpful recommendations. First, discuss with the community representative what the visit is about, what they want the experience to include. Introduce yourself, and explain how to get to the museum and where to stay. Provide any information you have about collections and archives ahead of time, and be sure community members and staff, both during and after the visit, are in agreement about what is acceptable to document and record and what is not.

Here are some examples of questions that can help museum staff prepare for a visit:

- Discuss who is participating in the visit, what they would like to see, and how the day(s) should be structured; ask whether any mobility or other comfort issues need to be accommodated for the visitors.
- Provide digital or printed copies of collections information ahead of time—not just of cultural items but also of associated documentation, photographs, archives, and conservation reports.
- Ask how items should be presented, and be transparent about what the visit will be like. For example, will items be placed on tables? Will community members be viewing items in cabinets or on shelves (figures 3.3 and 3.4)? Ask if any items should be covered or separated, or not displayed for view. Are there any kinds of items the group wants to avoid having contact with?
- Provide detailed information about where the visitors will stay overnight, how to get to the museum, and where to meet someone when they arrive; will lunch or other food be included in the visit?
- Provide information about who they will be meeting with—names, photos, and titles or brief bios with contact information (this helps for follow-up after the visit as well; community members often visit multiple museums, and having this kind of information helps with future communication).
- Ask whether/how community members would like the visit to be documented by museum staff: for the museum, the community, or both. Invite them to document their visit as they like as well.
- Ask ahead of time if they want to smudge or perform any ceremonial practices before, during, or after the visit (you may need to turn off sprinklers, identify quiet space, reserve a room to ensure there is no unexpected traffic during this time, and so on).
- Let them know if there are any Native ancestors or human remains in the building and where they are located.

When discussing what works well during a visit, two comments were repeatedly shared with me: don't hover, and don't be an expert. "Don't hover" means trust that community members are not going to harm items, and don't make them feel like they are being surveilled for potential wrongdoing while in museum spaces. Make them feel welcome, be enthusiastic and positive about their presence rather than wary. "Don't be an expert," many told me, means to listen first. Even if you have a great deal of knowledge about the items or archives being reviewed and are eager to share what you have learned, community members have connections and context to share as well. Let them take the lead and provide that context and knowledge when

FIGURE 3.3. Viewing items in cabinets during a collections visit. Artwork by John Swogger, 2025.

FIGURE 3.4. Viewing items on a table during a collections visit. Artwork by John Swogger, 2025.

appropriate and asked for. One Native artist put it like this: "Come with an empty cup."

When Native community members visit the museum, be sure to inform them if there are Native ancestors or human remains in the building, and let them know where they are located. Some individuals may not want to enter the building, others may avoid the specific room, and others will have no restrictions. If something unexpected does happen, be ready to stop for the moment or for the day, as community members may need to take steps to protect themselves from spiritual harm.

Another recommendation that recurred during my interviews was the idea that these visits are not just about work, they are about building relationships. They are about the purpose of the visit, and they are also about building trust, which requires learning who the staff are and their intentions. Get to know community members and be open to them getting to know you. It's important to connect with each other informally. One THPO said that we should not treat elders or ceremonial leaders like a stereotype or with too much reverence, and we should remember that they are people too. Or, as another THPO suggested, before the collections visit gets under way, "shoot the shit" with them! We laughed at the way he phrased it, but I hope it helps to repeat his recommendation so it sticks in your mind: be a whole person (not just a staff member with particular expertise), and engage with a community member as a whole person (not just as a knowledge keeper about an object in the museum).

Some other considerations during the visit:

- Try to make the spaces into which you invite community members feel human-scale and human-centered, as much as possible.
- Welcome them with coffee and snacks, introductions, and informal chat before getting down to business, unless they tell you ahead of time that that is what they want to do.
- Remember to let people know where Native ancestors are located in the building if they are present, and ask again if they want to avoid any kinds of items in collections. You want to avoid any surprises that may cause spiritual harm. (I am repeating this instruction intentionally because it should be discussed before and during visits.)
- Discuss the use of gloves during the visit; some community members prefer to use them, others not. Make them optional, and be sure to remind everyone to wash their hands before and especially after touching cultural belongings in case there is pesticide or residue that staff is unaware of.

- Attend to visitors' comfort; let them know where bathrooms are; make sure seating is available.
- Keep an eye out for fatigue, the need for breaks, and times when community members might need some alone time.
- Be an active listener—and be flexible and ready to change the agenda as needed.
- Also, don't forget that this may be the only time these community members visit your museum. It doesn't have to be all business- and collections-focused. Ask if they want to visit the exhibits or meet with museum staff with other specializations.

After the visit, be sure to document what was learned and promised, then follow through. Leave open the opportunity for community members to continue the conversation:

- Process any information and media that is appropriate to record in the collections information system and on the shelves; share copies with the community point of contact.
- Gather together the edited records or other materials that are new following what you sent prior to the visit and send them to the community members with a thank you and a list of promises you will follow up on if any were made during the visit.

The request for a collections visit can come from either a community or the museum. Keep in mind when you are hosting a visit that some community members may never have been behind the scenes in a collection space at a museum. Others may have dedicated years to traveling across the country and the world tracking down their cultural belongings; they may have a lot of experience working with museum staff and know exactly what they want to do during a visit. For example, staff from the Zuni A:shiwi A:wan Museum and Heritage Center in New Mexico are known for doing what they call "collections reviews." It is a well-defined process that began under the direction of Jim Enote, whose goal was "setting the record straight."[2]

Zuni cultural specialists reviewed collection items and their records to provide curatorial insights such as identification, materials, and use. They also identified reproductions or fakes, increased understanding about the items in the museum's care, and provided cultural care guidance. The cultural specialists asked a museum to print records, consulted and provided updated information, and then asked the museum to print the records again so they could review the changes (trust but verify!). Their primary goal was that the information be correct when young or future Zuni saw collections online or read descriptions in museum records.

These are just some ideas for how to be welcoming when you host originating community visits to collections. But welcoming goes beyond our individual behavior—it can be communicated in the structure and organization of the spaces and collections within the museum as well.

26

Collections Housing

Walking into a space that indicates an intention to respect Native ways of knowing can establish a welcoming environment without even having to say a word. How collection items are housed is important to their long-term safety and care. It can also communicate that the museum is willing to learn from and respect originating communities and their notions of how to appropriately care for cultural items. Visitors can see for themselves that staff members have gone beyond their school training, beyond their Western standards of collections management, to allow other forms of expertise to guide their practice. Where possible, consider making collections space feel less sterile and more like home—even small gestures in this direction make a difference, such as having artwork on a wall or providing comfortable chairs. Similarly, you can place a tablecloth over a worktable when serving snacks and coffee in other areas of the museum.

As noted earlier, language is important. Individuals can encounter names for themselves and the items that originate from their communities in numerous places—online in a website collection search, in the museum's database or card catalog system, and on the shelves, drawers, and mounts that house items. Names change over time, so it is a good idea to ask community visitors if they are correct or need updating.

Let's walk through the concentric "envelopes," as collection managers like to refer to them, in relation to collections housing. The building envelope is the first barrier for protecting collections—from pests to water to theft. The integrity of the "envelope," or seal, around the building is important to ensure the long-term stability and safety of collection items. A building that has a leaky roof or no HVAC system cannot adequately control the humidity and temperature, so it does not have a good building envelope. Along with the museum's website, the building's exterior is a big part of Native community members' first impression of the museum. Even the banner with the name of the museum can be off-putting if it is called a natural history museum. Some things you can control, some things you cannot. But it's good to be aware of how that first impression may be influenced by the building itself.

We often consider the exhibitions the only museum space that engages with the public and non-staff members. With increased community engagement with collections, more people are coming into the back of house. Thinking of those spaces as also areas of public/non-staff engagement has worked its way into newer museums' architecture. Examples of built-in architecture that newer museums designed to be welcoming to Native engagement with collections are a ceremonial space in the museum with a fire pit, an outdoor ceremonial space, vaults for community members to use as keeping places for items that remain under their control but benefit from the security and fire protections a museum might provide, and a space that looks like a living room for community members and staff to gather or share a meal before consultation. Perhaps you can repurpose space in your institution to serve some of these roles or create a space outside that is welcoming and private for ceremonial use.

Then you have the room in which collections are housed—what kind of space is it? Is it industrial, gloomy, bright, organized, filled with warm colors, cool colors, warehouse-ish? Can you bring a human scale and sensibility to a sterile workplace with community visitors in mind who intend to sit, talk, and spend time with collections and with you in this space? Imagine the space as a place where relatives are recalling memories and talking about the future together—how could you rearrange or adapt that space to make the conversation comfortable and to seem as though it was meant to take place here?

The next envelope is the cabinet, which can include drawers or shelves and may or may not have doors. I have seen a number of examples where the exteriors of the cabinets indicate cultural care (see the next section for more details), including posting maps of traditional land territories or Native language names for tribal affiliation of the items in the cabinet, muslin or vents on cabinet fronts to allow items to breathe, and signs indicating there are sacred items inside or restrictions on who should access the items within.

Within the cabinet, how items are situated and "mounted" really matters in giving an impression of how well they are cared for and valued in the institution. Imagine that you have never seen a treasured item that someone in your family made 100 years ago, and you have waited a long time to see it. When you arrive and peer into the drawer in which it is held, you find it tangled with and overlapping other items. You may not be able to change things about your building or even your cabinets, but the way items are arranged in space and organized on a shelf can be within your control. Even in a crowded, cramped, old room with ancient cabinets—if the items themselves have clearly been arranged to the best of your ability given the constraints of space, and they are mounted in a way that shows respect, it will go a long way. There are techniques to deal with overcrowding, like creating shelves within shelves using a particular kind of board so items are not touching even if they are stacked. Or if they need to be stacked, materials can be placed between items. The point is to do an audit of the items in collections, especially in preparation for a community visit, and be sure that the way items are housed conveys respect and care. If for some reason you cannot achieve this, then manage expectations—tell people ahead of time what they will see so it is not a shock, and be open to them providing guidance on how to remedy the situation.

A "mount" in museum speak can mean a couple of things. An "exhibition mount" can be a brass fitting that secures an item to the display wall (see chapter 19, "Interpretation and Display"); a "storage mount" is something that holds the item within a box or cabinet when it is not on exhibit (though we prefer to avoid the term *storage* more generally). A storage mount can be a box or construction from archival materials that provides housing for the item to reduce handling of the item itself, to keep an eye out for pests (white materials make it easier to see frass, or tiny bits of insect poop), and to ensure it is at a safe distance from other items to avoid it rubbing up against them.

Storage mounts can also communicate respect for other ways of knowing. For example, when we created a mount for a *rambaramp* in the University of Colorado Museum of Natural History (CU Museum), it was good for the item and respectful to the originating community of Vanuatu. We checked later with someone at the Vanuatu cultural center who agreed that the mount was done well. A rambaramp is an ancestor figure, an effigy of a person who has passed away, created through clay sculpted over his skull and a clay and wooden body whose markings resemble the man. In our research about the rambaramp, we learned that he is intended to sit in the men's house and be surrounded by people. His mount was constructed of wood, with a clear panel in front at his eye level and two muslin panels on either side. This respected the notion that he may be sentient or contain spirit, with a need to breathe and see, and also provided a window into the otherwise wooden box for preventive conservation inspection. It was good on both levels—for Indigenous ways of knowing and for Western standards of collections care. In another example at the same museum, a mummified eagle from an ancestral site in a cave was placed on a pillow in a blue board box, with a see-through cutout at the top of the box. The pillow was placed beneath the eagle's body to ensure it did not become misshapen over time by lying flat against a shelf. The care and attention to detail were also appreciated because this animal is revered. Whether community member or museum staff member, we felt something—about the eagle and the museum—when we saw how carefully, even lovingly, the eagle was cushioned. It is clear that the eagle was treated with respect.

For museums that continue to house human remains—whether Native ancestors or those from other marginalized communities whose bodies were not donated to science—we have learned from community members that a respectful way to care for them is to separate those individuals from the main collection into a quiet place where there is not a lot of activity. Ideally, they would be housed in a separate room, but if that is not possible then place them in a space divided out with curtains. The way those individuals are housed matters as well. When preparing their resting place on your shelves, think about a relative coming to visit them and how you might show respectful care in housing, placement, and materials. Think of the difference between encountering bones loose in drawers, mingled together, and individuals placed separately and carefully in clean boxes wrapped in muslin. Do the best you can with the resources you have to communicate respect in the mounts and housing of these individuals.

Next to consider is the organization of the collections space, beyond creating a separate area for ancestors or human remains. For many years, collections were organized by material or object type, either because cross-cultural comparative studies were the norm or because it was just easier that way. Putting all the arrows together in one place means you can place a lot of vertical shelves close together; if you organize by originating community, you may have arrows next to big pots. It may be more efficient, space-wise, to organize by object type or size. Organization by tribal affiliation is more prominent in museums today. We also learn from communities even more ways to organize collections, depending on the institution and the audience it serves. For example, the Makah Cultural and Research Center (MCRC) in Washington State used Makah language terms to provide a culturally relevant arrangement of its collections for community members and for learning about the Makah language.[3]

The point is to be intentional about the organization of collections; don't just assume it should be the way it is or that there is anything inherently natural about how to organize collections. As a staff member, consider your institution, its capacity and purpose, the audience you serve, and your engagement with originating communities (yours or others), and do an "audit" of the envelopes in your institution. What do the arrangement and layout of collections, the walls, and the orderliness of the space suggest about the purpose of and consideration provided to the items in your care? If you are a visitor to collections, consider doing this kind of "audit" to provide an institution with insight and recommendations to create a more welcoming space.

27

Cultural Care

During community visits to collections, there may be times when someone indicates that an item is sacred or requires special care due to cultural protocols. Or you may receive instructions for how to care for an item that has been claimed under the Native American Graves Protection and Repatriation Act (NAGPRA, 1990) and is awaiting its return home (see chapter 16, "Repatriation Law," and chapter 30, "Repatriation Consultation"). I refer to this kind of culturally informed guidance as "cultural care," following my colleagues at the National Museum of the American Indian. Cultural care is culturally specific; while this section provides some examples to introduce the concept, it is key to seek guidance from appropriate authorities in originating communities regarding this kind of collections care. In other words, absolutely do not take my word for it—I am not an expert or authority on cultural care practices. I can only share what I have learned along the way so that you might be more prepared to ask for (as a tribal member), or respond to (as a museum staff member), these kinds of requests in the context of community engagements with collections.

Cultural care is a form of stewardship that entails following an originating community's culturally specific guidelines, protocols, or practices for housing, displaying, interpreting, mounting, or conserving items. It may include how to appropriately create a quiet and set-apart space for Native ancestors, how to orient items in a drawer, or restrictions as to who can access a particular item. It is also helpful to seek guidance about which items do not require special care, noting in your records that they have been reviewed by originating communities and were deemed acceptable to display or share online.

As noted earlier, some Native peoples see particular cultural items as powerful or as other-than-human beings. They may offer to bless or protect you because you work with or near these items. They may have restrictions on what they can view or be around, depending on their tribal affiliation, societal role, gender, or age. They may need to conduct ceremony or ritual cleansing if they are inadvertently exposed to spiritual harm in their interaction with collections. They may need time and space to prepare for or recover from a visit with collections. Indicate where there are spaces for this in or near your building. Do not expect that every Native person will need to or want to do these things, but be sure to let them know they can request time or space to do so.

Community members invite museum staff to practice cultural care in their absence. Cultural care might be requested for items that are going to be repatriated or for those that remain in a museum's care. Community members often explain cultural care as both benefiting an item's well-being and protecting staff. Again, I can't tell you how to enact cultural care in your institution. That would be inappropriate—it requires meaningful consultation with originating communities. What I can do is provide some insight into and examples of cultural care so you are more prepared to invite or respond to such requests. For instance, cultural specialists may smudge or do a blessing while visiting to protect museum staff who are asked to handle powerful items,[4] such as taking a medicine bundle out into the sunshine to breathe. Other examples include being asked to orient arrows east to west in a drawer, to allow ritual feeding of a textile, to ensure that certain items are housed together or apart, or to restrict access to men who belong to a particular ceremonial society. Consider creating policy to guide staff in accommodating such requests.

It's important not to make assumptions about how this works for different tribes. The Tlingit Dakl'aweidi clan crest hat is not sacred, or *at.'oow*, unless and until a particular ceremony is performed on it. A replica is on display at National Museum of Natural History, with the community's blessing.[5] For others, like the Haudenosaunee, a replica or image of a False Face mask is considered to have the same protocols and restrictions as the original carving.[6]

There are many ways knowledge about and care of items are assigned as responsibilities within Native communities—for example, according to gender, status, or ceremonial role. These ways are reflected in the types of guidelines communities might provide about stewarding their cultural belongings. Notice the distinction between access and handling. Access is about viewing or being in the vicinity of an item; handling is about touching it.

Some general categories of cultural care come up repeatedly when working with different Native communities in collections. One is related to group membership. For example, perhaps a bundle or mask is used in a particular ceremony, and only members of the society who are the rightful owners, knowledge keepers, or practitioners of that ceremony are able to view or handle the item. Another example is gender, where, for example, only men or women can handle or access a particular item—this refers to museum visitors as well as staff who need to interact with the item to care for it. In many Native communities, during menstruation, women are considered to be particularly powerful. To protect the woman and the cultural items, women are asked not to be around powerful items during this time. In the Anthropology Section of the CU Museum, at one time three female staff gathered to compare when we would have our periods, trying to figure out when one of us could take bundles out for fresh air that month.

I would often tell students "don't start with no" when responding to a cultural care request. Instead, be true to your training and communicate your concerns. Allow for dialogue and mutual understanding—which often leads to something all parties can agree on that honors the intention of the original request. For example, during a repatriation consultation at the CU Museum, a Native community member suggested that red felt be placed under pipes that were housed in a drawer. Instead of saying no or arguing against this idea, collection manager Christie Cain expressed her concern for the objects based on her training. Each person was suggesting best practice in their understanding of proper care. Christie explained that the felt might catch on or snag the items and asked if she could place muslin cloth between the pipes and the felt. The cultural specialists agreed and said this would not hinder the intended purpose for the cloth's placement. At their request, sweetgrass was also added to the drawer (figure 3.5). Another example at this museum occurred when a cultural specialist wanted to place corn pollen on a textile for a blessing. The concern was that over time, the pollen might erode the fiber. The cultural specialist listened and determined that placing the pollen beside the textile would work. These examples would not happen at every museum or in every case—it was the foundation of openness, honesty, respect, and a sense of shared purpose in the care of these items that allowed for a way of addressing everyone's concerns that neither party may have imagined at the start.

FIGURE 3.5. Red felt and sweetgrass in drawer. Artwork by John Swogger, 2025.

If a tribal member offers cultural care guidance, be clear about whether you intend to follow the guidance and, if so, ask questions so the guidance is actionable and you can record it accurately in the database and on the shelf. Because we don't want to make assumptions about protocols, we need to be able to ask questions to ensure there is clear understanding of the protocols requested and how to implement them. This happened in my experience working with the Navajo Nation, to which we were repatriating medicine bundles. Our museum staff was asked to take bundles outside to get fresh air and sunlight each season while they remained in our care prior to repatriation because this community knows them as living beings. The tribe's repatriation officers told us that women are not supposed to handle these kinds of items. We asked whether they would prefer that a male graduate student from another department bring them outside. They said no, they preferred that we do so despite the protocols because they knew who we were. They conducted a blessing for our safety and left an offering for the items. So, there can be preferred manners of care, but there can also be exceptions. We asked questions to be sure we didn't make assumptions about how we should care for the items. Had we not asked, we would have had a male graduate student come in and handle the items.

To responsibly enact cultural care, you need to document the guidance adequately and record the name and role of the requester. It's important to know by whom and when instructions were provided because protocols can change over time. The issue of who has the authority to provide this guidance, or validate it, is significant; museums often rely on official tribal representatives like THPOs or tribal leadership to designate who has that authority. Once the cultural care has been recorded, it can be frustrating if it is incomplete or inadequate. A real-life example: a note in a collection record indicated that an item should be covered, without any indication of how or why. It is unclear whether that request is about people seeing or handling the object or because it is light-sensitive.

Learning how to respectfully ask questions that help staff collect actionable information for cultural care is essential. Otherwise, a community member may get the impression that the guidance will be followed but, in reality, museum staff may not have enough information to do so. So, sometimes we need to ask questions to ensure that we get it right. There is an art to asking questions, particularly when working in collections (see chapter 44, "Interviewing and Recording," for more on interviewing). It is important to respond to social cues, especially because visiting collections can be emotional experiences for originating community members. Respond to the situation at hand, and practice active listening. Active listening means being present, listening to what is said, being aware of non-verbal cues and body language, and avoiding interrupting the speaker or thinking ahead about your next question rather than staying in the moment. Then, when the time is right to ask questions, paraphrase what was said, and ask clarifying questions to ensure understanding. Staying in the moment instead of worrying about what you are going to say next does not come naturally to everyone—it took me a long time to be able to do this. Active listening is a muscle I strengthened through practice.

We often caution against leading questions when talking about interviewing and questioning people in social science and anthropology. A leading question might be "do you hate homework" versus "how do you feel about homework?" But regarding museum collections and cultural care, the concern is to avoid asking questions that seem to be prying or in search of sacred or protected knowledge when talking to community members. That's part of focusing on people's comfort. Both physical comfort and emotional comfort are important when engaging community members in collections.

It is not just your interactions and welcoming attitude that can help with inviting and responding to cultural care guidance. Mounts for items in collections can help as well. Mounts can help you enact cultural care. For example, let's say your museum has all female staff members and an item is male handle only. If you place the item in a blue board box, you can lift and move the box to get at other items on a shelf or do an inventory without having to touch the item. Perhaps an item should not be seen and is considered to breathe. Can you make a box from archival materials that has a top made of muslin? When you learn more about these ways of understanding collections, you ask new questions to guide your everyday museum work. For example, how can this mount enable access or restrict it? How can it communicate care and an intention to interact with community? Discussing a mount with the community member who is providing cultural care guidance can also be a way of asking questions. For example, if someone says the item should only be *viewed* by men, you might ask: is it okay for women to handle the item if they do not touch or see it? We could place it in a covered box; would that be okay?

You may or may not believe the same things as the Native individuals visiting collections who provide cultural care guidance. But you can honor and value their ways of knowing as best you can, treating items in a way that is culturally appropriate according to their community of origin. There is a lot to learn from and appreciate about enacting cultural care—building respect and trust between community and museum, showing value for each other's ways of knowing. I love how it changes how we do our work at the museum and our sense of purpose and commitment to stewardship. For example, when we follow guidance that asks us to talk to Native ancestors who remain in our care, whether in our mind or out loud, it helps us look beyond boxes and see individuals, people, longing to return home.

I also appreciate that the recommendations from communities for collections care are often also good practice according to Western notions of collections management. The first week of class, I would talk to students in my collections research course about being mindful when entering collections, that communities instruct us to be intentional and aware of what is on our minds when we work with and around cultural items and Native ancestors. Do not go in with frustration or anger. If it's been that kind of day and entering this space cannot be a respite, then perhaps it's not the right time to do this work. This is echoed in the standard object handling guide we provide to incoming museum studies students at the CU Museum. The final instruction on the handout says: "Be sure your mind is focused on what you are doing. Plan ahead—look for potential problem spots, determine what path [the item] will take, where it is going." While we may advise this for different reasons, we all agree that being present and intentional when working with collections is essential.

Finally, it is important to clearly communicate the guidance you receive to other staff, collections visitors, and the public. Develop a system for how you will record and communicate the information. You may develop in-house approaches, like signs on shelving and flags in your database, or a JPEG that says something like "not for public viewing" as the image for an online collection record. You can also utilize external solutions like the Local Contexts project, which was developed by two anthropologists who work closely with Indigenous communities: Dr. Kim Christen and Dr. Jane Anderson. Through a website, Local Contexts provides "Collections Care Notices," a set of standardized visual identifiers for museums to place in collections information systems and on shelves based on cultural care guidance received from communities. The website also provides resources for Native communities to develop their own labels, called "Traditional Knowledge Labels," or TK Labels, to identify protocols for access to and use of heritage materials that are digital and online. In this system, museums can post notices on their online records such as "open to collaborate," which invites originating communities to engage with the museum, and "attribution incomplete," which indicates that information about the item's cultural affiliation may be inaccurate or missing, inviting community members to notify the museum if it is related to them.[7]

28
Collections Visits to Communities

Sometimes, rather than community members visiting collections, the collection items travel to them. Placing items closer to home for community engagement can be a powerful and positive step in creating partnerships between museums and originating communities. For example, a museum may loan items to a tribal museum or cultural center for an exhibition. It is important to ensure the community understands that, depending on the size and location of the museum, loans can take a long time to process, and it may require considerable cost to ship the items to the tribal institution. This is one of those times when managing expectations and having a plan for funding and support is essential.

Depending on the resources of the tribal institution and the size of the loan, funds may not be available to cover shipment and other costs. Discuss funding sources as well as logistics when planning this kind of activity with originating communities, and be transparent about the process from request to approval to conservation to packing and shipping. Discuss the length of time the process will take and which institution is expected to cover specific costs, including insurance. Legal agreements should be written in plain language, and it should be clear whether handling is allowed under the agreement. Ideally, handling by community members is not only allowed but encouraged (see policy examples in appendix B). You should also be prepared for individuals to bring up repatriation during these discussions.

Loans tend to be for exhibition and display. There have also been instances of shorter loans for ceremonial purposes or educational programs when an item is couriered by museum staff to be used in a community event. One example of this kind of loan is when staff from the American Museum of Natural History (AMNH) took a carved wooden box called a chief's chest to Haida Gwaii for a potlatch in 2017. The box was then placed on display at the AMNH for the first time in thirty years.[8] Other examples include the University of British Columbia Museum of Anthropology agreeing to loan masks to a First Nations family for use in a potlatch in 1993[9] and the National Museum of the American Indian (NMAI) loaning dance regalia to the Siletz Tribe in Oregon for a ceremony in 1996.[10] I chose examples in the 1990s specifically so you do not come away from this narrative thinking these are new ways of doing things, though they may be more common in museums today. Museums like the UBC Museum of Anthropology, the Museum of Indian Arts and Culture, and the NMAI have been doing community collaboration and cultural care for decades.

Shared stewardship in general is another avenue for connecting communities to collections, whether through cultural care in the museum, as described in chapter 27, or through long-term placement of items in a community. The terms of a co-stewardship agreement can be more lenient than those of a typical loan agreement—more flexible in purpose, handling, length of time, environmental conditions, physical location, and more. This is about shared decision making regarding access, care, interpretation, and display of the items—whether they are located in the museum or in the originating community.

As noted by Cara Krmpotich and Laura Peers in their 2014 publication *This Is Our Life: Haida Material Heritage and Changing Museum Practice*, engagement with collections can outweigh potential changes to an item that may occur as a result of use.[11] Change becomes a part of the item's biography and tells the story of its value to and engagement with community. Conservators have a role to play here, letting community members know what items are more stable than others and what areas of a particular item are vulnerable so community members can make decisions about whether and how they want to loan or physically engage with an item.

29

Conservation

When I teach the course Introduction to Museum Studies, I always have my students read excerpts from Miriam Clavir's *Preserving What Is Valued: Museums, Conservation, and First Nations*, published in 2002. I love this book because it helps us understand more than the field of conservation—it exposes the assumptions baked into the knowledge we receive in museum-related classrooms and trainings. Clavir, conservator emerita and research associate at the University of British Columbia Museum of Anthropology, does a great job of explaining "preservation" not just from a Western and scientific point of view but also from the perspective of First Nations. We learn that cultural items can have a life cycle and that museums' efforts to freeze them in time arrests the life cycle; some items are intended to return to the earth when their purpose has been fulfilled.

Conservation is a museum profession dedicated to the preservation and repair of collections items through conservation "treatments." Conservators have science degrees—usually PhDs in chemistry or materials science—and they work with art, historical, and anthropological collections. They are often employed or contracted to ready items for display in an exhibit or to repair damage to an item caused by use-wear or a catastrophic event—for instance, if a building has a leak and the collections suffer water damage. When something like that happens, insurance may be used to pay a conservator to repair the items. *Preventive* conservation is not active repair; rather, it includes measures to reduce the potential for damage. Collections managers regularly use this approach, safeguarding the collections against environmental factors such as fluctuations in temperature and humidity and protecting them from dust and pests.

Collections managers and conservators go through training that is aimed at maintaining the collection item in perpetuity—in essence, something akin to freezing it in time from the moment of acquisition. The amount of conservation treatment considered appropriate varies according to the collection and intent—for instance, art collections may be restored so they appear in an original state, whereas for anthropological collections, it may be original use-wear that is important to preserve. For example, let's say a painting of a feather bonnet (often referred to as a headdress) has a scratch that obscures one of the tips of the eagle feathers in the artwork; a conservator might be contracted to hide the scratch and make the painted feather appear whole again. For a three-dimensional feather bonnet made of hide, fabric, and eagle feathers in an anthropological collection, if there is a damaged feather, it would be more likely that the original feather would be left in place and further damage prevented through pest management. However, if you ask a Native community member where the bonnet originated, they may suggest replacing the feather. After all, they repair their regalia all the time, and the intent is for the item to be beautiful and appear cherished and cared for.

Here is this section's recommendation: invite originating communities into dialogue about conservation because it is their heritage and because they may have alternate ways of understanding and implementing preservation or repair. Native methods of repair of cultural items existed long before the field of conservation developed. We see evidence of this, for example, in pitch seams on a canoe or resin on pots. Repair has always been a part of Native lifeways in maintaining the materials they create and use. In addition, the repairs are time-tested and traditionally from natural elements rather than factory-made chemicals. Working with Native specialists opens up the possibility of adding to the item's cultural biography through repair that is culturally and environmentally specific to the place from which it originated.

In her dissertation "Towards an Indigenous Museology," Dr. Jessie Ryker-Crawford (White Earth Chippewa Nation) provides a comprehensive review of conservation studies and methods and looks specifically at examples of repair in collections that were made by originating communities, before the items arrived at a museum. She gives an example of a repair patch on a Lakota dress and concludes that any discussion of Native-made repairs "must include philosophical matters as well as technical explanations."[12] Reviewing a small circular patch on a Lakota girl's buckskin dress, she notes the ring of beads around the patch. Western conservation and restoration practices are often intended to be reversible and unseen. This patch was ringed by very small beads, bringing attention to its repair as well as to the care, skill, and attention to detail it required.

Dr. Ryker-Crawford provides other examples of "Indigenous repair," including pitch patch repair on baskets; the shard plug method on ceramics, where a fragment of another pot is used to fill a hole with gypsum; hide and skin glue to repair a drum; various forms of rawhide lashings to mend cracked pottery; and various forms of basketry and textile repair. She explains that some traditional repair methods are passed down by people who care for ceremonial items, and sharing techniques outside of specific cultural practices is not appropriate. She cites conservators from the NMAI respecting Native consultant wishes that traditional methods for repair used by Native consultants during a consultation on collections not be disclosed beyond the staff members who were present, and some were not shared at all.[13]

So, if you intend to consult a conservator about an item that has been damaged before or after it entered your collection or an item needs evaluation for loan, exhibition, or repatriation, consider inviting a knowledgeable tribal member to the consultation. If you are unsure of how to find someone with the proper cultural knowledge, reach out to the Tribe's THPO office or cultural center and ask for a recommendation. Conservators may have Native collaborators they can recommend. I remember when I was working at the NMAI more than twenty years ago when an Anishinaabe group came to visit birch bark scrolls—sacred items that contain teachings. The NMAI conservators tested different techniques on birch bark test samples to prepare to unroll the scrolls, fully expecting to attempt one of these techniques when the community arrived. When they saw that the various techniques could not protect the scrolls from damage in the process of opening them, the community members did not ask for them to be unrolled but rather just wanted to be in the same room with them. This is what the NMAI team calls collaborative conservation: working with communities to determine the best course of action with the most appropriate technique and materials.

I found an article by the NMAI conservation team that included the birch bark consultation in which they reflected on the experience: "It is not necessary for us to know why decisions are made, but simply to realize and acknowledge that appropriate knowledge resulted in appropriate action for all parties involved." A favorite mental image I took away from the article is when conservator Susan Heald accompanied dance regalia back to the Siletz Tribe in Oregon to be danced in ceremony: "After every round of dancing, the floor was inspected to collect bits of shell or feather that might have fallen off the regalia, whether old or new, to be re-associated and repaired after the ceremony."[14]

As noted in the previous section, in the past, collection items were intended to be maintained on shelves in perpetuity. Museum staff used deadly poisons like arsenic to preserve organic materials such as feathers and textiles. This was a version of what scientists did with animals by placing them in formaldehyde. The chemicals arrested deterioration so the items would persist for future research and exhibition. Collectors and curators did not envision people wearing the feather bonnets, dancing with the masks, or playing the flutes in their collection. That is now a real possibility and a right under repatriation law, so it is important to research and test whenever possible whether items returning home may have been treated with chemicals. Conservator Nancy Odegaard and curator Alyce Sadongei (Kiowa/Tohono O'Odham) published a book in 2005 titled *Old Poisons, New Problems: A Museum Resource for Managing Contaminated Cultural Materials*, based on research testing for toxic chemicals and finding non-destructive ways to remove them from collections items. The book directly addresses NAGPRA repatriation.[15]

30
Repatriation Consultation

Community engagements with collections often lead to cultural care guidance as well as repatriation requests. Repatriation requests can be made in the absence of a visit or be proactively invited by museum staff. Repatriation is the transfer of ownership and return of cultural items and Native ancestors from museums to originating communities. The Native American Graves Protection and Repatriation Act (1990) and associated regulations guide this process, unless it is a Smithsonian Institution museum that falls under the NMAI Act (1989) (see chapter 16, "Repatriation Law"). Tribal historic preservation officer, NAGPRA liaison, and NAGPRA officer are the most common titles for individuals who are authorized by their communities to conduct repatriation with museums on their behalf. In this chapter I address the experience of repatriation consultation with these individuals and how to navigate consultations with respect and sensitivity.

We often hear about the NAGPRA law, its categories, and the implementation process. But we rarely hear about what consultation looks like, how it feels to be in the room, and some of the common challenges that arise. For that reason, one of my museum studies master's students, Claire Wilbert, created a two-day workshop focused on the consultation process for her final project. It was designed to fill the gap we saw in trainings associated with NAGPRA and what many museum staff were most apprehensive about. We also wanted to support tribal representatives who walk into consultation after consultation with often well-meaning but unprepared museum staff.

So that is what I will focus on here: laying a good foundation of knowledge about the consultation process to help set the conditions for positive experiences. However, no matter how hard you try to be welcoming, you never know what previous negative or positive experiences NAGPRA liaisons may have had with other institutions that influence how they show up to your museum. Museum staff may have hosted one or two repatriation consultations in a year, whereas NAGPRA liaisons may have been to dozens. Do your best to be welcoming, and avoid being defensive. Keep in mind that these individuals have taken on a heavy responsibility on behalf of their community's past, present, and future generations. The work of repatriation for these tribal members is never-ending and exhausting, and it can expose them to spiritual harm. It is also deeply meaningful and rewarding. Community members often refer to repatriation as contributing to community health and well-being.

I emphasize to museum studies students that it is important—especially in repatriation consultations but during engagements in general—to come to a meeting with tribal members with an open mind, with transparency and honesty about your concerns and point of view. Where I see engagements go wrong is when museum staff members assume they know what tribal members want and try to manipulate the consultation outcome to fit their predetermined goals. Staff might anticipate, rather than inquire and respond to, tribal members' concerns and desires and act accordingly. However, even if something is not what you think tribal members want to hear, if you are honest about your intentions and concerns, it will make for a better experience for everyone. For example, let's say you come into a consultation regarding Native ancestors assuming that the Tribe would say no to a request for destructive analysis, so you argue for the importance of keeping ancestral remains indefinitely for future scientific techniques that may be developed. Tribal members may feel manipulated or not heard and deny the request. Imagine if you had begun instead with your true intention: I would like to do a small destructive sampling to learn more about these ancestors' diet. Would that be something you would be interested in learning? We would share our data with you. The consultants may or may not say yes to delaying return of their ancestors so the study can be completed.[16] The point is to ask, don't assume. Allow outcomes to be emergent, to develop as a result of dialogue and shared understanding.

So, be honest and have an open mind—and make sure your ducks are in order. Gather as much information as you can about the collections selected for review; be transparent about what information you have, where it came from, and how reliable it is. Organize and provide as much of this information as you can to the NAGPRA liaisons ahead of time (this is an important act of transparency, but don't assume that everyone has read the materials prior to arrival). Also, be sensitive to community members' wishes to spend time with their ancestors or cultural belongings—perhaps they need space for ceremony, time alone with the items, or time apart from staff to converse. Much of what was discussed in "Community Visits to Collections" (chapter 25) also applies to NAGPRA consultations.

Keep in mind that NAGPRA liaisons do this kind of work all the time and with many museums. It's their job—you can rely on their expertise to guide you. If you are wondering, how should we organize the day? How should we arrange the collections on tables for consultation? Those are great questions for the NAGPRA or THPO officers! After the many consultations they have attended, they have preferences, know what works well, and can provide this level of detailed guidance. Consider asking: what are their priorities for viewing collections? How would they like the collections to be laid out? Would they like to see the entire collection or just the items they have identified for NAGPRA review? Do they want related archives or associated documentation put out as well? Whatever questions or apprehensions you may have going into a consultation, express them and let them guide you in creating a welcoming visit. Everyone has to start somewhere—a NAGPRA officer may be new in their position, so don't expect them to have all the answers. Regardless, respect and a desire for collaboration are expressed in the asking. If you are the NAGPRA officer or a THPO going to a museum, please do express your preferences because your doing so takes a lot of guesswork and anxiety out of the museum staff's experience in preparing for your visit. If done in a good way, as I have argued elsewhere, consultation and repatriation can become the foundation for longer-term partnerships and research projects that are mutually beneficial to both the museum and the originating community.

I have had many memorable repatriation experiences from my time at the University of Colorado. In every case, the first item on our agenda for a consultation visit was to have coffee and snacks and a discussion about how the NAGPRA liaisons would like to proceed for the day. We also provided documentation of our compliance with the law to date.

Every repatriation consultation is different. For example, THPOs or NAGPRA officers may come alone or with a group of people; cultural specialists or elders may be present or need to be consulted with back home after a visit; the delegation may come in agitated from a prior museum experience or in a great mood because the restaurant you recommended for their first night in town was a winner; you may have excellent or no information associated with the items under consultation; there may be very experienced people around the table or folks who are new to the process of repatriation. Whatever the case, the key is to be an active listener, read the social cues, and be flexible. You may have an agenda for the day, but don't try to stick to it. Let the community members lead when it comes to determining how best to spend their limited time with you and the collection.

This first example taught me a lot about trust and that the way individuals behave in the moment is not always about the consultation in progress. I had reached out to a community because I knew we had items in the CU Museum collection that were considered to be sacred and that we would repatriate them under the law if a request came our way. In other words, we were proactive, and when the THPOs came to do a review of the items it was an extremely positive experience. They reviewed the entire collection, offered a blessing, and provided cultural care instructions regarding items that would remain in the museum during the repatriation process. It was a wonderful experience. There were hugs, smiles, and an invitation to visit with the community later in the year.

On a second visit a year later, the THPOs requested an additional list of items to be pulled. When they arrived, the feeling was off—combative, aggressive, an item was handled in a less than gentle way. The dynamic of anticipating the other party goes both ways. In selecting these items, it seemed as though the liaisons expected me to object. But I stated my honest intention: a consultation is for us to determine what is appropriate to claim under the law, so our process is to listen to what you have to say; I have no intention of making any determinations until the process is complete. It was as if they didn't remember our previous experience together, that perhaps they even wanted a confrontation. I imagined that was because while their community was one of only a few that we were working with and it had a major impact on me, our staff, and the students, we were one of many museums they were working with. And those experiences were often not positive. I decided to debrief the noticeably stricken students afterward and provided a plausible explanation. It seemed to me that the tribal members had had a bad experience with another museum, and whatever they could not do or say there came out here. As I noted earlier, even if your institution is doing things in a good way, NAGPRA liaisons may be experiencing a variety of people and intractable institutions. Building and maintaining trust is difficult in this context and can sometimes be upended regardless of what you do. However, as if that second visit never happened, when the NAGPRA liaisons returned a third time to take items home, the hugs and smiles were back and it went great, thank goodness!

There are actions you can take that build transparency into the process. For example, change the database records during the consultation so tribal members see you taking their contributions seriously and don't have to trust that you will change the records later. During repatriation consultations at the CU Museum, we sat together in the workroom, and the collections manager placed a computer on the table, facing the NAGPRA liaisons. As we talked about each cultural item, she updated the record in real time (figure 3.6). Whether it was adding a Native language term, correcting a record, providing cultural care guidance, or flagging an item for a repatriation claim, they could watch the edits being made on the screen.

We do talk about trust and building relationships a lot when it comes to communities and museums. But it is not easy, and for good reasons. For non-Native folks who work in this field: you are never going to earn the benefit of the doubt. Trust is built on continual acts of good faith, especially in the arena of repatriation, which is at the center of the harm and pain of museum history and practice. Sometimes when I am working with Native communities, before I can introduce who I am or what I do, and even if I do that, I might get an earful about museums or anthropology or research or all of it and how terrible it is. And that's good! It's good to listen, to acknowledge, to welcome the reminding, the centering of Native perspectives in what are often felt to be hostile spaces. Even if we feel they are preaching to the choir, the act of making space for that teaching to be heard and acknowledged is important. (Though if it turns into verbal abuse, that's different, and you should remove

FIGURE 3.6. Editing collections information system records together. Artwork by John Swogger, 2025.

yourself.) Try not to interrupt, even if every fiber of your being is thinking, I know, I agree! It's why I am here doing this with you. I have felt that way—but hang tight. In listening and being patient and accepting, you acknowledge the other person's agency in identifying the pain, in reshaping the power relation that too often has been severely unbalanced and continues to be so.

Another example I want to share emphasizes the importance of active listening and honesty. Even with the best intentions, things can sometimes begin to go sideways in a repatriation consultation. When you get that sense, you feel a sudden shift, take stock and consider if there needs to be a side conversation or a dialogue with the visiting group to understand what is happening. In 2019, the CU Museum hosted a multi-day consultation with a consortium of tribes. As a standard practice, during the first day we would usually go over the law and its definitions together, but in this case we didn't have the chance to do that. So instead, we added it to our second-day agenda after community members had already begun to review items. The first day went well; everyone was working together and feeling positive and connected to each other and the work at hand.

The next day, our museum staff and NAGPRA consultants were seated at the head of U-shaped meeting tables with tribal members on either side. When our team started to review the NAGPRA categories as a matter of course, tribal members clearly became upset. The temperature changed quickly. In that moment, I realized that they might be thinking that we did not believe they knew the law or that this was a preamble to denying potential claims for items they had reviewed the day before. Neither was true. I immediately addressed what seemed to be going unsaid and explained that we do this at every consultation, that it was supposed to have happened yesterday, and that this was in no way a response to anything we experienced together yesterday. They confirmed that this had been their assumption and were relieved to hear the explanation. After that, the smiles returned! I was so glad we discussed the issue directly and immediately rather than letting hard feelings develop due to a misunderstanding. We could do this, in part, because of how we had engaged with each other the day before. Setting up good relations and identifying clear and shared goals help weather misunderstandings if they arise.

It is not just the interactions but also the outcomes of consultation that can be difficult. Laws and policies are in place for museums to determine whether to repatriate, and claims are not always approved by museum staff. Sometimes that is due to reticence, sometimes to lack of evidence to support a claim under the requirements of the law in both NAGPRA and the museum's deaccessioning policy. Even if a museum is proactive about NAGPRA, it doesn't always mean that its process and policy will lead to the outcome a particular Tribe demands. There may be conflicting evidence, other Tribes that are affiliated or making a similar claim, and other factors. It's complicated, and decisions are not always obvious under the law.

Something to always keep in mind about repatriation, or working with communities in general, is that things will happen in their own time, according to community priorities and capacity. My goal is to ensure that community members know—whether for repatriation or any other kind of project—that we have made a connection, our door is open, and we are willing and happy to work with them when the time is right for them. A phrase I often use is "we are happy to follow your lead." For example, I reached out to a community to let it know the CU Museum had a mask for which we knew it had made a general request to museums for repatriation. After preliminary research, we offered the option of making a claim and we would return the mask immediately, or community members could review the entire collection to potentially identify additional items for return under the law. We had digitized and shared records

FIGURE 3.7. Posed photo requested by Calvin and Elgin as we prepared to wrap items in red cloth for them to take home. They asked us to publicly share photos and tell people about our repatriation work together. Left to right: Christina Cain, Stephanie Gilmore, Calvin Grinnell, Jen Shannon, Jan Bernstein, and Elgin Crows Breast, 2014. *Courtesy,* Jan Bernstein.

with them, and they chose to do the latter. So, we obtained a NAGPRA grant to support a consultation visit with multiple related Tribes the THPO requested to have participate. During the visit, they identified a number of items they wanted to consider and discuss with elders back home. After a few months, we reached out and offered to assist them in writing a claim. I waited a year and reached out again. It is now more than four years later, and no claim has been made—but they know that if the right time comes for them to make a claim, the museum staff will be willing and eager to work with them on it.

One of the first repatriations I was involved in was with the Mandan, Hidatsa and Arikara (MHA) Nation in 2011. We repatriated cultural items to the MHA Nation in 2014. I learned so much from working with MHA Nation NAGPRA liaisons Elgin Crows Breast and Calvin Grinnell during that time and later during a series of collaborative projects. I remember clearly the day in 2014 when Calvin and Elgin invited us to wrap the items that were going home in red cloth; they then carried them out to their rental car in the museum's parking lot (figure 3.7). Calvin loved driving with his buddy Elgin by his side in a sporty red car. This was their preferred way to take the items home. Community members bring items home in different ways—sometimes in cars, as carry-on luggage on planes, through art shipping companies, and others. The community decides how best to do this, and National NAGPRA has grants to help with the costs.

I wrote at the start of this section that repatriation is a transfer of ownership. That means it is up to the Tribe to determine what happens to the items or individuals. Sometimes they want them to remain in the museum's care, but more often they want them to return home. The museum or repatriating institution has no say over what happens after repatriation; there are no conditions for return. And it is not our right or our privilege to know what happens with the items after they go home. We do not ask.

Sometimes, though, community members share that information with us. In 2018 Calvin Grinnell called to tell me what happened with the items that were returned, including that one is now a part of Sun Dance ceremonies. Another example is the return of a White Earth Nation drum from the Berkshire Museum, which the THPO explained was to be used to facilitate healing for young people struggling with depression and addiction.[17]

There are many stories of the role these important items play once they return home, some we know and most we will never know. But from the stories we have the privilege to hear, it is clear that these items have a significant role in cultural continuity and community health and well-being for present and future generations. It is a privilege and a special part of museum work to contribute to this process through repatriation.

Finally, there is a concern about returning museum collections to communities that has nothing to do with ownership or affiliation. Historically, when items were collected, the intention was that they would sit on a shelf forever and not go back into use. Toxic chemicals like arsenic and other pesticides were used to protect the items, but those chemicals make them dangerous to humans. That's why it is important for museum staff to wear gloves and sometimes masks when working with certain collections—textiles and perfect-looking feathers are usual suspects. Knowing that repatriated items will be handled and may be put into circulation and used by community members makes researching and providing a collection's history even more critical, especially with respect to the use of preservative chemicals. Consider including XRF (X-ray fluorescence) testing for toxic elements and seeking out conservators to assist in determining if there are toxic chemicals on items identified for repatriation. This kind of information is key so NAGPRA liaisons can make informed decisions regarding the handling and return of items to their community.

31

Catalogs and Online Databases

Similar to considering how to make community visits to collections at a museum more welcoming, you can apply the same process of reflection regarding how communities encounter collections online or in your database. In addition, I invite you to think about your online collections search not only as a place to be welcoming to communities of origin but also as a teaching tool for the general public about appropriate language for collection items and how to refer to communities.

Tools we see as neutral or objective, such as computer programs and databases, are not—they are culturally biased because humans created them, utilizing our own understandings of what seem to be natural categories and how things should be classified. Professional standards for naming objects and museum collection information systems are no different; they are based on Western concepts of classification. For example, many museums use standardized identification terms to be able to search and name objects. However, these terms are often biased toward tools, technology, and progress rooted in Western values and understandings of the world. It's worth looking at object type, cultural affiliation, and other categories in a catalog to see if the standardized terms need to be updated.

One of my favorite moments when I teach students is introducing them to Shelly Errington's "Two Centuries of Progress," the introduction to her 1998 book *The Death of Authentic Primitive Art and Other Tales of Progress*. It helps them see that some of our received, seemingly natural categories and understanding of the world are a result of historical events and social behavior. Errington explains that we take for granted that progress is measured and defined by advancement and complexity in technology and tools. But what counts as progress is arbitrary; this definition comes from Western philosophers and scientists. In the context of the history of anthropology and museums, this concept of progress routinely represented Aboriginal peoples as the lowest people on a ladder of progress. But, Errington explains, if progress were defined by complexity of kinship terms instead of tools, Aboriginal Australians would be at the top and Europeans at the bottom of the ladder. Dublin

Core is a set of Western-based classification standards that is embedded in most collections information systems and catalogs: it is a colonial structuring of knowledge about Indigenous things. There have been efforts to address this, but it is still the primary lexicon, or organized set of reference terms, by which collections are classified.

When people view collection items in exhibits, online, or housed on shelves, the cultural affiliation and object identification fields are often what they first encounter. These terms can communicate whose perspective is privileged. Most standard catalog systems carry colonial legacies of naming, from cultural affiliations (Eskimo versus Inuit) to object identification (fetish versus figure versus Native language term). Some efforts are local, such as a student project at the CU Museum to create a new reference list for culture terms in the database. National efforts include the Lexicon Task Force of the American Alliance of Museums, which identified a need for a more culturally appropriate lexicon for Indigenous collections, and the National Museum of the American Indian's cultural thesaurus, which is a living document, meaning it continues to be updated regularly because terms change over time and new information from communities continues to be added.

While it is important to record new or more appropriate names for peoples, places, and items—it is also true that things need to be findable, whether through access at a distance online or onsite in your database. Prior terms used for items and peoples need to be maintained in the record. For example, you might have all the spellings of Navajo, including the Navajo term *Diné*, in your database that populates your web search. If someone searches "Navaho," it will pull up the same records, but the names shown on the screen will be those the Navajo Nation prefers: Navajo and Diné. An item may have been classified as a fetish in the past, but the term that is at the top of the object identification field, and the only one that appears onscreen in the online search for "fetish," might be "figure."

Originating community members can provide words or names they use for items in the collection to add to the record. A Navajo person searching the CU Museum catalog would not think or know to use the term *fetish*, but they may search for records of *jish*. Both terms are in the database. A good example that comes from a tribal museum, whose primary audience is tribal members, is the Makah Cultural and Research Center. Its collection items are organized according to the root of the Native language term for each item.[18] For multicultural collections in larger institutions, this may not be feasible, but you can use the existing system in new ways to achieve similar results. For example, if you put the Native language term in the digital record and search for a root term, you could get a list of items categorized according to the Native language connection, not Western categories.

The standard fields in collections databases are also biased toward historical understandings of museums and collections, their purpose and audiences. For example, the database may separate archaeology and ethnography because the Western methods and subfields that created those categories of items and the kinds of information associated with them are different. Or there may be an entry field for researcher notes but not originating community contributions. At the CU Museum, we reallocated and renamed a field in the database to show that we value and provide space for community input.

An additional concern is how we know what we know in the catalog. In the past, a curator often input information as the authority. It's important that we know who provided the information entered and how they know. Was it a curator based on interviews or a particular scholarly article? A THPO during a visit? If it is a curatorial note, what is the degree of confidence? For example, I know this is a Mandan moccasin because it was purchased from the maker or at a nearby training post, gifted to an Indian commissioner during a treaty signing, the designs suggest this, and so on. It's important to document why you came to this conclusion. This is also pertinent to cultural care instructions; include who provided them and when, as these things can change over time. Was it the curator who knows from past experience or the community's THPO?

Once information and images are in a catalog or archives are digitized, it is often a short step to make that material available online. Online access is an excellent way for people to find and review collections from their communities, either for their own research or in preparation for a visit. For researchers, it may be possible to obtain needed information without having to see collections in person. However, be mindful of what information is shared. In archaeology, site location data are often not shared. For cultural items, there is also cause for restriction according to cultural protocols. If your catalog is web-ready and publishes to the web, ensure that items with cultural care or restriction guidelines are treated accordingly. That means not including images for some items and not including physical descriptions for others. For example, we have learned that under no circumstances should images of Native American burials or skeletons be made public without explicit consent. Items under NAGPRA claim or that have been determined sacred may also have restrictions on public accessibility (see Cultural Care above).

So, be sure you know how to turn on and off certain fields that publish to the web and provide contact information on your online catalog landing page. You are not always going to get it right or be able to ask each originating community to validate or contribute to the records. Make a conscious decision about your approach to online publishing, and define your policy and practice—do you err on the side of caution and show no images without consultation? Do you show most collection items, excepting those with explicit restrictions from consultation and well-known, specific classes of items such as medicine bundles and burial items?

Communicate to originating community members that you strive to get it right, and provide contact information for them to request a record correction or removal of photographs from view. It is important to monitor that contact so changes can be made immediately. For example, the CU Museum landing page for the Anthropology Section's collections search says:

> WELCOME TO OUR ONLINE DATABASE. The CU Museum of Natural History would like to acknowledge that we are located on the traditional territories of 48 tribal nations, including the Arapaho, Cheyenne, and Ute peoples who have historic ties to the land that currently makes up the state of Colorado. The Anthropology Section of the museum provides stewardship for cultural items and archaeology representing these nations, as well as peoples from across the world. We are committed to seeking guidance and ongoing dialogue with these communities. We ask that you view the items in this database with respect for the people who made and used them. If there is erroneous information or an image that should not be viewed, please contact us here.

Another example is the Local Contexts project's "Open to Collaborate" symbol, which can be placed in online collection records to invite communities to advise on collection attributions and identification or to request if something should be removed from the website.

Remember the idea of a "culture of learning"—if you make a mistake, apologize and share what you have learned. One of the students in my collections research class chose what was labeled a Hopi "replica" of a nineteenth-century "dance wand" for her semester project (see chapter 11, "For Example," for more details). We placed it in the student exhibit in the museum midway through the semester. Upon further examination, she saw use-wear—evidence of someone holding the item rather than marks from hanging on a wall, which is what was expected from something called a replica that had a hanging wire on its back. With my guidance, she reached out to the Hopi THPO office and learned that it was a sacred item. We apologized and took the *Marau Paho* off display immediately. This experience became a lesson shared in her public talk at the museum at the end of the semester.

32
Associated Documentation and Archives

For communities, anything the museum has related to them or their associated collections is of interest. Often, only cultural items are taken out for review by originating communities. When we consider "collections" to include not only three-dimensional items but also associated documentation, photographs, and archives, we can present a more transparent and complete record to community visitors. Museum staff may also find related information to improve object records.

The inclusion of all collections for review allows for provenance research, or seeking information about the context of collecting to determine the community of origin, the identity of the collector or donor, and the circumstances and ethics of the collecting encounter. This kind of information can help identify the originating community or help community members identify collections that were unlawfully or unethically obtained so they can request return. This kind of research may also help identify other institutions that have materials or information related to the collection. Providing communities with access to this broader range of materials can also provide opportunities for them to identify when, similar to some cultural items, there may be information or knowledge expressed in documents or photographs that is culturally sensitive and not appropriate for public sharing.

Associated documentation may include registration records, letters between collector and museum, videos of interviews with artists, and other items. These kinds of materials may or may not be organized systematically and are often grouped by collection item or collector. They are not accessioned materials the way archives are. Archives can have organizing systems similar to those of three-dimensional collections. The boxes and folders that house archives are usually made of special materials so that paper records, photographs, and glass plate negatives do not have chemical reactions or become exposed to other forms of deterioration over time.

Collections and documentation that are related can sometimes be divided among different institutions and private collections. For example, in working on a project to document a repatriation to the White Earth Nation, we learned that the items and photographs from the collection donor were at the museum institution where he had worked, but the testimonies he collected from community members were at a historical society in another state.[19] Through repatriation of items and scanned records of the testimonies and photographs, the THPO was able to bring those divided collections back together on tribal lands. Even within a single institution, collections can be dispersed. Recall my student Maddie King's research on cultural items from the Canadian Arctic collected by a former science professor at the university. Through her sleuthing, she tracked down other materials from the same expedition, including specimens in the botany collection and photos of community members in the university library archives.

Finally, photographs and paper archives can undergo similar community reviews to provide more accurate identification and determine whether they contain sensitive subject matter. Sharing those materials back in digital, if not the original, format is a wonderful way to give back to communities and support their authority and cultural continuity (digital sharing should not be called repatriation; see the next section).

33
Digitization and Digital Return

Museums are increasingly amassing digital files, whether images of collection items, recordings of community visits, scans of archives and documents, or video and audio recordings from interviews, public talks, or exhibit displays. Many see a collecting crisis in the future, much as in the past—only now, the concern is not over physical space but server space, along with standardizing file formats and metadata and the length of time a given storage technique is reliable (recent archival standards suggest re-saving materials on CDs every three years!). Will hardware and software become obsolete—unusable, unreadable? Unlike paper and three-dimensional items, digital reproductions and the increasing numbers of "born digital" items and artwork are creating concern for the long-standing assumption that museums keep things forever. That is, if you are going to start creating digital files in your museum, have a plan. Consider how you will digitize, save, back up, access, and share these materials. In other words, look into creating a digital asset management plan.

Similar to stewarding three-dimensional collections, there need to be plans for long-term storage costs and standardized information. You can look up standards for archival-quality image size and format; they are still in development for video. It is important to ask the purpose of creating digital materials and whether an archival copy is required: do you need a JPEG for a onetime copy that you can email or a TIFF file that is extremely large and meant to be stewarded by the museum long term?

A problem with digital material is that it is too easy to collect. If you have a video of a four-hour collections visit by an originating community, by all means send them a copy for their records. But would you ever watch the entire four-hour video again? If the answer is likely no, edit it into discrete chunks that are useful, like perhaps a ten-minute discussion and demonstration of how a basket hat is worn. Can you attach that to the basket's catalog record in some way? The point is to be deliberate and intentional about what you digitize, its purpose and its accessibility.

There are many places to begin digitizing collections if you have not done so before. This can be an opportunistic process or a systematic one. If you know that a particular originating community is coming to visit collections, that is an opportunity to prioritize those collections and documentation for digitization. Since this book is focused on Native perspectives on collections, if you don't know where to begin, my suggestion is to consider looking into whose homelands your museum resides on. Or perhaps look to the largest collections that may present an opportunity to connect with communities or to the most and least provenanced collections. Share reports of those items with originating communities.

For example, we wrote an Institute of Museum and Library Services (IMLS) grant to digitize some of the CU Museum's cultural anthropology collections. Our grant application stated, in part:

> The Ute, Arapaho, Cheyenne, Shoshone, and Apache have been prioritized for this project due to the fact that Colorado constitutes part of their traditional homelands . . . The extant digital records for the Ute, Arapaho,

Cheyenne, Shoshone, and Apache ethnographic collections (approximately 400 objects) are in various stages of completion, as most records do not include photographs, measurements, accession, or provenance information. Furthermore, additional data is dispersed throughout the Museum's digital network files, as well as in hard-copy card catalogs, ledgers, donor files, object files, tribal consultation files, and on historic object tags. The intended result of this project is to organize all of these data together in the Museum's digital database, Re:discovery Proficio, with the corresponding web interface, and then to share the data with the Ute, Arapaho, Cheyenne, Shoshone, and Apache tribal communities, as well as the research community and the general public.

As a result of this project, we were able to offer the Apache a full and complete record of the museum's Apache collections in preparation for a repatriation consultation. When an Arapaho community member was giving a talk elsewhere on our university campus, we were able to print the Arapaho catalog records with images, assemble them in a binder that included the digital files on a USB thumb drive, and present it to him after his talk, with an open invitation for him and members of his community to visit the museum.

Digital records also allow us to collect and connect intangible culture to tangible culture—connecting an audio file of a song with an instrument, or a field note about Bougainville Island with a photo. Digital records allow us to reassemble collections that are divided across departments or institutions or countries. An excellent example of this process serving communities is the University of British Columbia Museum of Anthropology's Reciprocal Research Network, formed in collaboration with First Nation communities. It is an online portal that brings together visually and in one (online) place collections from Pacific Northwest communities that are housed in museums all over the world. A Kwakwaka'wakw artist can now see, compare, learn from, and be inspired by masks that would take a lifetime and a great deal of money to go see in person. The portal can also help artists determine which of all these items may be a priority to find the time and money to visit in person, or it can help a community prioritize its repatriation efforts.

As noted in "Cultural Care" (chapter 27) and "Catalogs and Online Database" (chapter 31), it is important to review what you share digitally for potential cultural sensitivity. It is also important to keep in mind that cultural knowledge is embedded in the images, documents, and photographs you are digitizing. In the past, we would discuss concerns about intellectual property rights when sharing digitized archival records, photographs, or artwork. Today, there is a new language and movement among Native Nations for "Data Sovereignty." The Global Indigenous Data Alliance explains, "The rise of national Indigenous Data Sovereignty networks reflects a growing global concern about the need to protect against the misuse of Indigenous data and to ensure Indigenous Peoples are the primary beneficiaries of their data."[20] That framework is being applied to museums and the data they hold and share as well.

For my final note in this section, although I am not the only person who says this, I do not want to leave a discussion about digital return without saying it clearly and directly: do not use the phrase *digital repatriation* unless you are returning the originals and their copyright to their community of origin.[21] Providing digital replicas, whether two- or three-dimensional, is not repatriation; it is sharing digital copies. Sending scans of paper records is not repatriation—that would be returning the original paper copies from the archives. That said, providing digital copies can be an excellent way to be transparent, to make an institution that appeared impenetrable and secretive seem more open and accessible, and to support the return of intangible culture and knowledge. It can be a way to start a relationship with a community by giving first—sending copies of information you have about collections associated with that community (see chapter 38, "For Example," for a detailed description of how a digitization project at the CU Museum shared records back to an originating community). These digital materials can also be useful for visitors to access collections from a distance.

34

Researcher Access to Collections

Researchers here include anyone, Native or non-Native, who is seeking to engage with collections for research. A Native artist may seek to view pottery from their community to inspire new artwork; a Native or non-Native researcher may seek access to textiles to write about their construction and the history of trading posts in Arizona. In this chapter, my remarks are focused primarily on the latter group.

The availability of digitized records can sometimes fulfill researcher needs without having to arrange a visit or handle collection items. It may also result in a visit where you are asked to pull and display three items rather than the entire collection because the researcher was able to see the collection images ahead of time and make those determinations. In any case, if you are implementing cultural care guidance, there may come a time when a researcher is requesting access to view, handle, or photograph items that are culturally sensitive. Having a well thought-out policy ahead of time can help in these situations.

Do you have a policy for what a researcher can and cannot photograph? What if they are only photographing for research purposes and not for publication? If it is not okay to photograph an item, can they draw it? Can they have access to it at all? What if they want to do destructive analysis? If you are going to require that a researcher obtain permission from the originating community, whose authority will you accept—a research collaborator, or must it be a THPO officer? Many researchers have existing contact with originating communities, but the majority do not. They may feel uncomfortable contacting the originating community or not know who to contact. In the CU Museum collection information system, there is a series of images of items that the record states, at the request of the Tribe, you must contact the THPO office to view. A researcher searching in the database would see those instructions. Consider providing a sample request letter they can view as a model.

Too often, researchers study collections and never share what they learned with the museum they visited, let alone the originating community. I suggest that researchers commit to sharing the outcomes of their research with both originating communities and the museum. The information can also be placed in the collection's associated documentation and accessed by community members who search or visit the collection in the future. You might consider automatically emailing a THPO office when a researcher requests to work with collections that originated from their Tribe. Researchers have to fill out the museum's research request forms; consider stating on the form that their name and brief summary of what collections they are requesting access to and why will be shared with the originating community. Sharing this information with the originating community creates an opportunity for them to know what kinds of items are at the museum. They can also review what kind of research is being done, request a copy of the research, and express concerns, if any, about particular items being accessed, researched, or photographed.

Researchers often have to pay for the museum to provide digital records, audiovisual recordings, or object photographs. Those same materials are increasingly, and rightfully, being provided free of charge to their communities of origin. Museums like the Ohio History Connection are choosing not to charge originating community members for gaining access to or making copies of collections that are affiliated with them. The THPO of White Earth Nation wanted to obtain copies of collected testimonies from the community that were in Ohio's historical records to add them to the reservation's archival records. The historical society scanned the documents at no cost because an official tribal representative was requesting them. The same principle can be applied to language resources in university departments. You can create policies that define and explain different approaches to research requests. In fact, having policies about all of these commitments to community-oriented museum practice can both cover you when people ask why and ensure that the how and why of this work continue into the future.

35

Collections Management Policy and Shared Stewardship

Policies and standard operating procedures can set the conditions for a welcoming work environment and direct the future of the museum and its potential to have positive relations with originating communities. The discussions that lead to these documents can shape practice and ensure that if staff or community members leave their roles, the important work they contributed to continues in a good way. Build periodic review and revision into your policies and procedures to encourage a culture of reflection and learning.

Developing new policies, or adding to existing collections management policies, regarding access and public sharing is a great way to provide an informed and consistent response to research requests. For example, you may comply with NAGPRA as a law. But do you have a policy for how to enact it specifically in your institution? Is there a review process? Do you know the current law and regulations—for example, do you know what to do if a researcher requests access to Native ancestors or human remains, funerary items, or items under NAGPRA claim but not yet returned? What if a researcher wants to photograph culturally sensitive items? Are drawings okay but not photographs? What is your process for seeking guidance from originating communities before or when such requests arise? Developing a policy that anticipates requests about items that have cultural care guidance associated with them can be helpful and also signal to visitors what your approach is regarding originating communities and the care of collections.

Include in your policies a regular interval at which you revisit and revise them. The more we interact with communities, researchers, and our colleagues, the more we know. It's important to bake that openness to learning into your museum policies and procedures. Policies are also a great way to inform and get investment from institutional leadership. How might you invite relevant originating communities to guide these policies? Can you create an ad hoc committee or use this opportunity to build an advisory group?

Some areas of policy you might consider adding to the collections management policy include:

- NAGPRA policy: There is the law, but how is it enacted in this institution? Who is the decision maker; how are items approved for deaccession? Do you have a plan for international repatriation claims, photographs, publication, and researcher access?
- Cultural care policy: Are there requirements to enact cultural care guidance, such as confirmation from an official tribal representative? In their absence, do you include provisional guidance; if so, do you enact that guidance or await confirmation? If there is an access restriction and a researcher or community member requests access, what steps do you or the requestor take to determine whether access should be allowed?

Also consider whether you need to revisit your collecting policy: will you collect or accept donations of items that you know are sacred? Unassociated funerary items? Items with no provenance? Is community consultation recommended or required before adding new items to the collection? The point is to think ahead and be intentional in these decisions; let your policy help guide future actions.

You can also consider different forms of agreements to enter into partnerships or shared stewardship with communities. If there is a desire for a formalized partnership or written agreement to ensure accountability and to establish that everyone has a clear understanding of expectations and responsibilities, there are several approaches you can take. For example:

- Memorandum of understanding (MOU): outlines expectations, responsibilities, and accountability measures.
- Memorandum of agreement (MOA): outlines expectations, responsibilities, and accountability measures as well as funding committed.
- Memorandum of affiliation: acknowledges whose lands an institution resides on, thereby identifying a special relationship.
- Loan agreements: can be long or short term and are usually for the purpose of exhibition; terms of a loan often define required security and environmental conditions, include check-in visits by the loaning institution, and define conditions in which originating community members can handle the items.
- Care and trust agreement: after transfer of control through repatriation, this agreement indicates how the museum will care for the ancestors or items that remain in its custody.
- Shared stewardship agreement: whether items are located at the museum or in the originating community or both, this is an agreement by both parties regarding location, care, access, and handling of cultural items that is more flexible than a loan agreement and may include legal co-ownership.

If you have policies, share them online so the public can learn from your example and community members can see what is possible and what to expect in working with you (see appendix B for examples). You can also develop procedures, which are the steps you take to enact a given policy. Having policies that acknowledge this kind of work with and for originating communities is part of creating a welcoming workplace—one in which current and potential Native staff can see the institution's commitments to these principles and practices and all staff know what is expected of them in their engagement with collections and communities.

36

A Welcoming Workplace

Creating a welcoming work environment for Native peoples and allies can take many forms, including instituting proactive NAGPRA policies, displaying cultural care signs on collections shelves, developing exhibits and catalogs with Native language terms, and hiring more Native individuals. There are many ways to create pathways for Indigenous people to enter museum professions, including providing apprenticeship and training opportunities, hiring cohorts, developing more diverse and targeted recruitment methods, and rethinking job requirements.

A focus on retention is also essential and requires that the museum be a welcoming place for Native individuals after they are hired. Collections spaces can be difficult places for Native museum professionals and visitors. Not every Native individual has the same restrictions or concerns, but you can take some steps to provide the opportunity for the museum to be more welcoming and avoid spiritual harm.

I have already discussed much of what can create a welcoming space for Native staff, including how to show respect for originating communities and the collections in the museum's care. Here, I want to emphasize that bringing in diverse people to work in a museum is not enough; it's important to create the conditions for them to want to stay. This applies not just to Native staff but also to persons of color, people with disabilities, English as a second language speakers, and people from lower socioeconomic classes. Museums have a reputation and a history of being elite, English-speaking, white spaces. Having more diversity in the museum's management and staff means creating a space, exhibitions, and public programs that are more welcoming to all. Diversifying staff can also diversify and increase the museum's audience.

Recruitment for internships, fellowships, or hires is key. Museum staff often say they had few persons of color in their applicant pool. More often than not, this is a result of poor recruitment—either falling back on old recruitment habits or not thinking deliberately about how to target diverse populations with a job ad or intern application. Have a strategy for recruitment; do the research and networking to find out how to communicate with the population you are seeking to invite to apply.

As usual, I am focused on Native community members here because that is my experience. Consider these examples to think about and determine what may be right for the communities you serve—either located around your museum or represented in your collections. Regarding Native staff, here are some things to keep in mind (some points are repeated from earlier sections):

- Place signs at locations where there are Native ancestors or human remains.
- Invite individuals to discuss their needs—including physical and spiritual—in doing this kind of work. For example, provide time and space for ceremonial or cleansing practices. Ask if there are any ceremonies, feast days, or other important community events that may require them to be on leave from work. Institute flexible leave policies to accommodate these cultural obligations.
- Build networks with other staff both within and beyond the museum to create a stronger sense of community and support.
- Bring in groups of Native individuals when hiring (called cluster hires) or when designing internships (a cohort approach). Consider assigning mentors for new hires and interns. Refrain from asking or expecting Indigenous staff, fellows, or interns to generally represent Indigenous peoples or to be authorities on Indigenous matters.
- Create a Native advisory group for the museum or your department. This is helpful for Native staff in two ways. First, they should not become the persons others go to for information about what Native people would think or do about something. Their job is to be a collections manager, not a cultural adviser (unless that is what they were hired for; there is precedent for this). Second, doing this creates a group of Native individuals who can guide leadership and be fortifying for or accessible to Native staff in times of need.

Retention and a positive workplace culture can also be supported by providing opportunities for learning and professional development.

37
Teaching Museum Studies and Professional Development

Collaboration within the museum is important to the success of exhibitions and programs, as well as to working with communities outside the museum. Museum work relies on a group of individuals with different trainings, interests, goals, and audiences in mind. Understanding where your colleagues and museum professionals you are working with are coming from and how your interests overlap or diverge can aid in the collaborative process. The Museum and Field Studies program at the University of Colorado asks students to identify a track in the museum field they want to pursue, including administration, education, exhibit design, and collections management. The latter specialize in anthropology, biology, geology, or botany collections. The classroom includes a group of students with diverse experiences, interests, and career goals.

The Introduction to Museum Studies course at CU meets two days a week, one day for a two-hour seminar and the other for a fieldtrip to a nearby museum. When I taught the course, I reviewed the various professions in the museum field that developed over time. I started with curators, then collections managers, conservators, educators, exhibit developers, and others—all the way to the latest jobs advertised at museums, such as diversity and inclusion officers, tribal liaisons, and directors of decolonizing initiatives. The aim was for students seeking museum jobs to understand how each profession came about and why. I often joked as we started to read journal articles that "everyone craps on the curators!" They were the original museum professionals, and many successive professions either carved out and improved some aspect of the curator's original duties—such as label writing—or identified something missing and professionalized it, such as marketing.

This course was meant to be practical, and it included several projects. The first assignment asked students to research and present the history, use, and potential of a museum collection that interested them. The second was a "professionals project," which I go into more detail below. The third was a group project in which students created detailed plans for a new museum.

They received constraints such as budget and size of exhibition space, then determined what staff positions the museum includes. They described the museum's location, concept, and collection; identified its main audience and funding sources; and created a sample exhibit proposal. This assignment was meant to invite students to think holistically about a museum and how its mission, staff, and exhibitions are connected, as well as to provide them with an opportunity to flex or develop skills in a particular part of the planning. For example, a team member might want to spend more time practicing budgeting, creating a digital 3D model, or doing label writing. I was amazed at the innovative concepts for museums and creative exhibitions the students produced and how fully formed they were. We could really imagine them, and we all agreed that it felt like they already existed!

Reviewing Exhibitions Together

To prepare for their museum proposal, students were asked to complete an "Excellent Judges Review" of an exhibit of their choice. Developed by Beverly Serrell, this form of exhibit evaluation is meant to be conducted by museum professionals. Her handout guides reviewers to write down their impressions about whether an exhibition is comfortable, engaging, reinforcing, and meaningful through an individual rating process and then includes a group meeting to compare and discuss ratings.[22] It's a great way to give students a format in which to think critically and discuss together what they do and don't like about a museum exhibition, which can inform the way they design the exhibit for their project. I recommend this process of viewing exhibitions with your colleagues and fellow community members who intend to work with a museum. Whether you review formally and fill out a review with structured discussion like Serrell's or walk through an exhibit and chat over coffee afterward, having a shared frame of reference and thinking ahead about your preferences can aid in exhibition development and teamwork.

Informational Interviews

I always encourage students to think ahead, and to think strategically, about how course projects or master's theses can help in their career planning. For the museum professionals project, students selected a museum ethnography to read, reviewed job ads and created one for their ideal position in their field, received feedback from their peers and me on a résumé they drafted, and interviewed museum professionals whose jobs they admired. (See appendix E for additional pointers.)

Options for their book review included museum ethnographies about art, history, science, and anthropology museums. I wanted them to read about the everyday practice of museum work and discuss what they learned and how it influenced what they thought about their future in the field. I encouraged them to share their "aha moments" while reading the book or moments that left a strong impression, something they found particularly meaningful. Reviewing museum work in detail through these ethnographies also helped students develop questions for their museum professional interviews.

Informational interviews helped students concretely imagine the day-to-day experience of their chosen career and sometimes led to future internships. They are an excellent source of information and networking, whether you are a student, an early career professional, or someone who wants to make a career change. These interviews require some research to identify individuals who occupy the type of position in which you are most interested. The conversation should focus on the person's background, training, duties and responsibilities and their advice for prospective professionals in their field.

When you want to set up an informational interview, make it clear to your potential interviewee what you are looking for and how much time the interview will take. For example, if you are reaching out by email, I suggest using a specific subject line such as "invitation for informational interview." Briefly explain who you are, that you want to learn about how they entered the field and what their job is like, and that the conversation should take about thirty minutes of their time. Never offer your résumé or ask about a job; that is not the purpose or expectation of an informational interview. However, it's always good to have a résumé prepared in case you are asked for one.

Professional Development

An advanced degree is not necessary to learn and grow in museum professions, although it is increasingly sought after in job ads. There are many ways to engage in professional development and résumé building, including obtaining graduate degrees, attending conferences, pursuing trainings and certifications, doing internships, working with a mentor, asking people in your professional network about lessons learned, and more. There are many programs, online webinars, training institutes, and conferences—so it might be helpful to create a professional development plan each year. Select one or a series of opportunities that contribute to your career development goals.

You may wonder, as a community member, student, or both interested in museums and anthropology: what kinds of courses should I take? What degree is right for me? As a curator and associate professor of anthropology, I advised and taught master's students in museum studies, master's students in cultural anthropology, and PhD students in cultural anthropology. I tend to address the question of which degree concretely, so when a student asked me what degree to pursue, I often responded with something along the lines of: what do you want to be when you grow up, at least given what you know now? Of course this may change because an education will broaden your mind and may take you in a completely different direction—and that's to be expected!

If you are interested in pursuing graduate studies, here are some things to consider. If you want a museum professional career other than being a curator or you want to be a curator in a smaller museum and wear multiple hats, consider an MA in museum studies (you will likely need to choose a track, such as interpretation, education, or collections). If you want to be a curator or a professor, the PhD may be the way to go. If you are not sure, a master's in anthropology is the most versatile degree. Your thesis can specialize your credentials, and it will often count toward a PhD if you choose to pursue one later, which was my experience. But these are not the only routes to do this kind of work; they are just the typical ones *right now*. Increasingly, and encouragingly, museums are not necessarily requiring a PhD when hiring curators or research specialists to work with Indigenous collections, acknowledging the value and expertise of cultural knowledge acquired within one's community.

Graduate programs are different from undergraduate programs. Some museum studies programs, for instance, are better known for education or curation, others for the quality of their internship placements. Make sure the program you are going to enroll in specializes in the career you want to advance. You can ask to speak to a potential adviser and current graduate students and ask about job placements after graduation to learn more about a program. One of the things I loved about the museum studies program at CU is that students were résumé building while getting their master's degrees by working in a public museum on campus. Students in the Anthropology Section, for example, work as assistant collection managers, earning a stipend to help fund their education. Yes, they learn in the classroom—but they also work alongside their mentors and museum professionals to learn by doing.

You can seek out professional development in informal learning environments as well—from visiting museums to compare and learn how other institutions do similar work, to attending conferences in your field, to shadowing someone for a day. There are general museum conferences like those of the American Alliance of Museums, career-specific conferences like those of the American Institute for Conservation, local and regional conferences like those sponsored by the Colorado-Wyoming Association of Museums, and conferences that are focused on tribal museums like those sponsored by the Association of Tribal Archives, Libraries, and Museums (I regularly attend the last one to learn what I should be teaching and to connect with tribal museum professionals and their institutions). Some conferences are more lecture-like; others have hands-on activities and certificates.

Museum staff and cultural center staff can also create professional development opportunities for others—perhaps you want to be a mentor, host an intern, or provide a workshop on pest management for a smaller museum whose staff are local volunteers. Mentoring and internships are key parts of museum learning and professional development, whether in teaching/university museums or standalone museums. These are ways important lessons and practices developed from everyday work in collections and with Native peoples can be passed on. These are also ways we can shape the future of museums, their purpose and practice.

Internships

Professional development can include seeking out or being a mentor. A mentor is a role model and guide. A mentor can be a professional at your institution or elsewhere, someone who guides you through a professional conference, an intern supervisor, an academic adviser, an elder, and more. I tell the students I advise and mentor that they are driving the car and I am the navigator. They tell me where they want to go—what studies they want to pursue, what career they want to achieve—and I do everything I can to get them there. I find that ideas and learning flow both ways in mentoring Native and non-Native emerging museum professionals, which is why it is so enjoyable.

I encourage interns and research assistants to develop work plans. An intern will be more productive, be able to work more independently, and feel more secure in their role if they have a plan with clear expectations. It is best to work together to make a work plan but to also be flexible. A plan might be as simple as a description of the project and a list of steps to get there or a list of short projects with descriptions and rough deadlines for their completion. Invite your intern to fill out the details of the work plan, and then go over it together and make adjustments. This helps give you an idea of what they know and how they problem solve and break down the steps to accomplish a project.

As a mentor or intern supervisor, there may be opportunities to guide the intern in how to cope with challenges in the workplace. Ultimately, you want to encourage open and honest communication so they can ask, can I look forward to learning something new when I complete this project? Or, I need a personal day. Maybe they have done three inventories in a row and are losing interest—a moment to reassess the order of projects. Perhaps they have had a death in the family, and you can explain what a personal day is. Or perhaps a task brought them in contact with sacred items that made them feel spiritually harmed, but they didn't feel comfortable speaking with you about it.

Be prepared for the possibility that Native interns or mentees may discuss concerns about being at risk for emotional or spiritual harm when working in museum collections. A tour can be a good way to leave the door open to have this conversation. If you are working with Native interns, research assistants, students, fellows, or visiting professionals, a tour of the museum's spaces is a good opportunity to let them know that cultural practices are welcome. Explain where smudging or ceremony, if needed, can take place for staff or visitors. Do not assume this is something every Native person does, but be sure people know that these practices are welcome within the museum and that this is part of the museum's values of supporting other ways of knowing and practicing inclusion.

Some things to keep in mind, and perhaps to bring up during an introductory meeting with a Native intern, are whether they need to avoid certain areas or collections in the museum. It is very important to openly discuss possible cultural sensitivities someone may have (mentor or mentee). Are there any restrictions to keep in mind when planning projects for the intern to work on? For example, are there specific collection items that they cannot view, handle, or be near? How can you protect them from inadvertently coming into contact with those kinds of items? Make a plan. It can be as simple as using sticky notes on cabinets, alerting collections staff to these restrictions, and letting the intern know when certain items are placed in the open for community consultations. If Native ancestors or human remains are housed in the building, know where they are. Regardless of who you are with, always alert someone when they are about to enter a room with ancestral remains, so they can choose whether to enter. Due to cultural protocols, a mentor or an intern may not be able to enter. You will need to find an alternate place to meet people or view items.

In addition, discuss with your intern or mentee opportunities for professional networking. For example, is there an appropriate conference for them to attend? If so, would you consider working with them to create a paper or presentation that would enable them to participate? You will likely be asked to be a reference for them in the future. Be sure to keep notes on their work and accomplishments—this is a good reason to ask them for brief reports throughout the mentoring process.

Additional Training

There are also online resources and webinars that you can review to continue your professional development. The iPINCH, ATALM, and National NAGPRA websites provide recorded presentations; the National Preservation Institute and Beloit College Center for Collections Care offer training; and the Getty has a conservation program specifically for increasing diversity in the field of conservation.[23] These are just some examples; the point is that if you know what kind of learning you want, you can probably find resources to support your goals. If you are unsure whether a program is reputable or a good investment, reach out to networks or listservs in your field and invite recommendations.

The broader takeaways here include the importance of building a professional network and community to support each other and advance our shared values, as well as being open to new ideas and continued learning. In planning your career development goals, include opportunities for you to learn from others and to share what you know by giving presentations or workshops. Teaching others is a great way to better understand, reflect on, and learn from your experiences (as this book suggests). Either way, engaging in professional development provides opportunities to create community among museum and cultural center professionals and to increase support and implementation for the approach to museums embodied in this book.

38

For Example

Bougainville Primary Source Book

I have used examples in a number of publications of how a repatriation to the Mandan, Hidatsa and Arikara Nation led to many collaborative projects over time. While that might be a great example to close this section, its scope and scale may seem overwhelming if you are just starting a project. However, at the beginning, I was just starting, too, and I did not anticipate that over ten years of collaborative work together would result from our first engagement. A repatriation consultation unexpectedly led to years of positive relations and meaningful projects—from a video documentary working with elders, to a citizen science project working with tribal college and grade school teachers, to conducting workshops about filmmaking with youth, to a comic book about repatriation. All because I asked after our first repatriation consultation, is there anything else you'd like us to do with or research about this collection?[24]

I want to focus here on an example that may feel more approachable, more feasible, and perhaps more similar to something you may experience at either a small museum with few resources or a large museum where the size of collections means you don't always know everything they contain. The CU Museum Anthropology Section is best known for housing Southwest pottery and Navajo textiles. Research by curators and professors engaging with the collections has primarily focused on Southwest and Plains materials and communities. But the collection contains items from all over the world. In my cultural anthropology course on collections research, I invited students to choose items from anywhere in the world for their semester research paper and subsequent exhibition and public talk. In 2017, Isabella Vinsonhaler decided to direct her research toward collections from the Pacific.

Until Isabella began investigating the Pacific items donated by Conrad "Bud" Johnson, we had no idea of the amount of documentation associated with items from Bougainville Island. Once we learned this, it became clear that we needed to connect this collection to its originating community. Remember—we had no prior knowledge of the details of this collection or anyone at the university who specialized in this specific region, but we were still able to create a meaningful connection, learning experience, and return along the way. This is an example of what a museum can do with limited capacity and knowledge about a collection that it wants to share with an originating community. I list the series of steps in the process that evolved here, as an example to think with.

The CU Museum has a collection of more than 300 items from Bougainville Island, collected in 1949 by Johnson, who was a CU student on leave and a soldier doing geographic surveys in 1947. Bougainville Island is geographically part of the Solomon Islands but is politically part of the Autonomous Region of Bougainville (previously North Solomons Province) in Papua New Guinea. Bougainville is the largest island in this region. World War II had a drastic impact on the island. We learned that during the war, bombs resulted in loss of life and cultural heritage. The island's population declined by 25 percent after the war, and foreigners outnumbered islanders three to one. A civil war from 1988 to 1998 further devastated the island and its people. In 2019, Bougainville's referendum for independence passed; negotiations in 2021 determined that, if ratified by Papua New Guinea's parliament, independence will be granted by 2027.

In 2017, Isabella shared what she was learning about the Johnson collection from Bougainville Island and the fact that there was a large amount of associated documentation, including letters to the museum, detailed field notes about collecting encounters and collected items, and named makers of the items. Later, we found associated photographs in our archives and at the Denver Museum of Nature and Science. That same year, I assigned a museum studies graduate student, Jane Richardson, to digitize the collection. She inventoried, photographed, and updated records for the items and scanned all associated documentation.

In 2018, I emailed Dr. Jerry Jacka, my closest contact who worked in the Pacific; he is a professor at CU. He put me in touch with Dr. Paige West, who had closer connections to Bougainville Island. Dr. West introduced me by email to Dr. Jeffrey Noro and Mr. Junior Novera, who were the manager and co-founder, respectively, of the Kainake Project. This project is dedicated to creating and sharing knowledge to empower people to preserve and develop their natural and cultural inheritance through community solutions on Bougainville Island. They expressed excitement over the return of knowledge associated with Johnson's collection, and we began working together. Once we digitized the collection and updated the records, we could post everything to the web through our collections information system. Dr. Noro and

Mr. Novera reviewed the collection and told us that there were no items that were inappropriate for public viewing.

One of the remarkable things about this collection is that Johnson's field notes from 1947 were respectful and detailed. They included the names of specific people and places, as well as how items were collected, how they were used by community members, and even how one item was repaired by a fellow soldier. His photos included places and people and material culture; sometimes the photos included the author and other times they were portraits of named people. There was one photo of the author, in his twenties, that stood out to me: he was standing with his arm around the shoulders of an Islander, both smiling. When we share archival materials with communities, we sometimes have to prepare them for offensive language or photographs that treat people like specimens. That was not the case here.

In 2019, undergraduate student Jack Piephoff worked with me to research and prepare what we called a "Primary Source Book" to send to Dr. Noro and Mr. Novera to share with other Bougainville Islanders. The printed and bound book included: (1) the Conrad "Bud" Johnson collection of photographs from the Denver Museum of Nature and Science, (2) images of all of the items in the Conrad "Bud" Johnson collection at the University of Colorado Museum of Natural History, and (3) copies of all associated documentation related to the Conrad "Bud" Johnson collection at the University of Colorado Museum of Natural History, including his field notes and letters to the museum.

With the support of Dr. Jacka, Dr. West, Dr. Noro, and Mr. Novera, we applied for and received $763 in funding from the Association for Social Anthropology in Oceania to print and ship the primary source books through the association's Grant to Return Indigenous Knowledge to Pacific Island Communities (GRIKPIC) program. The books were received in 2019, one of which Dr. Noro presented to the curator of war history at the Papua New Guinea (PNG) National Museum and Art Gallery and other museum staff, including museum director Dr. Andrew Moutu (figure 3.8). Dr. Noro emailed me a photo and explained:

> We have been invited to make a presentation [about this project] during a parliament seating at a date yet to be set. I will let you know when that happens. Our presentation of a copy of the book to the PNG National Museum and Art Gallery went well. As a result of this, a member from our community has been invited to attend a museum conservation training at the PNG national museum from the 24th–28th June 2019. The training will be

FIGURE 3.8. Presenting Bougainville Primary Source Book to Papua New Guinea National Museum and Art Gallery. *Courtesy,* Jeffrey Noro, 2019.

provided by the University of Canberra, Australia. This is a great indication of how this collaboration could evolve in the future, where communities become active participants. The below [figure 3.8] shows our presentation, where I'm handing the book to the Curator of War history and other museum staff. The Director, Dr Andrew Moutu is second from left.[25]

Mr. Novera expressed to us in an email (November 9, 2018) that the materials in the Bougainville Primary Source Book "are vital for the communities and people of Bougainville to rediscover and trackback on their history. It is unfortunate for us that nothing such as you have in your museum can be found today on Bougainville. That is why we are so privileged to connect and collaborate on this project." Dr. Noro told us in an email (November 10, 2018) that he was "delighted to be able to collaborate with you on this museum project because we feel that historical information as this is critical for Bougainville, both as tangible and intangible . . . though this collaboration with you, we may be able to create systems and processes for digital and print repatriation of collections back to Bougainville. There are many collections from Bougainville that are stored in museums around the globe, and thankfully have been preserved. Sadly, we have lost many of these. So repatriation is a great way to regain some of [this] lost knowledge."[26]

In 2019, we also reached out to a broader community of Islanders through social media because we wanted to share the materials digitally with them. Dr. Noro and Mr. Novera told us that Bougainville Islanders often use Facebook, so Jack and I created a Facebook page titled "Bougainville Museum Collections Abroad."[27] We provided a link to download the Bougainville Primary Source Book PDF, and Jack posted Johnson's photographs and their captions. Although it is now a static page that provides resources without additional posts, the number of followers continues to grow. In 2024 the page had 3,300 followers, an increase of 600 from the previous year.

I also oversaw an independent study with graduate student Manuel Ferreira in 2019 to develop an exhibit for the CU Museum about Bougainville, Johnson, and the collection. Due to the Covid-19 pandemic, the exhibit was never installed. However, we were able to convert it later, with the help of Jack and graphic designer Jennie Dillon, into an online exhibit, which we opened in 2022 and shared with the community on the Facebook page.

I tried to find Bud Johnson's relatives and descendants to include their perspective in the exhibit; I called Johnsons in Colorado and California, to no avail. Mona Lambrecht, CU Heritage Center curator, put me in contact with their family at Ancestry.com. Three years later and after the exhibit opened, in September 2022 I received a phone call from Johnson's daughter, Barbara! She and her brother loved the online exhibit. I invited her to post something at the Bougainville Museum Collections Abroad Facebook page, where she wrote: "I grew up hearing stories from my father about his time on Pacific Islands when he was in the army but I didn't realize exactly why he was there and what he was doing . . . he built a Bougainville style outrigger canoe in the 1960's. He used wood and screen for the frame and had it coated with fiberglass . . . Everywhere we moved from the 1960's on, my father moved that outrigger with us . . . My father would have loved all of this."[28]

To accompany the exhibit opening, Dr. Noro gave a public talk in May 2022 via Zoom about our collaboration and the Kainake Project. In his concluding remarks he noted that it's important to create tangible outcomes from this kind of work: "What we have been able to achieve with University of Queensland, and now the University of Colorado and the book project, I think there's so much more to learn from each other. Moving forward, Junior [Novera] and I have been working with the Bougainville government to include some of this experience in Bougainville's policy and legislative frameworks. So these are not just community actions happening in isolation, they can make an impact on the future."

39
Questions to Guide Practice and Additional Resources

Some basic questions when working with museum collections that originate from Native communities include:

- Are you accepting that this is the way things are and have always been, or are you reflecting on and intentionally making decisions about your work in the museum?
- Are you being respectful to originating communities in how you care for, interpret, and display these items?
- Are there ways you can collaborate with originating community members in a meaningful way to ensure this?
- Should particular items or images not be shared with the public?
- How can you contribute to a workplace that is welcoming to Native visitors and staff?

These questions prompt us to seek guidance from the originating communities themselves, when possible. However, as museums, institutions, and researchers increasingly reach out to Native communities, we need to understand that their capacity, resources, and time are limited and respond with compassion and patience.

Contacting Tribal Cultural Specialists and Museum Professionals:

- **ATALM** (Association of Tribal Archives, Libraries, and Museums) has bios of all presenters at the end of each annual conference booklet at https://www.atalm.org/ and a list of tribal museums and cultural centers at https://www.atalm.org/node/504.
- **National Association of Tribal Historic Preservation Officers** provides a regularly updated contact list at https://members.nathpo.org/thpodirectory.

Working with and Teaching about Native American Collections:

- *Preserving What Is Valued: Museums, Conservation, and First Nations* (Clavir 2002).

- Caring for American Indian Objects: A Practical and Cultural Guide (Ogden 2004).
- This Is Our Life: Haida Material Heritage and Changing Museum Practice (Krmpotich and Peers 2013) is about the collaboration between the Haida and the Pitt Rivers Museum documented in Everything Was Carved.
- "Teaching Collections Management Anthropologically" (Krmpotich 2015).
- Weapons of Math Destruction: How Big Data Increases Inequality and Threatens Democracy (O'Neil 2016) is about how our turn to algorithms can lead to, rather than eliminate, discrimination.
- Cataloguing Culture: Legacies of Colonialism in Museum Documentation (Turner 2020) is a critique of the colonial ideologies embedded in the cataloging and data systems that organize ethnographic collections.
- Everything Was Carved (video) at https://www.prm.ox.ac.uk/haida.

PART 3 NOTES

1. *Everything Was Carved* (video).

2. Much has been written about collections reviews by Jim Enote and others. I select here a recorded presentation at the Japan National Museum of Ethnology because it is a detailed visual demonstration that includes a transcript: *Demonstrational Lecture of the Collections Review Research.*

3. Bowechop and Mauger, "Tribal Collections Management at the Makah Cultural and Research Center."

4. Smudging is the burning of sage, cedar, or sweetgrass; the smoke is considered to be cleansing and is often fanned with feathers or hands toward oneself or another person or within a space.

5. Hollinger et al., "Tlingit-Smithsonian Collaborations with 3D Digitization of Cultural Objects."

6. Shenandoah, "Haudenosaunee Confederacy Announces Policy on False Face Masks." Thanks to student Ashley Muggli for bringing this reference to my attention.

7. Local Contexts, "Grounding Indigenous Rights."

8. American Museum of Natural History, "Press Release."

9. Clavir, "Reflections on Changes in Museums and the Conservation of Collections from Indigenous Peoples."

10. Johnson et al., "Practical Aspects of Consultation with Communities."

11. Krmpotich and Peers, *This Is Our Life.*

12. Ryker-Crawford, "Towards an Indigenous Museology," 140.

13. Johnson et al., "Practical Aspects of Consultation with Communities," 204.

14. Johnson et al., "Practical Aspects of Consultation with Communities," 207, 206. I appreciate that NMAI conservators have published many articles about their work process and case studies over the years, providing a model for others to learn from.

15. Odegaard, Sadongei, and Associates, *Old Poisons, New Problems.*

16. See, for example, Pacers, "Kenaitze Tribe Allows DNA Testing on Dena'ina Remains"; Kenaitze Indian Tribe, "DNA Project Connects Dena'Ina Past and Present."

17. Jaime Arsenault, personal communication, April 29, 2021; August 27, 2024.

18. Bowechop and Mauger, "Tribal Collections Management at the Makah Cultural and Research Center."

19. Shannon, "Drawing Together."

20. Global Indigenous Data Alliance, "CARE Principles."

21. See chapter 38, "For Example," for a detailed description of how a digitization project at the CU Museum shared records back to an originating community.

22. For a handout that guides the review process, see https://serrellassociates.com/images/uploads/img/EJFramework_8.5x11_copy_.pdf; see also Serrell, "Judging Exhibitions."

23. National Preservation Institute, "Trainings"; Beloit College, "Center for Collections Care"; Association of Tribal Archives, Libraries, and Museums, "Locations of Native Nations and Cultural Institutions"; UCLA/Getty Interdepartmental Program in the Conservation of Cultural Heritage, "Andrew W. Mellon Opportunity for Diversity in Conservation"; Intellectual Property Issues in Cultural Heritage, "Intellectual Property Issues in Cultural Heritage."

24. Shannon, "My Cry Gets Up to My Throat."

25. Jeffrey Noro, personal communication, June 18, 2018.

26. Dr. Noro uses the term *repatriation* here, but he is referring to digital sharing. While we told him we were open to receiving an international repatriation request, he never asked for anything to be repatriated.

27. Shannon and Piephoff, "Facebook: Bougainville Museum Collections Abroad."

28. Barbara Johnson, reply to a Facebook post dated September 4, 2022.

FIGURE 4.1. Perspective. Artwork by John Swogger from *Kumeyaay Comics: Our Past, Present, and Future*, 2024.

Part 4
Collaborative Research

This section is designed for anyone, in any discipline, who intends to work with communities as part of their research practice—whether in the museum or beyond, whether in anthropology or not. I dedicate this section to Native community members: I hope this inspires researchers to be more informed and focused on "doing some good," in your estimation. I have carried that phrase with me since reading Sam Yazzie's (Navajo) conversation with authors Sol Worth and John Adair in their groundbreaking 1972 work, *Through Navajo Eyes: An Exploration in Film Communication and Anthropology*. I loved and learned from that moment in the book when Mr. Yazzie asked, "Will making movies do the sheep any harm?" Worth said it would not. Then Mr. Yazzie asked, "Will making movies do the sheep any good?" When Worth replied that it would not, Mr. Yazzie responded: "Then why make movies?"[1] It is a good question for collaborative research to go beyond efforts at consent to do no harm and instead aim for proactive consent to join together to do some good.

I also hope this approach and models for collaborative research encourage communities with ideas for projects to reach out to universities, museums, students, and researchers when you have projects of interest. Below are ways you can invite them to practice with you. There are many existing texts that define and describe social science research methods, including collaborative methods; here, I want to highlight additional things to think about when doing collaborative or community-based research.

What I have found over the years is that any researcher doing community-based or collaborative research ends up advocating for very similar methods and practices. Although developed in the context of the museum, what I learned early on from the process of community curating guided me in general in my own anthropological research. I have used something like it, for example, as a method for creating a non-fiction comic book. Participatory action research and community-based research practice are names for structured approaches. I think what makes all of these methodologies similar, at their core, is the fact that a group of community members helped guide the process and insisted on being integral not just to the information gathered but also to designing the project and its outcomes.

While this book focuses on partnering with Indigenous peoples because that is my experience, the lessons we learn about how to work together in a good way are applicable to all originating communities whose items are housed in museums. They are also applicable in the field of anthropology and in social science research in general. Actually, they are good guidance for any research discipline, whether researchers are working with Indigenous people or not. A biologist who wants to study sturgeon on tribal lands or a doctor conducting a medical study on cancer will also benefit from community members' expertise and investment.

What you will learn in this section:

- How to center values and community in your research practice
- How to think creatively about seeking consent and determining what is appropriate to record and publish
- How to design, budget, and write grants for collaborative research projects
- How to communicate your project and its outcomes effectively to your community partners and the broader public
- How to teach the values and practice of collaboration and public scholarship to the next generation.

40
Values-Centered Research Practice

I often cite a quote from Regna Darnell in her book *Invisible Genealogies* (also cited in this book's preface) where she says, "For a long time Native Americans have been teaching anthropologists how to behave in a civilized fashion and respond to local communities' needs and concerns."[2] I think it helps explain why museum anthropology in North America has led us in collaborative, experimental directions. In our work together, our community partners motivate us to develop new ideas, to think outside our academic box. Their demands that we create something that is relevant to their communities and that reaches beyond the academy drive us toward diverse and creative ways of sharing our research.

Collaboration in the museum and in the field is best when guided by "virtue ethics."[3] In other words, rather than rules or protocols, the project and its associated relationships are founded in shared values. The values often cited in Indigenous research methodologies include respect, relevance, reciprocity, and responsibility.[4] When you embark on collaborative research, be conscious about identifying the values that guide your work and relationships with others and then discuss them with your research partners—not just the core values of your project but also how they will specifically be enacted in your work together.

Recently, I was reviewing a graduate student's grant proposal to do collaborative research with a Native community. The project is excellent, and the student already has ties to community members. However, in her methods she emphasized that she will build relationships of trust with community members as part of her method. The phrasing and directionality didn't sit well with me, so we talked it through. You may want to build a relationship with community members to create a more collaborative and meaningful project, but that is not in your control. You can earn trust by showing up, following through, and being accountable for the things you promise. This opened a good discussion among the committee members at the student's defense, where one faculty member with an outstanding reputation for collaborative research said that relationships didn't really start for her until after she had completed her dissertation and came back to present it to the community: showing that she had done what she had said she would do. So yes, relationships and trust are central to collaborative research, but they are earned. And they are not always earned in the first project you do.

We also need to acknowledge that not all projects or relationships are meant to last forever. If you cannot promise to make a lifelong commitment, then don't. I have heard students talk about intending to have long-term relationships with communities. Some anthropologists maintain their connection to one community throughout their lifetime. Others, like myself, work through "projects" with multiple communities (this is more often the case with museum-based anthropologists).[5] I maintain connections to communities, but my research work with them does not continue for decades. Again, relationships and trust emerge from the work. Sometimes it is appropriate—given your time, where you live, the kind of job you land in—to commit to a lifelong engagement. Sometimes it is not, whether due to your constraints or the capacity of the community you are working with. The most important thing is to be clear about expectations; be honest about your commitments and the length and purpose of the work you are doing together. Follow-through and keeping promises matter.

The "4Rs" that Indigenous scholars advocate should guide research with Indigenous communities are a great way to keep values and relationships front and center as you design, implement, and share your research. There are some great resources on these principles that prompt us to think critically about the work we intend to do, ask questions, and plan intentionally for ethical and collaborative research. Below are some of the ways I use the 4Rs to guide my practice:

- **Respect:** In Indigenous thought and theory, respect is focused on being in good relation with all living beings or, as Anya Montiel (Mexican and Tohono O'odham) puts it, "Respect acknowledges . . . connection between all beings and life-forms . . . respect also centers on being a good relative and descendant."[6] When applying this in collaborative research, I think about
    - Respect for Indigenous or other ways of knowing that can guide our practice in meaningful ways—for example, the idea that some collection items are living beings.
    - Respect for the expertise of others, which includes inviting community partners to help plan the project from the start and providing compensation for participation when appropriate.

- Respect for individuals and their knowledge, which also means that research is not about studying a people or a culture; it is about something we are looking at and analyzing together.
- Respect for community partners' time and efforts; being honest and open about intentions, resources, and availability; and understanding that life brings changing circumstances and the importance of being flexible.

- **Relevance:** This demands that research be desired and meaningful to communities.
  - Relevance is determined by community partners and means sharing authority—whether in the shaping, directing, or funding of the research.
  - Relevance prompts us to provide ongoing communication about a project's progress to ensure that as the project or circumstances change, relevance continues to be up for discussion. Communication strategies may include regular meetings, newsletters, and social media posts.
  - Relevance can be ensured by directly inviting community partners to work with you in developing the structure and process of the collaboration, writing grants, developing budgets, determining the outcomes and the formats in which they are shared, and so on.

- **Reciprocity:** This is about mutual benefit.
  - Reciprocity demands that we be creative in the way we structure, carry out, and share our research with communities. At the very least, discuss with community partners what they think mutual benefit looks like. The best way to determine benefit for the community is to engage members in how to structure the project because then it will be baked in from the start rather than simply being one outcome of the project (like a report or video). If they are involved in structuring the project, there may be suggestions for how to get youth involved, how to include local businesses, or perhaps how to go on tribal radio to talk about the outcomes of your work together.
  - Reciprocity invites us to think about what we can give or leave behind that increases capacity sharing between us and the community.[7]
  - Reciprocity provides us with creative ways of thinking about what we can give (for example, a hard to find history book about the community, funding for local research assistants to participate) or leave behind (a facilitator's guide to a workshop, an edited video of oral histories).

- Reciprocity ensures that we ask people we interview if they want a copy of the recording.
- Reciprocity demands that whatever we learn or produce based on the research is shared with the community.
- **Responsibility:** This is about being accountable to yourself and others.
  - Responsibility means being held accountable to these principles by treating others with respect and developing research that is relevant and mutually beneficial to communities with whom you work.
  - Responsibility means following through and keeping your word.
  - Responsibility means setting clear expectations for the project and for those who are working on it: define roles and responsibilities, individuals' availability, the project time line, budget, and the length of relationship between project partners (for example, is it a semester-long class project, an individual's lifelong research focus, or a multi-year commitment between a university and the community).
  - Responsibility means you disseminate findings to the community.
  - Responsibility means you conduct research and record, store, and disseminate information in an ethical manner.

There are many more articles and books from Indigenous scholars about how to appropriately conduct research than when I began doing so in 1999, and I recommend seeking them out. One passage that stood out to me was from the authors of the introduction to *Indigenous Research* who explain "research as relationship." I appreciate the way this perspective invites us to think broader than just the project, the work, and the now: "Indigenous research methodologies can be understood as processes for establishing, strengthening, and coming into closer relationship with knowledge. However, other relationships—between researcher and their research participants, between the land the research is taking place on and all its inhabitants, among the people who learn or read about the research once it is completed, between the ancestors and future generations—must all be honoured."[8]

These values were exemplified in a dissertation project with Aboriginal media organizations in Australia by my PhD student William Lempert. His work was deeply collaborative. Something he wrote about, a moment during an annual Christmas party with the Aboriginal media organization he had been volunteering with, struck me as emblematic: "In addition to the white elephant gift exchange, everyone received a mug with a nickname on it. I was surprised when mine was announced as 'sure, no problem.' This evoked a big laugh from the group and became a jokey nickname for some time afterwards."[9] You can imagine what a delight it was for me to hear this! "Sure, no problem" was his common response to requests for help, whether to be a camera operator or to take out the trash. It represented to me community members' confirmation that he was practicing the 4Rs.

41
Collaborative Research Design

Collaborative research can be university-, museum-, or community-based. It is founded in the commitment to shared authority, where community members participate in decision making and determining the research questions, methods, and outcomes. The joys of collaborative research and shared authority are many—as are the anxieties at times because it means you alone are not in control of the pace or completion of the project. Shared authority means the community has the prerogative to end participation at any time. Allowing for communities to "structure their own participation"[10] in the research process and remaining flexible and open to changing priorities and directions for the project are key to this kind of work. In this section, I provide some guidelines I think with and some lessons learned from community-based projects.

I have referred elsewhere to collaborative research as "tentative anthropology."[11] For me, reflecting on the collaborative process with research partners is part of the project and its write-up. I also believe that our theory and methods are deeply co-constitutive; how we structure our methods and relations in the field influences the knowledge we produce and the theoretical possibilities of our work. Part of that reflexive process has led to my developing a tentative approach to research with and in Indigenous communities. Tentative is defined as experimental, unsure, uncertain—not definite, hesitant. This approach is based on the history of anthropology and museums and Indigenous peoples and on my experiences in the field. It means that my work at times feels anxious and that I have doubts. I sometimes wonder if I should continue. But it also means that when it clicks (and you know when it does!), it feels like we are doing the right thing. To me, success means that community partners feel the outcomes of our work together are appropriate and meaningful to them and that how they are represented "feels right" according to their experience, that we do not just have consent but also encouragement and support from the people with whom we work. It feels like we are on a good path, and we are walking it together.

Collaboration, as well as the terms *decolonizing* and *community*, are concepts that point to the values we embrace in our work, but they are empty terms until we define them meaningfully and in detail to ourselves, our community partners, and those who read about our work together. We need to be clear about who is involved, how we work together, who makes decisions, where the funding comes from, and who has control over the direction and outcomes of the collaboration. Be specific. Be flexible. And follow through. Plans change—sometimes because of community partner needs or capacity, sometimes because of yours. Maintain good communication to weather the changes in a good way.

Another thing to keep in mind is that while for the researcher the project is a front-and-center priority, for community members it is one of many responsibilities. Family and community obligations will be prioritized, as they should, over research project goals or time lines. It's important not to take this personally or feel undermined in your work but rather to expect these kinds of developments in the course of collaborative work. Community members have a lot of responsibilities; plan and allow for things to happen in their own time, when they are ready. This means expecting time lines to be responsive and flexible and having contingency plans if you are on a time line you cannot control, such as a grant or a degree completion deadline. For example, perhaps a master's thesis talks about the planning and execution to date, describes why the project was not completed as a form of scholarship about community-based practice, and includes next steps to complete the project so community members or another student can take up the work. In recent years, I have found granting agencies to be understanding and amenable to requests for extensions for collaborative projects. So don't be afraid to ask for more time if you need it.

There is a spectrum of the level of collaboration and power/authority sharing in collaborative and community-based projects. As I tell my students, community-based research is not always the best design for a project. For example, if a community asks you to secure copies of archives from a national museum for its language program, that's not community-based research, but it is collaborative research. It's important to ask the best way to accomplish the goals of a project and to be mindful of the capacity and resources research partners have—including your own, whether you are part of the community driving the project or a researcher collaborating on it.

You may have an idea for the kind of work you want to do as a researcher and invite community members to participate and help shape it so it is mutually beneficial. That is collaborative research. For me, community-based research means the project takes place in the community and is community directed. Community partners determine the project's primary goals and methods. Community-based research can be part of cultural or museum anthropology work or any kind of research, whether social science or otherwise. Work that begins in a collection can lead to other projects within the originating community.

Students are often looking for ways they can apply themselves to earn their degrees. For years I have had this daydream of a clearinghouse of research projects proposed by communities that university undergraduate and graduate students could review to see if there was one they wanted to take on for their thesis or dissertation projects. That would provide students with a sense that their work is desired and directed and give communities a greater sense of control in identifying what they need in advance. Once matched, they could work together to determine a refined research focus and methodology. This daydream came from my experience of asking members of the Mandan, Hidatsa and Arikara (MHA) Nation whether there was anything more they would like to do after we repatriated items from the University of Colorado (CU), and they asked me to do an oral history project. They selected and gathered the people I should interview and determined the focus of the resulting documentary. My concerns of being a researcher and being exploitative were replaced with a sense of purpose to fulfill a need that I did not identify but was happy to attend to. That was my first research project with MHA Nation, which led to a series of others. One of which was not so successful . . .

Each time I wrote an article about collaboration, the editor would ask that I emphasize not just the process and positive aspects of collaborative research but its challenges or failures as well.[12] That is because we often look to collaboration as an antidote to the historically colonial or extractive nature of research with Indigenous communities. But it is not easy or always successful. All collaborations risk failure, and my work has been no different.

One example that started with such promise and ended a failure was a citizen science project I did with my students and MHA Nation at the height of the fracking boom in North Dakota. However, some great lessons were learned along the way. The tribal college was doing air-quality monitoring due to concerns over the effects of increased truck traffic and hydraulic fracturing in the region. Tribal educators expressed interest in working together with us on an outreach project in which students could participate in additional monitoring as a learning activity. While we started the discussion with the tribal college professors, they said the project needed to be implemented in middle and high school classrooms. So we did listening sessions with teachers and learned about questions they and their students had about their changing environment due to fracking. The tribal college provided continuing education credit to the teachers for their participation. But the problem was this: we had established good working relations with the tribal college but not with the grade school teachers, who we only met with twice.

CU graduate students worked on a series of lesson plans that included monitoring air and water quality and movements of animals in the region, as well as social science questionnaires and an activity to critically analyze media. Data collected from air- and water-quality monitors and trail cameras were to be uploaded by four different schools in the region so students could analyze trends across the reservation. An undergraduate student wrote an article for the tribal newspaper. The project in progress was covered for a radio segment on Prairie Public, North Dakota public radio.

We packaged the kits and brought them to the schools in 2016. After the graduate students delivered the kits, we never learned how or whether they were being used. We should have followed up after the kits were delivered to see how they were being used and whether we should make adjustments. Unfortunately, due to other pressing projects—even within the same community but with different participants—and students graduating, we did not follow up. That was on me as the person who was consistently present in the relationship between the university and the community over time. In any case, we should have been working directly with the teachers from the start rather than partnering with one group to serve another, even if within the same community.

Another project that was community directed with highly motivated individuals at MHA Nation was a pilot project to develop a short comic for language learning that would include stories about how animals find food in the winter, with translations in Mandan, Hidatsa, Arikara (Sahnish), and English. After three years, we all agreed it was time to end the project. Community partners consistently stated that they wanted to do the work. There was no deadline to use the grant funds, so we waited for the time to be right. But in the end, we realized that the new positions community members held and for me as well, the capacity wasn't there in the same way it was when we had written the grant. This was not a failure in concept, design, or execution; people just simply couldn't prioritize it, and that was okay. It is sometimes important to let community members, whose capacity has changed and yet who still want to fulfill their commitment, know it is okay to let a project go.

As I have noted elsewhere, when people you are partnering with work on a project in your absence, you know you're on the right track with the project and its goals and that everyone is motivated to participate. This happened during the film production workshops that CU students, my colleague Dr. Christian Hammons, and I conducted with MHA Nation community members in 2016.[13] Community members redirected us away from a documentary project about the oil boom to creating and conducting week-long film production workshops. Afterward, two community members who co-facilitated the workshops with us used the guide we left behind to teach similar workshops at a nearby reservation. This also happened on the comics project with Kumeyaay Nation community members. Tribal historians gathered and recorded their conversations to develop content for the narrative. They sent me a copy, and I transcribed it and sent it back to the project director, who edited it into a script for the comics artist to use. He did not have to do that, he wanted to because it was a skill he wanted to develop (for more on this project, see chapter 47, "For Example").

A note about authorship. When working collaboratively with people, it is important to ensure that the way you credit them is accurate and acceptable as well. There is a range of approaches for how to acknowledge community partners in a project's writing or outcomes. Sometimes community partner contributions are included in acknowledgments, often when one person does all the writing. Others include "with" statements, as in the authorship of the book *Voices of a Thousand People*, which says "Patricia Pierce Erikson, with Helma Ward and Kirk Wachendorf"; each of the latter two is the coauthor of a chapter in the book. Or, there may be community-authored callout boxes within a text.

I assisted MHA Nation emerging museum professionals by editing a book chapter based on a conversation they recorded among themselves. It was authored by them and "with" me. I developed the questions with their feedback. They recorded and I transcribed and edited the conversation for length. Then they further edited and approved the final text. For the comics I work on, coauthorship rests with community partners, and I am listed as a co-producer. This is all to say, remember to consider not just what you do together but also who will write up the work, what the process for review might be, and how each partner will be credited in the written outcome.

An exercise that may help you start to design your project is to diagram it (see appendix C). Consider, where does the community enter into the project (conception, methods design, later)? What if they say no; are you prepared? Where are the decision-making points? What aspects of decision making are up to the community partner? Do you have a plan for sharing the results of the project with the community? That should be part of the project discussion from the beginning. Grant applications are increasingly including requests for "broader impacts"; sharing results with the community is one way to fulfill that requirement.

Below are some things to consider when doing community-engaged work that I often double check at the start of a project. There are many excellent resources about how to conduct this form of research; this is just my shorthand of things to keep in mind:

Start with giving: Before you ask for something, consider if there is something you can offer first. For example, if you are interested in working with a community on an exhibit, consider sharing all the information you have about the collections in your museum that are related to that community.

Follow the community's lead: When talking with community members I am partnering with, I often use the phrase "we will follow your lead on" whatever decision is to be made or the pace of the project, to make clear that we will listen first and do what they believe is the most appropriate and best process for working together.

Move at the speed of trust: When working in collaboration, especially in research, it takes time to build trust. Consistent follow-through and transparent, direct communication are key. So is getting to know your research partners; consider arranging a shared meal or some way to bring people together before jumping in to your work together. Don't rely solely on texting and email. Call, check in—even when you don't have a project update or need.

Be flexible in process, time line, and outcomes: Collaboration means you are not in control and that there are emergent outcomes.

Communicate concisely and clearly: Make a plan for providing updates, and ensure that there are clear and agreed-upon expectations, responsibilities, methods, and outcomes.

Design for mutual benefit: Collaborative and community-based research projects should mutually benefit all participants, and they should be part of determining what that benefit may be.

Leave something behind: After the project is complete, consider what you might leave behind to provide documentation or increase capacity sharing. For example, if you conduct a workshop, perhaps leave a guide on how to conduct the workshop in your absence; if you conduct oral histories, hire a local student as research assistant to assist or run the camera; or, if you created an exhibit at an institution a distance from the community, consider creating a similar pop-up or traveling exhibit that can be hosted in the community's cultural center or school. Here are some examples from projects I have worked on:[14]

- *MHA Citizen Science Curriculum* (Shannon, Polmear, and Duhe 2016): This project created materials focused on the concerns of teachers and students at the MHA Nation during the height of fracking activities. The materials can be adapted for any community experiencing this phenomenon, so we shared the curriculum with the senior museum educator at the University of Colorado. It included teaching kits with lesson plans and activities for units on these topics: Introduction to Fossil Fuels and Hydraulic Fracturing, Air Quality, Water Quality, Animal Behavior, Public Health, and Media and Its Impact.
- *MHA Collaborative Filmmaking Project Workshop Guide* (Shannon, Kambeitz, and Hammons 2016): After we did a series of week-long video production workshops at the MHA Nation, we distributed a teachers manual and associated slide presentations online at the project website that included videos community members made during the workshops and afterward.
- *A Guide to Facilitating Comics Workshop* (Shannon and Swogger 2019): This guide is based on John Swogger's comics workshops after he provided a series of them to the Mandan, Hidatsa and Arikara (MHA) Nation; community members can lead their own workshops, or individuals can work on the drawing exercises at home using this resource. We produced two versions of the guide, a PDF and a Word document, so people can modify the guide to suit their needs and, hopefully, have some fun!

- *Guide to Creating Community Engaged Comics* (Shannon 2022): This guide is self-published and is available online at no cost. It includes information about process, budgeting, and additional resources for creating comics in collaboration with communities. See appendix G for an excerpt.

Collaborative research is risky and challenging and exciting and full of learning that goes both ways. Active listening, honesty, and flexibility are key to community-based research. Collaborative research also helps you consider and discuss from the start what you can offer and leave behind, how you will communicate, and how decision making will happen while still being open to change and emergent outcomes. Grant writing can be the opportunity to start this conversation.

42
Grant Writing for Collaborative Projects

Securing funds is necessary for most collaborative projects, whether from your institution or an external source. You need a plan to show a supervisor, donor, or foundation what you intend to do, that you have the knowledge and resources to succeed, and how much it will cost. Some good news: in recent years I have seen an increase in requirements for "broader impacts," where the research is not just intended to contribute to the researcher's career but the project must also serve a community or broader public in some way. Further, working in cooperation with Indigenous peoples is valued in grant applications. Sometimes it is even a requirement, depending on the program.

In general, I think about grant writing as—yes, this sounds corny—making daydreams come true! It is a process of taking something you really want to do or create and figuring out the concrete steps and resources needed to make it possible. It's a great skill to develop no matter what your role or position, not just for seeking funds to support the work but also for practicing the art of transforming ideas into the details of feasible practice. This can be very satisfying because even if you don't receive the grant you applied for, you have a roadmap for your project and language you can use for other grants, for sharing a detailed project plan with your collaborators, or for creating a website about your project. Grant writing is a very practical and useful genre of writing as well as a project planning tool.

But! There is grant writing, and then there is grant writing for collaborative projects. Collaboration can happen at many steps in a project's development and execution. It's important to know what time availability, human capacity, and the budget allow for. Are you engaging community partners in planning the project? In grant writing? In developing the budget? Grant writing with community partners results in a stronger project plan and greater investment from your collaborators. It also means you need to start the grant writing process very early.

Even if you have funding in hand, writing something similar to a grant proposal, something that outlines your process and includes how you intend to spend your funds, is a great way to create a document that all partners can review, edit, and agree on. This ensures that everyone knows what they are signing up for, and it makes the roles, responsibilities, and expectations clear. In some cases, a more formal letter of agreement or memorandum of understanding may be crafted between your institution and a tribal entity as part of transparency and accountability to each other as well (see chapter 35, "Collections Management Policy and Shared Stewardship").

When doing collaborative projects, invite community partners to inform and review the budget, and be mindful of how much of your project budget directs funds to support those partners. When you invite community members to review the budget, they get a sense of the limits of your resources. It also allows them to direct you to costs or opportunities you may not have thought about.

General Tips for Grant Writing

Match the mission—*do your homework*: Don't just read the grant description; read the organization's mission as well. Be sure to connect your project to that mission—use important phrases from the mission and the grant description to shape the way you talk about your project.

Directly address grant requirements—*make it easy for reviewers*: If the grant provides a list of things you need to address, make sure you address each item in turn. Don't leave it up to the reviewers to find the answers—make it obvious that you have addressed all the questions/requirements.

Formatting—make it easy for the reviewers: Format the grant so reviewers can quickly find what they are looking for and the formatting is easy to read. That goes beyond following font and margin guidelines. Are there questions in the grant that you need to answer? Then underline the questions or highlight them in bold. You may want to highlight your main research question or project goal.

Research and citations—make it easy for you: Review an example of a successful grant to the organization, if possible, and consider the word limits. Are citations expected? You can use a citation manager (some, like Zotero, are free). That makes it easy to create in-text citations and a bibliography, and you can save notes and tag articles by topic. Further, with the click of a button at the top of your web browser, a program like Zotero can grab all the citation data from the WorldCat catalog or university library page or any other site. You don't have to enter in all the details, but definitely double-check them; they aren't always automatically entered correctly.

Input and feedback—you don't have to work alone: You can't be an expert on everything. Find people whose work you respect and ask them for input on your project plans. If you are working with a team or doing collaborative work, you intend to implement the project together, so why not design the project together? Invite people into the project planning and grant writing process, if doing so is appropriate and their time allows. Before submitting the application, ask someone to read it and get feedback. A set of fresh eyes can be very helpful. In addition, especially with collaborative research, having clear expectations for everyone's roles and responsibilities is key. Who will manage the project's milestones, write up the reports, manage the budget, guide the research, do travel and meeting logistics, store the data, and other duties? Grant writing is a great excuse to begin those discussions early and be certain that everyone is on the same page, ensuring that people are committed, that they feel their skills are contributing to the success of the project, and that they understand their responsibilities if the project is funded.

Reviews and resubmission—keep trying. If you are not successful, ask to receive the reviewer comments. They are very helpful for reapplying for the same grant or applying for other grants. It is rare to be awarded a major grant on first try.

SUMMARY OF KEY POINTS

Do Your Homework	Make It Easy for Reviewers	Make It Easy for You	You Don't Have to Work Alone	Keep Trying
Write in a way that follows the grant requirements and the organization's mission.	Format the document so it is obvious where you are answering each grant question.	Seek out a successful example of a grant application; note whether citations are expected, and use tools available to cite and update references.	Seek input for developing the project, and ask for feedback before submitting your application.	Ask for reviewers' comments; submit the application again if your time line allows.

Grant Writing for Collaborative Research Projects

Depending on the project, a budget can include many different categories and line items. There are some standard categories for budgets, such as travel, housing, a per diem, and supplies. In this section, I want to highlight categories that are specific to collaborative research to give you some ideas of what you might add to a standard budget. Whether you can include different kinds of budget items largely depends on the size of the grant or fellowship you are applying for. For instance, with a small budget, perhaps funding for food for community meetings is all you can budget for. For a medium-size grant, perhaps you can include honoraria for community members who provide interviews. For a large grant, you can seek stipends to hire community members in positions like research director and research assistant. (For a sample grant at the $20,000 level, see appendix D.) I would also suggest including a project coordinator to assist in logistics for large, complex projects that have high levels of funding.

It is important to confer with community partners to determine the funding priorities so they understand why decisions were made to fund some things and not others. Perhaps there is a promising high school or college-age community member they want to support, and community members suggest that a stipend and official position in the project is what they most want the budget to be directed toward. To save money for this purpose, project partners may choose to organize potlucks for community meetings instead of allocating grant funds for catering.

The American Alliance of Museums has helpful guides for collaborative museum work, including "In Good Relation: Reimagining the Grant Process for Community-Based Projects" by Kate Hadley Toftness and Lois Taylor Biggs (Cherokee Nation and White Earth Ojibwe). The authors describe how they have built relations with specific funding partners, working with program officers to build trust and understanding for the changing needs of collaborative projects over time. They suggest including funding for "research outside of universities, museums, or archives; travel to and from displaced or otherwise marginalized communities; unrestricted funding lines for supporting community partner programs; compensation for knowledge sharers; and, gifts for project contributors."[15]

When we think about doing collaborative research or exhibit development, we usually only think about the community that is featured as a partner in our work. However, there are many opportunities to work with Indigenous peoples beyond the development of content. Make directing funding to community-based or Native-owned businesses a priority. This may require some extra networking and research on your part, but it is worth it. For example, for the comic series I co-produce, we work with a tribally owned printing company in California. If you need to contract a film production company for a video short you are creating for an exhibit, make sure you get your request for proposals out to Indigenous companies and videographers. Or perhaps you can hire an Indigenous consulting firm to facilitate your meetings (we did this for the large project with Mesa Verde National Park mentioned in chapter 11).

Engaging Indigenous-owned businesses creates goodwill when collaborating with Native communities. You can do this by asking around for recommendations, searching for outstanding media produced by Indigenous people and looking up who produced it, or sending requests for recommendations to tribal contacts who can pass it on through their networks. Whether for film production, catering, printing, exhibit design, website development, or something else—ask yourself if there is an opportunity to engage with a Native or community-based business as part of your commitment to collaboration and reciprocity.

Sample budget items for which to seek Indigenous businesses include:

- Transportation
- Lodging
- Event hosting
- Catering (team meetings, events)

- Exhibit designers
- Film or video production team
- Location scouting/manager
- Local film or audio crew
- Website development
- Marketing materials
- Exhibit fabrication
- Murals/art/photography
- Meeting facilitation
- Research assistants
- Project blog/videographer

When working with Indigenous peoples, it is important to compensate community members for their intellectual contributions to the project. This is not paying for information; this is compensating people for the time they take away from their other responsibilities to participate in the project. And it acknowledges these individuals as expert consultants. Consider this: non-Native guest curators and museum consultants are paid for their time when they contribute to creating museum exhibits. So too should Indigenous people who work on a museum or research project. This may not always be possible, though. Perhaps you are a graduate student who did not receive funding for your collaborative research project, or you are a curator at a very small museum. Then consider other ways to compensate community partners, such as offering the use of your facilities for free, taking them out to dinner, writing something for the tribal newspaper, and so on.

Working with community members on grant proposals and budgets may also provide an opportunity to discuss and prepare for cultural protocols that may arise during the project. For example, purchasing tobacco or groceries may be appropriate if working with elders. If you are relying on institutional funds, be sure to talk with administrative staff and leadership about expenses unique to community-based work. Prepare them for what to expect, and ensure that the expenses are acceptable under the institution's policies. Institutions have protocols too, especially when it comes to transferring money. Be sure to prepare community members and let them know if, for instance, they will need to fill out a W-9 form to receive honoraria. We often fail to discuss these kinds of details in the excitement of forming a partnership and daydreaming about what we will do together. Grant writing can be a great opportunity to be sure that everyone understands not just the collaborative process for the project but the logistics as well.

43

Research Review and Informed Consent

If there is one takeaway from this section, it's to get creative! Don't let existing structures or processes stop you from advocating for what you think is the best way to seek consent and conduct research, whether you are a community member or a researcher. Think broadly and ask questions about how best to communicate about a research project with community members. Doing this led me in some new directions, such as sharing information about research projects on tribal radio and Facebook.

When a researcher is part of an institution, like a university or a museum, there is usually a requirement for the project and methods to be approved by what is often called an institutional review board (IRB), a human subjects review board, or something similar. As the name suggests, special checks are in place when research is done with people. The unfortunate labeling of them as human subjects is a result of this kind of board having originated in response to medical research. However, social scientists need to go through the same process of showing that their research methods are well planned, that individuals are informed of the research that is taking place and consent to participate, and that participating will not harm any individuals.

Another layer of research review can also happen when working with Native Nations—they may have their own research review boards that determine whether a particular research project can go forward on reservation lands or with members of the Nation. They may seek to determine not just that the research will not do harm but that it will also do some good for the community. When I first reached out to the Mandan, Hidatsa and Arikara (MHA) Nation, it did not have a research review board, so I provided IRB materials that I had prepared for my university to the tribal college for review and feedback. This is a reminder to use plain language in IRB documents, something that is welcomed by the IRB team as well as community members. When working with a Native community, ask whether it has a research review board or established review process. I was pleased to see this question in my university's IRB questionnaire as well.

Native community members who may be working on a project with their own community, as one of my graduate students did, may need to do additional review. In addition to research review, they may also be required to seek approval from an elders' council or other form of tribal leadership and publicly present their work to the community. To support Native graduate students doing work with their own communities, advisers have some work to do. I educated the other faculty members on the student's committee about the added obligation to community and the dual audience for the thesis (academic and community), which required a different form of writing. They were happy to review the student's work with this in mind, and the thesis was a success by all accounts.

The IRB process is a good way to think deeply and to think ahead about the methods that are most appropriate for a given project. Here I focus on interviews as an example for obtaining consent and for recording and sharing research. I am going to suggest that to create your methods plan for the IRB process, which comes early and before research proper begins, you ask community members how best to document the information you are gathering. Because the IRB process is based on medical research, there is often an emphasis on paper documentation. It is really important to keep in mind, however, that the IRB process is flexible, and you should feel empowered to ask for what you think is most appropriate given the context of working with a particular community.

When I was a graduate student, a community partner insisted, for the success of my project, that I not use signed paper forms in my research.[16] While discussing how I planned to conduct ethnographic research for my dissertation, Joe Podlasek (Lac Courte Oreilles Band of Ojibwe), then director of the American Indian Center in Chicago, told me it would be problematic to ask community members to sign forms. Before this conversation, it had never occurred to me to ask the IRB to adjust the requirements for consent. Joe's request prompted me to call IRB staff at my university to discuss his concerns and the negative connotations signed forms have for Native community members. The IRB staff asked me to submit a request to waive written consent and granted my proposed accommodation that I developed in conversation with Joe. This experience shaped the way I seek and document informed consent to this day.

Based on this experience and my work since, I suggest bringing research partners into the conversation about methods—including informed consent procedures—so they are part of determining culturally appropriate ways to discuss and distribute information about, and to seek consent for, a research project. When community partners are involved in research planning, they will likely answer the question about how they will benefit as they guide you to create a more reciprocal approach.

My second suggestion is, don't assume that IRB staff will be unwilling to consider accommodations to the standard requirements. Faculty and students in anthropology often talk about the IRB as if it is a thing or a faceless institution, but it consists of people—you can call or email them! Ask for what you need to make your research successful and in line with the spirit of IRB protections, keeping local cultural contexts and ethical practices in mind. In case you do end up taking a collaborative approach to research design, here is an example of language I use in grants and IRB documents to indicate that our plans often change on the ground as we continue to work together: "Flexibility and sensitivity to issues of power and knowledge sharing are key components in any collaborative endeavor involving Indigenous communities. All partners realize that the project structure is subject to change with increasing input from community members, but we also believe the project as outlined to be a feasible and productive guide to our process. Respecting different knowledge systems and allowing partners to determine the nature of their participation are key to implementation and sustainability."

A signed form is intended to document or record evidence of consent. There are multiple ways to do that through other means, including during audio and video recordings. There are also some advantages to recording consent orally rather than on a preprinted page. The individual's stated consent and whether they want a copy of the recording cannot (without editing the original file) be separated from the recording itself, unlike a piece of paper. An audio recording also allows the interviewee to ask questions about and dictate acceptable uses of the recording if they wish, and they can provide conditions the researcher may not have thought of or have placed on a predetermined list. Here is an example of the language I included in an IRB application regarding verbal consent:

> This project will use verbal consent and, when appropriate, video or audio recorded verbal consent. Consent will not be documented in writing.
> First, there is no more than minimal risk of harm to participants. Second, signed documents have a particular negative symbolism in Native American communities and can produce unease. Consent will be clearly

and repeatedly sought verbally throughout the research. When audio or video recording, consent will be documented on the recording by an affirmative response to the interviewer who will ask before and after the recording is started, "Is it okay for me to record this?" Therefore, we request IRB approval to waive written consent.

This approach is not appropriate for all projects and circumstances—not even in my own dissertation project![17] In other cultural and institutional contexts, research participants preferred to sign consent forms. Rethinking IRB applications and forms as more than just hoops to jump through can provoke us to think deeply about the purpose behind this process and plan our research design accordingly. So, my third suggestion is to think broadly about how you seek informed consent. It can and should occur in many ways beyond a signed form. We often think of consent as occurring one to one, explaining our project to each individual we meet. But you can also reach out more broadly, if appropriate to the cultural context in which you are working.

IRB research protocols separate recruitment and informed consent as distinct activities, and the templates can suggest that consent is a onetime question instead of an ongoing practice. However, in my research context, community outreach is not primarily about recruitment—it is intended to contribute to the "informing" part of informed consent in ways requested by community partners. For example, I have introduced myself and projects I am working on to communities by being interviewed on a tribal radio station, writing and distributing newsletters and blog posts to keep everyone updated, creating Facebook pages for projects, and contributing articles to tribal newspapers so community members not only know who I am and why I am there but also that they are invited to give feedback on the project itself.

The IRB and the forms we fill out for research approval can make it seem like the researcher alone is in control of the project. But without the people in the communities where we work, there is no project. Collaborative research with Native communities offers one model for creating more reciprocal and respectful research relations and outcomes. Community-based research in other contexts might lead to different methodological innovations and models for sharing authority. I believe that anthropological research design and methods can be made more effective and creative when developed in dialogue with the people with whom we work.

44
Interviewing and Recording

When you are conducting or participating in research, consider how information being shared is recorded, stored, and distributed—and in what formats and for what reasons. It is okay to ask a researcher if what seems to be a casual conversation is part of their research. Interviews, informal conversations, phone calls, and more are part of the way researchers communicate with community members to learn about a topic. Cultural anthropologists also use a method called "participant observation," or participating in the activities we are learning and writing about. Ethnography is both the practice and the written product of doing all the methods combined that provide a sense of "being there," describing everyday practices and relations and interactions of working with and in communities. Community here is broadly defined and does not just refer to Native peoples—for my dissertation, museum staff was also a community I worked with. Other disciplines like history, education, and journalism have since taken up ethnography and participant observation as well, but they began as hallmark approaches in the discipline of cultural anthropology, which continues to center these methods as well as to adapt and change with new ones.

It is common in cultural and museum anthropology research to talk one on one with community members about the research topic, whether through more formal (structured) or less formal (semi-structured) interviews or as part of a natural conversation (participant observation). When you interview a group of people simultaneously, it can be called a focus group. Sometimes these interviews are recorded; other times a researcher may take notes or remember and write notes about the conversation later. For these reasons and more, informed consent is important. In the prior section, I talked about seeking consent in novel ways. Here I focus on the interview itself as an example of seeking consent, and I offer tips from my own experience.

Recording Interviews

As I tried to show in the preface, interviewing can and should go both ways. If you are being interviewed, you should feel able to ask the researcher questions too. If you are the interviewer, be prepared to answer the same kinds of questions you are asking. This situation may not come about, but it is important to be understanding and open to the possibility. Especially when working with Native community members who have historically been maligned through extractive interview practices, the researcher should be equally open to inquiry. If you are doing life history interviews, for example, don't be surprised if someone wants to know where you come from or what growing up was like for you. This is not a suggestion to tell your life story or make the conversation all about you. It is an invitation to be aware of social cues: sometimes an interviewee will prefer a one-sided interview; other times a two-sided conversation is preferred.

Be open to the unexpected if you are an interviewer, and if you are an interviewee, don't hesitate to direct the researcher to information or knowledge you think is relevant and important that they did not ask about. One way to be open to this is by asking at the end of each interview: is there anything else you'd like to add? In my work on an oral history project with elders in North Dakota, that question led to the key insight that only individuals over sixty-five would have: that the oil boom felt a lot like the times when their homelands were flooded by the United States government and they were forced to relocate. That question allows for insights that are not anticipated or cannot be known by the interviewer, and it provides an opening for the interviewee to direct the conversation somewhere meaningful to them. What also often happens is that after the recorder is turned off and some moments pass, more occurs to the interviewee and the conversation continues. If that happens, be sure to ask afterward if it's okay to include the added information in your documentation and writing or if it was meant to provide background context and not be recorded. I have also had interviewees ask for the recorder to be turned back on when something more occurred to them.

For documenting informed consent during interviews, I believe it is essential that recorded consent and the audio file be one and the same. Often, we are prompted to collect signed consent forms, and that is okay. But I would offer, regardless of whether signed forms are part of the requirements, that during the interview or conversation two things are reiterated while recording: first, be sure to include the person's name at the start of the recording and ask if it is okay to record; second, before turning off the recording, ask if they want a copy. Papers can get lost, and digital or other forms of the interview can circulate without the document associated with it. Following the steps here ensures that consent and your promise are attached, so to speak, and inseparable from the interview file.

As for the interview itself, here are some tips I often share with graduate students:

- Make sure the person being interviewed is comfortable and that the background noise level is low (especially if recording for publicly shared media; for example, listen for a moment: does a noisy refrigerator need to be unplugged? Is an overhead fluorescent light buzzing?).
- Consider where to do the interview, and ask for suggestions. Should it happen while walking the land? In someone's kitchen, so they feel more comfortable? Outside their home, so they feel more comfortable? At a café, community gathering, or elders' luncheon? Is there enough privacy for the nature of the conversation? It depends on the individual and the project. For example, we once set up an interview station outside a tribal college classroom where we hosted a screening of the first draft of a documentary in case others wanted to contribute.
- Consider whether you should share questions or topic areas ahead of time with the interviewee; seeing questions ahead of time can help with oral histories, for example. If the recording is for public dissemination, it can be helpful and less stressful for your interviewee to have a conversation before the interview to go over the questions and discuss the topic.
- Ask before turning on the recorder if it is okay to interview; explain that you will ask again.
- Once the recorder begins, ask the person's name and if it is okay to record.
- Allow for stretches of silence. Don't jump into the next question when the interviewee takes a breath or pauses; allow them time to think and add more information. It is better to wait too long and be asked if you have another question than to miss rich detail or a deeper memory.
- At the end of the interview, ask if there is anything else the person would like to add.
- Before turning off the recorder, ask if they want a copy. If they do, put that on your to-do list and make sure you follow up and send them the recording.

I also talk with students about paying attention to whether emotion is part of the story or a surprise. I explain by sharing my experience from when I was conducting interviews for the MHA Nation oral history project. In one interview, when an interviewee started to cry, I could tell that it was part of how she wanted to relay the story and her experience, so I left the video camera rolling. She continued with the interview. During an interview with someone else, I could see it was a surprise that she became so upset while talking about the past, and I immediately turned off the camera and pointed it away. Active listening and attending to social cues can be the difference between highlighting someone's story as they want it to be viewed and making them feel embarrassed or exploited.

Interviewing during Collections Reviews

For those who work in museums and may think reading about interviewing is not relevant to your work, if you are working with originating communities in collections, interviewing is an important part of collaborative museology. It can be part of collections reviews, asking an artist about their work in the collection, or talking to originating community members about an item featured in an exhibit. For collections reviews in particular, when community members want information to be recorded in the object record or they have cultural care guidance to share, it is important to be able to record that information accurately and check with them to be certain that it was adequately documented. Below is a recap of what I discussed earlier in chapter 27, "Cultural Care," with some additional logistical considerations.

Here are some things to think about and tips for interviewing that I presented in a workshop for museum staff about hosting community visits to collections. Although staff members are not technically "interviewing" while hosting visits to collections, they do need to ask clarifying questions as information is shared. A big part of this in the context of collaborative museology is considering how we can, for example, respectfully ask questions that help staff collect actionable information for cultural care. Otherwise, a community member may get the impression that their guidance will be enacted, but museum staff may not have enough information to do so.

As noted earlier, active listening means being present, listening to what is said, being aware of non-verbal cues and body language, and not interrupting—but when the time is right, asking questions or paraphrasing what was said to ensure understanding. Avoid asking questions that seem to be seeking ceremonial or protected knowledge when talking to community members about collections.

Another thing to consider when hosting communities in collections is how the tools of documenting the visit might affect the feeling in the room. Whether you are taking notes on a notepad or a laptop or recording with an audio-digital recorder or a video camera, each method can affect the comfort and tone of the conversation with community members. Sometimes they may insist on having the visit recorded; other times they may want nothing recorded, not even notes, by staff at the host institution.

Similar to informed consent during research, it is important to have consent to record during a collections visit as well, even if doing so is not governed by an institutional review board process. Ask prior to the visit how and what the community members would like to have recorded, and find out if they will be recording the visit. Let community members know what the recording will be used for and whether it might be shared publicly—for example, whether it will be for internal use only for notes and then deleted, internal use only for records, available to researchers but not the general public, or a source for public sharing in a website or exhibition. Let them know that they can ask you to stop recording at any time. In fact, there may be a time when you sense that the recording is causing discomfort though they have not said anything—check in, and ask if they are still okay with recording.

There are different reasons for recording the information shared. For the museum, reasons may be to transcribe and ensure accurate documentation in the records, to represent the collaboration in an exhibit, to record Native language terms, or perhaps to have visual information that shows how to handle or wear an item. For a community, perhaps they want to share the experience with a classroom back home, in a cultural center exhibit or documentary, at a conference, or in their own records. Whatever the case, ask about recording ahead of time, if possible. If community visitors want to record, make sure you know your institution's policies (and whether they need to change for this context).

In the CU Museum, the collections manager and I were asked by a visiting Native researcher if he could share cell phone photos of moccasins in the collection on Facebook. We chatted briefly and said yes. It was an effective way for the broader community to see the items, and we loved reading the discussion in the comments, which also confirmed identification of the item.

Expect that community members will want to share the collection and their experience with their colleagues, friends, and family. It was possible for us to make this decision on the spot in our small museum because we were the decision makers for image rights. For those who work in larger museums, it is important to anticipate this kind of request and to know—and if necessary change—the museum's policies.

Finally, a note about visual recording. When we hosted a repatriation consultation with Native American Graves Protection and Repatriation Act (NAGPRA) liaisons from Navajo Nation, they allowed us to record our conversation with them about how the consultation should proceed as a teaching tool for our museum studies students. We realized later in viewing the footage that a sensitive item on the table during the discussion was partially visible. We edited it out of the video before sharing. If you are museum staff doing a collections review and you learn that some items are culturally sensitive, be sure to review the recording. Ask if you should delete, edit, or black out areas of photos or video segments that include those collections items. More often, if there are culturally sensitive items in the room where visual recording is taking place, you will be asked to turn off or point the camera away from the items.

45

Sharing Research Results

As has become clear throughout the chapters of this book, being mindful of what is appropriate to share publicly is an important part of collaborative research and collections engagements with Native communities. Western museums and scholars operate under the assumption that all knowledge is shareable and that the purpose of museums and scholarship is to share that knowledge with as broad an audience as possible. However, that is not the view of Native communities, where certain kinds of knowledge are a privilege, often passed on and protected by select knowledge keepers. Therefore, it is important not to share some kinds of ceremonial or specialized cultural knowledge with the public—even if that knowledge has been published in the past. Respecting Native knowledge and ways of knowing means ensuring that we honor these protocols.

Regardless of what you share publicly, bringing the results of research back to community members who participated is essential and should be discussed and planned from the start. This might be in the form of a finished thesis, updated collection records, a presentation about research results, or some other way community participants suggest. I always advise giving copies of recorded individual interviews to the interviewees for their own use. Even though they give us permission to use recordings for research or museum purposes, it is ultimately their knowledge, and they should be able to use the material as they see fit. I have really valued and enjoyed thinking creatively with community members about how to communicate what we accomplish and learn together, which led me to design a new anthropology seminar in 2020.

46
Teaching Collaborative and Public Anthropology

I want to share my thinking on why teaching collaborative and public anthropology is so essential in the university and to our community partners. It has been encouraging to see the academy embrace science communication and public scholarship in recent years as well. Today, many academic departments accept public scholarship in their tenure and promotion evaluations. In addition, we are increasingly seeing diverse formats for communicating anthropology and research more generally—podcasts, multimodal journal sections, videos, blogs, and more—aimed at scholars and the public.[18] This kind of work is why I love being a museum anthropologist and why I think anthropologists in and beyond our subfield should look to museum anthropology for models to think with and literature to turn to as we bring the values of experimentation, collaboration, and public-oriented scholarship to the center of our discipline.

The major association for the discipline in the US, the American Anthropological Association (AAA), distributed the "AAA Guidelines for Tenure and Promotion Review: Communicating Public Scholarship in Anthropology" in 2017. The AAA defines "public scholarship" as "that which is in dialogue with non-academic as well as academic audiences, and that is informed by anthropological scholarship and knowledge." In these guidelines, the AAA acknowledges the importance of public scholarship and recommends that tenure and promotion committees review their existing guidelines. To guide this review, the AAA offers a series of considerations, starting with: "*Acknowledge the value of public forms of communicating, writing and publishing as scholarship. Some of this scholarship involves experimentation and risk-taking or requires rapid responsiveness. Some of this work is crucial in terms of community and public engagement, and in numerous instances it includes scholarship that blurs boundaries between research, teaching, and service. We encourage departments to familiarize themselves with this new ecology of writing and publishing.*"[19]

I think museum anthropology is where exciting, experimental, and risk-taking work is happening in anthropology: specifically, at the intersection of the public, Indigenous communities, and anthropologists. We have been doing this work with community partners for years, so I think we need to advocate more for our role in contributing to and leading this shift in the discipline's vision.

As noted earlier, museum anthropologists regularly produce anthropology for the public in the museum. We work with exhibit developers and design specialists who require us to be succinct and to communicate with the general public using accessible language. We work in consultation and collaboration with diverse museum staff, originating community members, and design professionals. Whether due to the intersection of various perspectives and disciplines or of historical and contemporary social and political dynamics, our work is by nature a risk; we seek to establish trust, but failure is always possible.

Beyond advocating for museum and public anthropology, I have also called out to science communicators and science journalists to commit to increasing public literacy in social sciences, to feature more *social* sciences in reporting in the hopes of increasing empathy in society. Earlier I mentioned that grant writing can be excellent for thinking through project plans; it can also lead to publication even if you don't get the grant. In this case, my colleagues and I did a lot of research about journalism and anthropology to apply for a National Science Foundation (NSF) grant. When we learned that we didn't get the grant, we published our background research as a commentary in a journal for science communicators.[20]

What I learned through doing this research is that the lack of anthropology in news is not just the fault of journalists; it's also because of anthropologists' shortcomings. Journalists talk to some social scientists, such as economists and psychologists, but they know little about how anthropologists might contribute to their stories. On the one hand, journalists don't seek out anthropologists, even as their craft is moving toward providing more context and narrative. On the other hand, anthropologists fail to provide digestible material to journalists. Our NSF grant proposal was intended to address this disconnect through training and online resources.

Anthropologists have often been working in a region or community for years and can offer broader context and insight to frame what is being reported on in the moment. This could provide more nuanced understandings of issues that affect our society, giving greater context and insider perspectives on stories related to, for example, refugee crises, increasing educational outcomes, Indigenous rights issues, and more efficient energy systems.

Topics like immigration at the US-Mexico border provide a glimpse into the potential for communicating anthropology to a broader audience. In 2018, the popular show *Radiolab* produced a three-part series about the US-Mexico border featuring the research of anthropologist Dr. Jason De León. It was a timely and important show and an excellent example of relevant and engaging public communication of social science research. It was also pure happenstance. *Radiolab*'s director of research explains: "I sat next to a pleasant stranger on a bus from New York to DC. Her name was Lynn Morgan. She's an anthropologist. I told her that I found the field fascinating, and asked her to tell me about the youngest and most interesting folks working in the field today. She told me about a book, *The Land of Open Graves* by Jason De León. That conversation was the seed for a story that took me and the rest of the Radiolab team a full year to report and produce, and ultimately became Radiolab's *Border Trilogy*."[21]

We need a more systematic and sustained process for promoting powerful stories from anthropology research through science media so these kinds of stories are reported on as a result of more than just a chance encounter. Anthropologists and university instructors also have work to do—such as responding to journalists' calls for social scientists to communicate stories rather than topics or issues.[22] Accordingly, I designed a course at the University of Colorado called Collaborative and Public Anthropology. As noted above, I see these things as inextricably linked because part of the reciprocity of collaborative research is sharing the outcomes of your research with the community.

For museum or cultural anthropology, I usually write about process to provide models for how to conduct collaborative research and lessons learned from our experience. When I write about a project, the first question I ask myself is: what audience do I want to speak to about this? My first answer is: the community I worked with, which requires a different kind of writing—or media production—than that for a peer-reviewed journal article. For academic articles, I ask *which* disciplinary audience I want to speak to. Just as we published that commentary in a journal for science communicators, I wrote an article about teaching museum studies in the *Collections* journal for collections managers instead of publishing it in something like *Museum Anthropology*, which is my discipline.

In the course I taught, students were communicating their dissertation projects in blog posts, comics, podcast episodes, five-minute recorded talks for social media sharing, and more. When we communicate our work with the public, that public can include research partners, students, and family members. One student told me that when she shared her video talk with her mom, her mother said it was the first time she really understood what her daughter was doing in graduate school. That meant so much to me because doing this kind of communication work is about building relations, trust, and understanding—not just with the communities with whom we work but with the public, and that includes our own relatives as well.

The graduate seminar addressed community engagement, introducing the values, history, and contemporary practice of collaborative anthropology as a form of knowledge production and ethnographic practice. We reviewed decolonizing methodologies, different collaborative research models, and how to design a project.

The seminar also addressed public engagement, teaching students how to communicate their research to the communities with whom they work and the broader public through a series of in-class workshops and media assignments. Students experimented with different media and their affordances, including blogs, podcasts, videos, and comic books. Each student completed a public blog post, a pitch to an online publication, a major media project of their choosing, and a five-minute TED-style talk about their research that was recorded and shared online.

Course learning objectives included:

- Define and understand how to identify and design collaborative and/or public anthropology projects.
- Understand the relationship between collaborative and public anthropology.

- Assess the factors that contribute to a desire for public engagement in anthropology as well as the obstacles to this engagement.
- Identify examples of anthropological research that has contributed to the public good.
- Identify examples of the need and possibility for engaging the public with anthropological knowledge.
- Discuss reasons for and actions that can be taken by anthropologists to facilitate public engagement.
- Identify, plan, and practice various forms of communicating your research to the public.
- Publish some aspect of your research online to a public audience.

The reading list included articles and media-making resources, plus these texts:
- *Understanding Comics: The Invisible Art* (McCloud 1994)
- *The Chicago Guide to Collaborative Ethnography* (Lassiter 2005)
- *Our Lives: Collaboration, Native Voice, and the Making of the National Museum of the American Indian* (Shannon 2014)
- *Going Public: A Guide for Social Scientists* (Stein and Daniels 2017)
- *Lissa: A Story about Medical Promise, Friendship, and Revolution* (Hamdy and Nye 2017; see also University of Toronto Press ethnoGRAPHIC series)
- *Elements of Indigenous Style: A Guide for Writing by and about Indigenous Peoples* (Younging 2018)
- *Savage Kin: Indigenous Informants and American Anthropologists* (Bruchac 2018)
- *Decolonizing Methodologies: Research and Indigenous Peoples* (Smith 2021 [1999])

Student projects were based on their master's and dissertation projects. Their TED-style talks included combining Indigenous oral traditions with archaeology and why there are problems using carbon dating on the Plains (Carlton Gover), why small-scale farming is a labor of love and the need for specific changes to the US Farm Bill (Melanie Matteliano), and why people with diabetes are hacking medical equipment to improve the quality of their lives (Paige Edmiston). Comics created for the class included the story of a pot that demonstrated Mexico's central role in world history (Kristin Enright) and how drone pilots commuting to and from war each day has consequences for the individual and their family (Georgia Butcher). Paige Edmiston made a podcast pilot using the Sorting Hat from Harry Potter to explain how medical students are matched to their first jobs as doctors, and Scarlett Engle created a public website to share information about the process of collaboration she was documenting between twenty-six Pueblos and Tribes and Mesa Verde National Park (see chapter 11, "For Example").

I was really proud of the students' commitment to the class and the work they produced. I have always felt that publishing, putting my ideas out there in the world, is difficult and stressful, and I am sure many feel this way. Doing so for a broader audience can be even more nerve-racking. The students stretched beyond their comfort zones and embraced the challenges and rewards of sharing our research plans and outcomes with communities and the public. They were able to explain their projects clearly and compellingly in plain language, preparing for the "elevator speech" as we say! After the course ended, one student went on to teach a similar course as a new assistant professor, and another published a revised version of her course assignment in the digital anthropology magazine *SAPIENS*.[23]

The general takeaway from this course is that what we teach (in the university classroom and elsewhere) communicates what we value in our field and shapes what the next generation sees as possible and probable. For me, that includes collaborative methodologies and disseminating research beyond the academy—and including a plan to do so from the start. During this course I shared some of my own collaborative and public anthropology projects as models and lessons to learn from, including fun moments (I loved co-hosting *SAPIENS: A Podcast for Everything Human!*) and some difficult lessons, too. An example of the latter is the citizen science project with a tribal college, mentioned earlier, that delivered some excellent environmental monitoring equipment and lesson plans, and was featured on North Dakota public radio, and then fizzled out. There were positive lessons, too—actual daydreams that came true—such as a comics project I designed in cooperation with Kumeyaay Nation members, which I describe in the next chapter.

47

For Example

Community-Engaged Comics

The Kumeyaay Visual Storytelling Project (KVSP) is one of the most collaborative and well-balanced projects—in terms of both power and control of resources—I have had the opportunity to develop and participate in. Even the name of the project reflects community-directed guidance. Originally called the Kumeyaay Comics Project, we changed the title after receiving guidance from tribal historians. I go into detail below about the project, how it was structured, and our work to date. It represents a methodology that John Swogger and I call "community-engaged comics" (see appendix G).

Community-engaged comics are a form of collaboration in which the result is a comic and so much more. The comics are a means for community engagement, for community members to discuss and build together what they want to communicate and how. Community partners direct the project from conception to implementation to evaluation, and they are in control of content and distribution. We conduct community-based workshops and presentations and public events as part of our work together. Comics are distributed via PDF for free and in print through a non-profit, **tribally owned business**, Tribal Print Source in California.

NAGPRA Comics was the precursor to the KVSP and the reason why Kumeyaay community members approached us to do a comic with them. *NAGPRA Comics* is a community-based, collaboratively produced comic series that tells true stories about repatriation from tribal perspectives. We work with Native American communities to share their experiences with the law, from their point of view. Each comic issue is developed differently, according to the community we are working with.

The first draft of *NAGPRA Comics* **failed**. It was a storyboard that a colleague and I created for our talk at a symposium, "Indigenous Storytelling and the Law," hosted by the Center for Native and Indigenous Studies and the American Indian Law program at the University of Colorado in 2017. Each CU faculty member was asked to invite a colleague to coauthor a talk. I had not worked with Anishinaabe-Ojibwe archaeologist Sonya Atalay before, but I admired her work and had been in the audience when she was on the National NAGPRA committee while Native community members gave testimony seeking support for their repatriation claims. I always tell my students that it never hurts to aim high; the worst thing that happens is someone says no and, hopefully, feels appreciated in the process. I asked Sonya if she would coauthor a talk with me, and she said yes. This started a years-long collaboration that continues to this day. We agreed that we didn't want to speak to our discipline alone. We wanted to reach a broader audience, so eventually we landed on comics and partnering with archaeologist and comics creator John Swogger to communicate our research.

Sonya and I had created a draft storyboard of testimony we both witnessed a tribal member give to the National NAGPRA committee; a transcript was publicly available at the National NAGPRA website. The individual whose testimony we represented liked the storyboard and the idea of the comic, but his Tribe's research review board did not approve it. They were concerned that comics or a graphic novel would be a disrespectful way to address issues of sacred items and traditional knowledge and also that their knowledge could be seen as fictional if depicted in this medium.

We learned a lot from this experience, and it was why we started using the term *graphic narrative* rather than comic book or graphic novel. But that wasn't the real problem. We didn't have an existing relationship with this community; there was no concrete example we could point to, and there was no trust. To represent true and difficult stories in this medium, trust is important. But this first attempt sparked an idea that we continued to pursue. The first issue of *NAGPRA Comics* was successful because of the existing relationship between Sonya and the coauthors, and we are so thankful that they trusted us to take a chance on this medium. What started as a one-off for a symposium has grown into a series with two issues published and more in process.

Our first comic was *Journeys to Complete the Work . . . and Changing the Way We Bring Native American Ancestors Home*. It was coauthored with Shannon Martin and William Johnson from the Ziibiwing Center of Anishinabe Culture and Lifeways and Anishinaabe elders Sydney and George Martin (see figure 1.1). The focus was a critique of the 10.11 regulations under the NAGPRA law regarding Native ancestors who were not culturally affiliated and the fact that the regulations did not require that the associated funerary objects be returned (the new 2024 regulations address this issue). An example of applied comics as well as scholarly research, we explained the law, highlighted community perspectives and activism, and included references and recommendations for action. We launched *NAGPRA Comics* and this first issue at the 2017 Indigenous Comic-Con in Albuquerque, New Mexico. Since then, we have presented the work to the American Anthropological Association, the Association of Tribal Archives, Libraries, and Museums, the Society of American Archaeology, and the Graphic Justice annual conference, among others.

The second *NAGPRA Comics* issue, *Trusting You Will See This as We Do: Tribal Sovereignty and the Return of Sacred Objects and Objects of Cultural Patrimony*, was created in collaboration with Mandan, Hidatsa and Arikara (MHA) Nation community members to highlight two instances of repatriation of cultural belongings, one before the passage of NAGPRA and the other more recently at the University of Colorado Museum of Natural History. Because community members are in control not just of content but also distribution, this issue is available only to clan members associated with the repatriated items at this time.

What amazes me about *NAGPRA Comics* is their accessibility. I was impressed with how this research outcome traveled across many communities, age groups, and institutions. We learned from word of mouth and an online survey on our website that the first issue was available in tribal museums and cultural centers, assigned in high school classrooms and archaeology graduate courses, passed out at conferences, and more. It felt like we were really on to something. What I saw in the summer of 2023 while working on a comic with Kumeyaay community members sealed the deal for me to continue in this medium: we were sitting at a table in the Sycuan Cultural Center, and one of John's comics happened to be on the table. A girl around age seven picked up one of the comics and started reading. No invitation was needed. She saw something that she felt was meant for her. How exciting! John and I looked at each other with wide eyes and smiles.

NAGPRA Comics are not really projects; they are coauthored works that have been supported through a combination of small grants and institutional research funding. The Kumeyaay Visual Storytelling Project is a full-on *project*—with more moving parts, more structure, and more outcomes. John and I met Kumeyaay Nation members Mike Connolly Miskwish and Stan Rodriguez while we were on the panel "Recovering Indigenous History through Comics" at San Diego Comic-Con in 2019. Inspired by the success of *NAGPRA Comics*, Mike and Stan asked us to consider making comics about their Kumeyaay Nation to respond to the need for more accurate and Indigenous-centered accounts of California history. Here, I want to discuss how we structured the project as a case that brings together many examples of what you have read earlier in this book.

Kumeyaay Visual Storytelling Project

We started discussions about this project early, and **community members were involved in developing the grant and its budget**. I worked with John Swogger, Campo Kumeyaay tribal historian Mike Connolly Miskwish, and Jewyl Alderson from the San Diego County Office of Education to develop the project's structure for the grants. Content development was designed to be similar to community curating in museums, and we noted that in grant applications. We were awarded a California Humanities for All Grant on our second try, which went to Mike; Campo Kumeyaay Nation managed the funds. I was awarded a Whiting Foundation Public Engagement Fellowship to support the project, and the funds were managed by the university and me. So, not only did we co-structure the project, but control of funds was distributed between the university and Native Nation for shared authority that is both conceptual and budgetary. (For an infographic outlining the team and goals of the project, as well as one of the grant proposals, see appendix D.)

PROJECT TEAM

Content development team
- Ethan Banegas (Luiseño-Kumeyaay), San Diego State University (SDSU)–American Indian Studies, San Diego History Center historian
- Mike Connolly Miskwish (Campo Kumeyaay Nation), Kumeyaay historian
- Lorraine Orosco (Kumeyaay-Ipai), education executive director for the San Pasqual Band of Indians
- Dr. Stanley Rodriguez (Kumeyaay-Iipay, Santa Ysabel), instructor of Kumeyaay language and director of the board of Kumeyaay Community College

Production team
- Jen Shannon, curator and associate professor of anthropology, University of Colorado
- John Swogger, archaeologist and comics creator
- Jewyl Alderson, director of systems of support, San Diego County Office of Education

ROLES AND RESPONSIBILITIES

Project/research director (Banegas)

- Coordinates content development with tribal historians
- Leads vetting sessions and community-based events

Project coordinator (Shannon)

- Manages the project
- Provides research assistance
- Documents and organizes information provided during project meetings
- Tracks the budget and grant requirements

Creative director (Swogger)

- Designs comics layout and artwork
- Engages with local artists
- Conducts comics workshops

Educator liaison (Alderson)

- Connects to and advises curriculum developers
- Designs teacher institute day

As the project coordinator, I scheduled meetings and provided the team with notes and resources. I worked closely with project director Ethan Banegas, a member of the Barona Band of the Kumeyaay Nation, who led the content development team—which included Ethan and additional tribal historians Mike, Lorraine, and Stan. John was the creative director and Jewyl was the educator liaison; the two of them and I made up the production team. I also created a project website that includes a description of the project, our bios, and updates about our progress.

Since this project began in 2021, our team did numerous Zoom sessions together, tribal historians worked together to develop content, and we all met in person for two weeks in July 2023 to review and edit draft scripts and comic panel layouts and to present at San Diego Comic-Con (figure 4.2). We met again in November 2024 to launch the comic and post it for free online. Beyond the comic and the website, we conducted comics workshops at the tribal college and community recreation center, developed a traveling banner exhibit that is free to host, and developed plans to help teachers use the comics in their classrooms. Digital copies of posters, the banner exhibit, and lesson plans will be available online in 2025.

For Example | 209

FIGURE 4.2. Kumeyaay Visual Storytelling Project team reviewing draft comic at the Sycuan Cultural Center, July 2013. Lorraine Orosco and John Swogger. Author photo.

PROJECT OUTCOMES
- Forty-four–page comic book (2024)
- Project website (2022)
- Community-based comics workshops (2023)
- Grade 8–12 lesson plans (2025)
- Traveling banner exhibit (2025)
- Educational posters (2025)
- Summary report of project evaluation (2025)

The comic and its format have evolved over the course of our collaboration. In its final form it is in two parts: "Beyond Gaming" is a conversation among the tribal historians as they walk through a community gathering based on a script Ethan developed from conversations he recorded with them and informed by a community-based oral history project he completed in 2020. "Our Past, Present, and Future" is a series of two-page spreads that can be converted into posters in which the tribal historians highlight historical moments that help contextualize the discussion at the gathering. Sources for this half of the comic included Mike's book *Kumeyaay: A History Textbook*, Vol. 1: *Precontact to 1893* (2006) and Sycuan and Barona cultural center exhibits.

The comic is circular in that its layout is designed so that either of the two parts can be read first. Key lessons the tribal historians communicate in the comic include "it matters who writes our history," the importance of "challenging and changing the language and point of view you might find in most other resources," and that "when it comes to changing and adapting our culture you have to ask: are you staying true to the original intention when you make changes? . . . Are your heart and mind in the right place?"

In 2023 we had the opportunity to **share the model for our project publicly** in our San Diego Comic-Con session titled "Honoring Kumeyaay Nation Past, Present, and Future through Visual Storytelling." Each of us had a chance to talk about an aspect of the project to date. The session was reported on by the *San Diego Union-Tribune*, from which the quotes below are taken.[24] Stan began the panel by reminding the audience that the conference was taking place on Kumeyaay lands, followed by Mike sharing his thoughts about why who is telling history matters. He said: "California is such a great example of not only historical distortion but of marketing and branding . . . In the 1890s, when they came in and invented this fictional history, the missions had been defeated . . . The Native people outlasted them, they were crumbled into ruins, and in the 1890s the chambers of commerce and the railroads put money in to rebuild them. These are zombie missions that they built in order to be tourist attractions."

I briefly described the structure of the project, and Ethan explained what the comics are about and why telling this history was meaningful to him personally: "My whole life, I knew powwow culture, but I knew very little about peon . . . It wasn't until 2007 that our gatherings [at Barona] returned, and this momentous event provides the setting for our comic book, where the audience will learn our traditional game of chance called peon." John and Ethan reviewed the process of going from discussion to script to comics panels. Then Jewyl talked about the development of lesson plans and future teachers institutes she will be hosting to connect teachers to the Kumeyaay and to show how to use the comics in class.

Jewyl, who was moderating, asked what this project means to the panelists. Ethan said, "[It shows that] we're much more than casinos." Stan replied, "Our story is not being taught . . . It's important for our people to learn because if it's not, it's a romanticized lie." Lorraine replied, "I love that we put contemporary pieces into our story . . . I want to encourage our young people, our future historians, our future educators, to be inspired to continue the work and feel proud about us being from San Diego." She also said, "This is an opportunity for us to tell our story in our words."

On November 15, 2024, we launched the comic at the Barona Cultural Center. It was important that we first share the comic on Kumeyaay lands, in an event specifically for Kumeyaay people. We started the evening by un-boxing and handing out the comics. Bird singers followed, then dinner, presentations, and time for questions and answers from the audience. More than sixty community members attended. In response to a survey, people's comments about the "big idea" they took away from the event included:

> "The ability to be creative while teaching history" (age 18–24).
> "Native history is part of everyone's history" (18–24).
> "That people should know about Native American history and culture" (25–34).
> "Trying to get the real story into the school system" (45–54).
> "Kumeyaay people/my people are awesome" (25–34).
> "Tell the truth of our history" (25–34).
> "Teach the real Kumeyaay story from the Kumeyaay people" (55–64).
> "That the real history needs to be told" (35–44).
> "I liked the speech and comic books" (under 18).
> "I love reading and I collect Native books, everything was amazing" (under 18).
> "I had an awesome time" (under 18).

A fun part of the evening was when a boy raised his hand to give his evaluation out loud: "I don't like this comic . . . [pause for dramatic effect], I *love* it!" The following night we did a similar event at Kumeyaay College, which is featured in the comic in a section titled "We Teach Our Past, Present, and Future." It is also where the four tribal historians first gathered to discuss and record the story that became "Beyond Gaming." Once again, the evening ended with a boy raising his hand to make a comment; he pointed to a page in the comic that showed kids playing peon and said he liked the page because he plays peon, too. After the event concluded, a young man approached Mike and told him he wants to become a tribal historian. It was a good weekend!

Although our grant-funded project concludes in 2025, it has sparked new opportunities and collaborations for each of us. For example, the tribal

FIGURE 4.3. Comic launch at the Barona Cultural Center, November 15, 2024. From left, Ethan Banegas, John Swogger, Mike Connolly Miskwish, Jewyl Alderson, Jen Shannon, Lorraine Orosco. Author photo.

historians are co-curating an exhibit based on the comic for the La Jolla Historical Society, which applied for and was awarded a grant to fund the exhibition. We are all looking forward to seeing *Kumeyaay Comics: Beyond Gaming/Our Past, Present, and Future* interpreted as an immersive museum exhibition![25]

48
Questions to Guide Practice and Additional Resources

Here are some questions to guide research design and teaching that embody the values of honesty, respect, reciprocity, and shared authority:

Research

- Why are *you* doing this research or project? What does it mean to you personally?
- Why are you doing *this* research or project? What is its purpose?
- Who does your research benefit; what does it illuminate, and to whom?
- Are community members invited into decision making? If so, where are the moments of impact community partners will have on the project's direction?
- What are your plans for sharing the results of the research with the community?
- What are the most appropriate formats to communicate and disseminate information about your project?
- What is at stake in how and what you present to the public?

Teaching and Publishing

- Who are the authors in your syllabus; do they represent a diversity of perspectives and peoples?
- Have you included not just the benefits but also the challenges of collaborative work? Have you provided opportunities to discuss both successes and failures?
- How will you acknowledge the work of collaborators on the project or publication?

Collaborative Anthropology

- *Decolonizing Methodologies: Research and Indigenous Peoples* (Smith 2021 [1999])
- *The Chicago Guide to Collaborative Ethnography* (Lassiter 2005)
- *Community-Based Archaeology: Research with, by, and for Indigenous and Local Communities* (Atalay 2012)
- *The Community-Based PhD: Complexities and Triumphs of Conducting CBPR* (Atalay and McCleary 2022)

PART 4 NOTES

1. Worth, *Through Navajo Eyes*, 4.
2. Darnell, *Invisible Genealogies*, 29.
3. Colwell-Chanthaphonh and Ferguson, "Virtue Ethics and the Practice of History."
4. McGregor, Restoule, and Johnston, "Introduction."
5. Some anthropologists have written publications about one community for twenty years, based on one year of fieldwork. Others, such as Keith Basso, have returned to the same community again and again over their entire lifetime. Early examples of anthropologists who

worked with multiple communities in a more project-style approach include Hortense Powdermaker and Sol Tax.

6. Montiel, "Respect, Reciprocity, and Responsibility."

7. I received a suggestion to move away from the phrase *capacity building* to *capacity sharing* from an anonymous reviewer, who kindly noted that the latter better defines the approach I write about here; I have since introduced that reorientation and updated phrase to colleagues, staff, and students (and thanked the anonymous reviewer each time).

8. McGregor, Restoule, and Johnston, "Indigenous Research," 11.

9. Lempert, "Palya Futures."

10. An excellent phrase that I have cited and used often, from Rowley et al., "Building an On-Line Research Community."

11. Shannon, "On Being a Tentative Anthropologist."

12. Ray Silverman asked this of all the authors, including me, in his edited volume *Museum as Process*. On page 1 he cited Ivan Karp's observation that collaboration often brings failure and that failure can be splendid, productive, meaningful. Silverman cited an often-used phrase for many who work with communities—that process is more important than product—and introduced the notion of slow museology, where working in collaboration means a project will take more time but is worth it. That has certainly been my experience (and thank goodness for granting organizations that understand this). Silverman, *Museum as Process*.

13. Shannon, "On Being a Tentative Anthropologist."

14. Shannon, *Guide to Creating Community Engaged Comics*; Shannon and Swogger, *A Guide to Facilitating Comics Workshop*; Shannon, Kambeitz, and Hammons, *MHA Collaborative Filmmaking Project Workshop Guide*; Shannon, Polmear, and Duhe, *MHA Citizen Science Curriculum*.

15. Hadley Toftness and Taylor Biggs, "In Good Relation."

16. Some of this section is taken from Shannon, "'Dear Concerned about Consent' (Response to 'Yours Sincerely, Concerned about Consent')." Reproduced with permission.

17. Shannon, "Informed Consent."

18. This commentary is based on an excerpt of my AAA conference paper, "NAGPRA Comics: Risking the Media for the Message," presented November 17, 2018, in San Jose, California, at the session "How Experimental Are You? Museum Anthropology as a Catalyst for Shaping the Discipline," organized by Gwyn Isaac and Jennifer Kramer; and on a post I wrote in 2019 for the AAA blog titled "Museum Anthropology Has a Lot to Offer Public Anthropology!"

19. American Anthropological Association, "AAA Guidelines for Tenure and Promotion Review."

20. Shannon et al., "Anthropology, Empathy, and the Need for Social Science Communication."

21. Nasser, "The World's Biggest Scavenger Hunt."

22. Baron, *Escape from the Ivory Tower*, 41.

23. Edmiston, "What's Behind Match Day's Algorithm?"

24. Quotes from the panel session are from two news articles: Mapp, "Comic-Con 2023"; Monteagudo, "At Comic-Con, Kumeyaay Tribe Reveals Plans to Counter the 'Romanticized Lie.'"

25. Banegas et al., *Kumeyaay Comics* 1.

Conclusion

Reimagining Anthropology and the Museum

Reimagining the Museum

This book is intended to introduce some of the ways Indigenous communities have guided us to reimagine the museum's purpose toward centering cultural continuity instead of object perpetuity, as well as reimagining the relationship between museums and originating communities. When we take seriously other ways of knowing and relating to the items that are cared for in museums, when we focus not only on objects but on all the people connected to them past, present, and future—originating communities primarily but also museum staff and visitors—it helps us think differently about our work and our relations with other people and with the items in museums.

    The concept of shared stewardship, which has been practiced for decades at institutions like the University of British Columbia Museum of Anthropology and the National Museum of the American Indian, has come to the fore in recent years—most recently at the national level through the new Smithsonian Institution Shared Stewardship and Ethical Returns Policy. Talk about how leadership and who is in charge matters! The Smithsonian

Institution-wide policy of Shared Stewardship and Ethical Returns was implemented in April 2022 under the direction of the head of the Smithsonian, Dr. Lonnie Bunch III, former director of the National Museum of African American History and Culture, and Undersecretary Kevin Gover (Pawnee), former director of the National Museum of the American Indian.

Museums are increasingly open to digital return and knowledge sharing. We are moving in the right direction, but there is more work to do. I do tend to be an optimistic person and can occasionally wear rosy glasses, but I also feel that in general, these are optimistic times for change in museums, for Indigenous communities, and for increasing access to heritage materials in museums. There is momentum toward, but not universal adoption of, these ethics and approaches. I believe we are in a moment: now is the time to catch the current wave that is propelling these approaches and initiatives forward. It is a great time to start, or to increase, implementing these approaches because there is more societal and leadership attention on and openness to these efforts than ever before.

As we reimagine the museum and its relation to originating communities, we start to see the museum differently. I believe a museum can be a safekeeping place where items can come into collections and also go out through repatriation, shared stewardship, or loan for community use. It is a place where communities can house their treasures without relinquishing them, where we can work together in ways that benefit us all now and in the future. I also believe a museum can be a (social) science communication center and a cultural center, a public space and a classroom, a site for inspiring awe through art and for hosting scavenger hunts for kids; it can be a lab for experimentation and a community gathering place. All these things are possible in a museum, especially a university museum (and it's why I loved working in one!). Museums are remarkable places when they work in concert with Indigenous communities and are made responsible to their future generations.

Collaboration and ethical museum practice is about building and maintaining good relations—with each other and with the items and beings in collections. As Jan Bernstein put it during an Indigenous Collections Care working group meeting, this is a turn to a focus on human-centered museum practice. Micah Parzen, director of the Museum of Us in San Diego, California, discussed a similar concept in a meeting—for him, it's about how we treat museum staff and starting the work internally before extending outward. Either way, thinking about museums as human-centered or relationship-centered instead of object-centered is one way to reorient how we make decisions and do our work in these institutions.

Reimagining Anthropology

Some people may say that cultural anthropology is an antiquated and colonial discipline, and that it should end—why not look to other disciplines instead, like sociology or ethnic studies or geography or history? Well, I am not ready to give up, in part because anthropology continues to reckon with its past (it embodies that idea of a culture of learning)—so much so that I've heard undergraduate students from other disciplines express exasperation at the constant reflection on and discussion of this "terrible past" instead of simply moving forward with new ideas and practices. But doing this is necessary; it teaches reflection, social construction (we made it this way, we can change it), and valuing other ways of knowing. I began as a biology major in college and added anthropology as my second major in part because it matched my values: seeking understanding from other points of view, learning from other ways of living in and knowing the world, and reflecting on our own past and present and future with an open mind. These are valuable approaches to learning and engaging with others: reflection, empathy, social change.

There are many different kinds of anthropology and many different areas of interest in the field beyond Native peoples and their past and current practices and lives. However, that is the oldest form and stereotype of the discipline. This is not a new proposition in our field, but I want to emphasize it here: I suggest we reimagine cultural anthropology as a field that engages with and serves Indigenous communities instead of studying them, that encourages research and theorizing alongside our community partners, that presents an opportunity to position community partners as project directors and co-creators of research questions and methods, and that allows us to imagine more experimental approaches and provide more accessible outcomes of our work together. Collaborative anthropology can be difficult—cooperation, the process, and the time line are not always in our control. The great thing about collaborative anthropology is that it commits to ethical practice and shared authority, and this can provide a deep sense of meaning and enjoyment when working with others toward a common purpose. Collaboration doesn't always work out, but when it does, it is a powerful and positive experience.

The Impact of Collaboration

Collaboration between museum staff and originating communities has had significant and positive impacts on museums but also on the field of anthropology and research practices more generally. As collaboration and community-based research become more valued, taught, and expected, we also need to ask ourselves what other kinds of impact this increased engagement might have.

One thing that keeps coming to my mind as we advocate for collaboration in so many realms of museum, academic, and research practice is the burden this places on Native communities. Collaboration can be taxing in both time expended and physical and emotional labor. When the Native American Graves Protection and Repatriation Act (NAGPRA) was enacted, new tribal positions had to be developed to meet the demand—to receive and prioritize requests and lists of collections coming in, to respond to inadvertent discoveries, to manage the responsibilities associated with the law, and to interact with the dead and their associated funerary items. Some Native Nations have created research review boards to centralize the review of proposed research projects. Other communities have developed centralized or organized committees or offices like these to meet the demand, but not all communities have the resources or the ability to do so.

We need to think about the consequences of our increasing calls for advising, consultation, collaboration, and partnership with communities in all these arenas—for repatriation, for applying duty of care under the new regulations, for work in museums, and for research projects. Don't let this concern stop you from inviting people to collaborate or asking for advising, but do come prepared (part of the reason this book was created), and be patient and compassionate—understand that Indigenous communities need to prioritize how they spend their limited time. The decision to participate or not is up to community partners, but also consider ways to ease the burden of labor, although not the burden of authority.

When museums, and sometimes researchers, want to collaborate with communities, they often go to the Tribal Historic Preservation Office or cultural center first. Those are great places to begin, to ensure that people know what you are interested in; perhaps these tribal officials can suggest others to work with you if they do not have the interest or capacity to do so themselves. Seek out tribal research review boards to see if they are available as well. One Native colleague suggested that enlisting Native consultants to help guide museum projects is another way to go, to spread out the work and the support for individuals in the heritage sector.

For communities, there are ways you can seek labor assistance as well. Graduate students are always looking for meaningful topics for their master's or PhD theses. Consider partnering with a local university to develop a program in which you identify research that is of interest to you and the university recommends researchers to partner with you. Students often struggle with defining a research project. I can assure you that having help with that, as well as knowing it is wanted and can be useful, will be of great interest to many students.

Many recent guidelines for museums say the museum must consult with the originating community. This may not be sustainable, as these requests increase exponentially over time. So, what's next? Is it appropriate for museums to share with each other what they learn from communities? How can we be fully collaborative and also mindful of community capacity and interest in the work? These are big questions moving forward and ones I hope will be answered by following the lead of communities and what they would like to see develop in these fields.

Relationships between originating communities and museums should endure longer than those between individuals from each group who create positive relationships in the present. We need to take a generational perspective—something we learn from Indigenous communities and that is also part of museum planning—to think long term and be responsible to future generations. Focus on good relations today and also on policy and collections care documentation and other initiatives that ensure that the good work now continues and is honored in the future.

A Big Tent

Teaching anthropology and museum studies has been a great privilege and honor in my life; it is where I have primarily located my commitment and actions to the movements for change in museums and anthropology and society more generally. What we teach the next generation can impact other institutions and future generations as our students go out into the world and pass on what they know. So, my own approach has been less one of critique and more of seeking to better understand and document process. I focus on communicating in a way that will keep others listening, especially those who don't know or don't agree with the practices described in this book. Some may see my approach as not strong enough; they may think my form of advocacy and practice doesn't critique or disrupt enough. But I believe there are many different roles for all of us to play in making and supporting change in anthropology, research, and museums. We need people who write theory and academic papers as well as those who focus on practice and write blogs and white papers. We need people who protest and talk to reporters, and we need people who edit labels on museum exhibits and add a second language to online exhibits.

I have learned so much from students and have expected much of them as well (and they do not disappoint!). I often say that the futures of both museums and anthropology look bright from what I see in the next generation: students coming into the university now, in my experience, take for granted that repatriation and reciprocity and community engagement should be integral to what we do.

Finally, I believe we can maintain a big tent in following the lead of Indigenous communities with respect to more ethical practice in museums and anthropology. There is room for people of many different approaches, abilities, experiences, and skills as long as we all maintain a sense of humility and a culture of learning.

Embracing a Culture of Learning

Our language in museums, similar to the language preferred by originating communities, changes over time. "Diversity, equity, and inclusion" has been frequently discussed in recent years. Committees and job positions dedicated to these values have been on the rise in museums, universities, and elsewhere. Like decolonization, these terms highlight a need, give people a goal to aim for, and also need to be specifically defined. Again, actions are more important than words. I believe institutions like the University of British Columbia Museum of Anthropology and the National Museum of the American Indian have been doing the work of diversity, equity, and inclusion for decades, even if it was not called that. It was just the right way to do things.

So, a caution to new students and generations coming up: be sure to look at the actions and work of those who came before you. Just because something didn't show up in a word search based on the language you know, just because it wasn't labeled the same as the work you are committed to (and kudos for taking up that work up!), does not mean it wasn't happening. There is much to learn from those who came before—talk to them through informational interviews, chats over coffee, and other ways. A lot of this work is not new, but it is much more common and more commonly valued, institutionally supported, and visible now. This is wonderful! Of course, it is not present in all institutions and not everywhere, so there is still much to do.

So much has changed in our field, even during the time it took to write this book—and that is largely also due to the generations coming up now. For those who have been working in this field for a long time, the members of the next generations have great perspectives to share and learn from, including new ideas and methods for how to communicate and accomplish our shared goals. Together, we can keep experimenting and working toward the common values of honesty, respect, reciprocity, and shared authority. We can learn together from our mistakes and share what works. I hope this book can be a resource to spark ideas for consideration on what to do or think about in the day-to-day work of making these goals a reality.

Epilogue

Dear reader,

I began writing this book as a professor at the University of Colorado. I am writing to you now from Washington, DC—the traditional territories of the Nacotchtank or Anacostans, which neighbor the ancestral lands of the Piscataway and Pamunkey peoples. Today, around 4,000 Native people live in the area we call the District of Columbia, and a national museum and a Native veterans' memorial are situated next to the seat of US power, the United States Capitol building.[1] In 2023, I received a grant to start an outreach and engagement office at the National Museum of the American Indian, working with inspiring tribal museum professionals and Smithsonian colleagues. I continue to advise graduate students, which brings me joy, and to work collaboratively with Native communities to tell true stories about history and repatriation from their perspectives through comic books.

In April 2024, I co-taught a four-week online continuing education course with Dr. Jessie Ryker Crawford (White Earth Anishinaabe), who was the academic dean at the Institute of American Indian Arts. The course, Culturally Informed Collections Stewardship, was part of a series of classes at the

Beloit College Center for Collections Care. Beloit College's Logan Museum of Anthropology director Nicolette Meister designed, wrote a grant to support, and administrated "C3." This course included students and practitioners, Native and non-Native museum professionals, and Nicolette herself. It was a wonderful example of knowledge sharing and building a sense of community around shared values. As we said at the end of the course, we are in a *moment*. We are in a time when ethical and collaborative museum and research practice is rising, supported, and valued—not everywhere, not evenly—but we *are* in a moment, and now is the time to seize it.

I also continue to be inspired and informed by current and former graduate students. Much of what I wrote in this book was a result of conversations. In fact, the paragraph describing grant writing as a form of making daydreams come true was a direct quote of something I said to a former graduate student who was considering taking on a new job as a grant writer. I often say my thinking and processing happens in the space between me and others, in dialogue. It's good to know yourself and how your best ideas emerge. Students past and present have been significant in my figuring out the big takeaways and how to share my experiences working alongside Native community members. Teaching really is a particular kind of thinking process. It meant I was never just doing research or community-engaged work but also reflecting on that work and thinking about what lessons I could bring to the next project and to the next generation going forward.

On the flip side, community-based work is about being patient and listening. Now, anyone who knows me knows that I am excitable and energetic. I come from an Italian family who talks a lot and talks over each other (with love!). Slowing down and listening were skills I had to practice and hone over time. I am still working on them. I remember in 2001, when I was interviewing elders in Igloolik who spoke Inuktitut and the translator suggested that I wait and allow silence before asking another question—it was excellent advice that I have shared in every methods course I have taught since. What a gift it was for him to clue me in. For each of us, some things are intuitive and others take practice. Identifying the difference is helpful in doing collaborative and community-based work.

As I was transitioning from working at the university to the national museum and from writing during work hours to writing outside work hours, my wonderful editor at the time, Robert Ramaswamy, said: "There are no emergencies in publishing. And we don't need to be creating stress by pretending there is one; we should work on a schedule that makes the most sense for you." I was like, what? I have always needed deadlines to push me, to make me get the writing done. But in this case, I found myself wanting to spend time with this narrative and with you, the reader. Because the narrative was based on my teaching and practice, I could dip in and out along the way, continuing to think about and practice the commitments in this book. This has been a conversation I have enjoyed having with you intermittently over these years, and I very much appreciate that you are here, reading this now.

Thank you for being part of a movement to change the way we work with each other and with communities in research, anthropology, and museums. Ideas and practices for doing this work will continue to evolve. I hope this can be a foundation for feeling more prepared, asking respectful questions, and considering how you can continue to carry this movement forward in new ways.

Jen Shannon
August 31, 2024

CONCLUSION NOTE

1. For more information, see Association of Research Libraries, "Land Acknowledgment."

Appendixes

You will see in these appendixes some examples of guides I created in the past. For each of these practice-oriented documents, my primary aim is not to tell you what to do or suggest that you use these particular documents. I want to show how teaching about/working in collaboration led to these forms of writing. They are meant to serve as examples for you to think with and encourage you to create similar and other kinds of resources in service of, and to give back to, the people with whom you work. It is also my way of shedding light on the other kinds of writing we do at a university when we are committed to community-based research.

Appendix A

Sample Project Newsletter

CU@MVNP Newsletter

July 1, 2021   Issue Number 5

A PARTNERSHIP TO REDESIGN THE CHAPIN MESA ARCHEOLOGICAL MUSEUM

Staff at Mesa Verde National Park (MVNP) and faculty and students at the University of Colorado (CU) Museum of Natural History are working together, in collaboration with Pueblos and Tribes associated with the park and archaeologists, to **redesign the Chapin Mesa Archeological Museum (CMAM)** exhibits. See CU@MVNP Newsletter #1 for more info.

Did You Know?

MVNP entrance is free for members of the 26 associated tribes. Please let park staff know where you are from so they can welcome you to the park! Contact Jennifer Beaudoin at 970-529-5034 for more info.

-Content Development-

Native Interpretation
Woody Aguilar (San Ildefonso)
Tim Begay (Navajo)
Betsy Chapoose (Ute)
Gloria Lomahaftewa (Hopi)
Theresa Pasqual (Acoma)
Gary Roybal (San Ildefonso)
Octavius Seowtewa (Zuni)
Kristy Sholly (MVNP)
Richard Smith, Sr. (Laguna)

Archaeology
Woody Aguilar (San Ildefonso)
Samantha Fladd (CU)
Donna Gloawacki
Tim Hovezak (MVNP)
Gay Ives (MVNP)
Chris McAllister
Theresa Pasqual (Acoma)
Susan Ryan
Laurie Webster

History
Marietta Eaton and from MVNP: Kay Barnett, Lizzie Dickey, Amy Ireland, Tara Travis, and Kristy Sholly

Natural Resources
Pat Kociolek (CU)
Tova Spector (MVNP)

CONTENT DEVELOPMENT UPDATE

The content development groups are creating "content packets" that summarize their work to date, including descriptions of topics they feel are important to consider for potential inclusion in the CMAM exhibits. They will inform the October meeting (see below).

The **Native Interpretation Working Group** has been meeting monthly online since January via Zoom. Kristy Sholly, Chief of Interpretation and Visitor Services at the park, has joined the group. Recent discussions have included migration and movement and how behavior is and was related to people's relationships to the land. Tara Travis, Supervisory Museum Curator from the park, discussed cultural items in the park's collection with the working group. The working group is currently reviewing the draft content development packet which summarizes the priorities of the group and will guide exhibit designers.

The **Archaeology Content Development Working Group** is reviewing the first part of the content packet. The resources section is being assembled by Dr. Fladd and will be sent out for review by the archaeologists in the next few weeks.

Content development teams for **History** and **Natural Resources** are also preparing for the October meeting by pulling together information from interviews that CU and MVNP staff conducted with subject matter experts.

For the **New Park Film**, by Boyd Productions with filmmaker Jonathan Sims (Pueblo of Acoma), Governor Vallo (Acoma Pueblo) and Madeline Naranjo (Santa Clara Pueblo) have been selected as the primary speakers on camera. The filmmakers did a site visit at the end of May and began conducting interviews in June. The first draft of the script will be available for review by the Native Interpretation Working Group this fall. Please direct questions about the film to Jonathon Sims (noreservations@gmail.com) and Amy Ireland (amy_ireland@nps.gov). Photo: Madeline Naranjo on camera for the film.

OCTOBER MEETING FOR CONTENT TEAMS

All of the content development teams will meet during the week of October 18th at MVNP and in Cortez to visit the CMAM, review museum collections, and discuss content for the CMAM exhibits in dialogue with each other. Through examining the similarities, differences, and unique perspectives that come from each content team we hope to develop innovative exhibits grounded in mutual respect and multiple ways of knowing and connecting to Mesa Verde.

FIGURE A.1. Sample project newsletter, page 1.

PUBLIC PRESENTATIONS

CU faculty and staff and community partners have given presentations about this ongoing MVNP project in several venues, with additional presentations forthcoming:

December 1, 2021
"How should we proceed?: Redesigning an archaeology museum at Mesa Verde National Park" panel about community outreach to be presented at the International Conference of Indigenous Archives, Libraries, and Museums (ATALM) in Washington, DC.
– Joseph "Woody" Aguilar (San Ildefonso), Elysia Poon (SAR), Tony Chavarria (Santa Clara MIAC), Scarlett Engle (CU), and Jen Shannon (CU)

March 12, 2021
"Collaboration is Theory in Motion: Redesigning the Chapin Mesa Archeological Museum at Mesa Verde National Park in Partnership with Twenty-Six Pueblos and Tribes" at the University College London forum for Heritage, Participation, Performativity, Care."
CLICK HERE FOR VIDEO
– Joseph "Woody" Aguilar (San Ildefonso) and Jen Shannon (CU)

April 8, 2021
Presentation to CU Exhibit Development class – Gloria Lomahoftewa (Hopi) and Sheila Goff (CU)

May 5, 2020
"Towards a More Inclusive Mesa Verde National Park"
CLICK HERE FOR VIDEO
– Scarlett Engle, CU PhD student, for a class project

TESTING OUT IDEAS AT THE CU MUSEUM

Led by PhD student Scarlett Engle and undergraduate Kaia Noone, with assistance from CU curators and Sheila Goff, the CU Museum will host a small "prototype" exhibit to test audience response to different ways of presenting the idea of "multiple ways of knowing." We will share more about this exhibit and its outcome over the summer and fall of this year.

UPDATE FROM UROP RESEARCH ASSISTANTS

The Undergraduate Research Opportunity Program (UROP) team is a group of undergraduate students who provide research assistance to the Archaeology and Native Interpretation content development working groups. This past academic year Maddie King, Sean White, and Anna Cohen graduated from the university. Each reflected on their UROP experience: **Maddie** said that "having the opportunity to work as a UROP Research Assistant for the CMAM Project taught me the importance of collaborating with Native American tribal representatives from the very beginning of the curatorial process;" **Sean** "learned about the critical collaboration and listening needed to create something as important as a museum exhibit; in our work we focused on as many points of view as possible in order to properly show the amazing nature of MVNP;" and **Anna** noted, "through research in archives and electronic materials, I learned to underscore the importance and recognition of contemporary Native populations." Congratulations to these students and a sincere thank you for their research assistance!

Two new UROP students joined the project this summer. **Kaia Noone** is a fourth-year undergraduate student majoring in Anthropology with a minor in Women and Gender Studies. She grew up in Denver, Colorado. In the future, she aspires to continue to work with and empower underrepresented communities. **Grayson Higsley** is a fourth-year undergraduate student double majoring in Classics and Anthropology with a focus on History, Art History, and Archaeology. He has lived in Colorado for most of his life and plans to go to graduate school in order to pursue a career in museum studies or archive work.

NEXT STEPS IN THE PROJECT – OVERVIEW

Below is a basic overview of the project. This is subject to change according to circumstances and tribal community input, which is engaged throughout the process. We are currently at step 5, moving to step 6 in October of this year. The project has been progressing smoothly despite the restrictions due to COVID-19. Many thanks to all who have continued to stay invested and participating in this process over the past year.

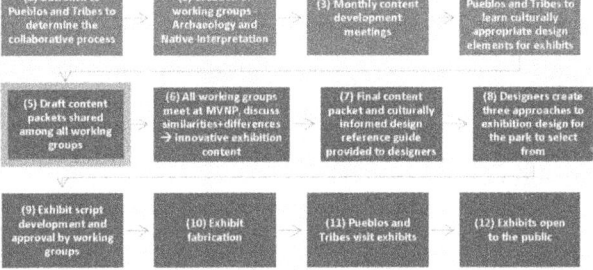

Please share this newsletter so everyone is included and informed

Click Here for all newsletters and reports to date. Have questions, concerns, or want to provide feedback? We welcome your input - please contact Jen Shannon at 303-919-5022 or jshannon@colorado.edu, or Sheila Goff at Sheila.Goff@colorado.edu. Thank you!

FIGURE A.2. Sample project newsletter, page 2.

Appendix B

Example Policies and Guidelines for Inspiration

We don't have to reinvent the wheel. There are a lot of great examples to draw inspiration from in mainstream and tribal institutions. Below is a selection that centers Indigenous communities, their perspectives, and their needs in museum practice. I consider them great examples to think with.

Seek out the research, collections, loan, and repatriation policies from museums like these, which are known to work closely with originating communities and to have progressive policies:

- American Philosophical Society Center for Native American and Indigenous Research.
- Autry Museum of the American West.
- Robert S. Peabody Institute of Archaeology, also known as the Peabody Andover museum.
- School for Advanced Research Indian Arts Research Center.
- Smithsonian Institution Shared Stewardship and Ethical Returns Policy; each individual Smithsonian museum has its interpretation of the policy on its own website.
- Smithsonian National Museum of the American Indian.
- University of British Columbia Museum of Anthropology.

Ask tribal museums and cultural centers who present at conferences about their policies to provide insight into museum practice preferred by originating communities, such as the Alutiiq Museum, the Seminole Tribe of Florida Ah-Tah-Thi-Ki Museum, and the Ziibiwing Center of Anishinabe Culture and Lifeways.

Sample Policies and Guidelines

- ***Indigenous Collections Care Guide*** provides a framework to respect and re-center collections stewardship practices around the needs and knowledge of Native American and Indigenous community members: https://sarweb.org/iarc/icc/.
- ***Memorandum of Affiliation between the Musqueam Indian Band and the University of British Columbia***: https://aboriginal.ubc.ca/files/2011/01/UBC-Musqueam-MOA-signed1.pdf.

- **Memorandum of Understanding between the Penobscot Nation and the University of Maine:** https://umaine.edu/nativeamerican programs/wp-content/uploads/sites/320/2018/05/Penobscot-Nation-UMaine-MOU.pdf.
- **The Protocols for Native American Archival Materials**: http://www2.nau.edu/libnap-p/protocols.html.
- **Routes to Return**, Amy Shakespeare's online guide to repatriation policy and practice in Europe: https://routestoreturn.com/.
- **School for Advanced Research Guidelines for Collaboration** have separate guidelines for museums and Native communities: https://guidelinesforcollaboration.info/.
- **Smithsonian Institution Shared Stewardship and Ethical Returns Policy:** https://ncp.si.edu/SI-ethical-returns (each Smithsonian museum has a web page explaining its procedures to implement this policy).
- **Standards for Museums with Native American Collections (SMNAC)** includes recommendations for the seven function areas identified in the American Alliance of Museums' Standards of Excellence: https://sarweb.org/iarc/smnac/.

Appendix C

Workshop Your Project

This activity is based on a workshop I gave twice at the University of California Merced, which has a Research Center for Community Engaged Scholarship and a Community Research and Service minor degree program.

BE PREPARED TO ARTICULATE PROJECT VALUES, GOALS, and MOTIVATIONS.

MOTIVATION: *The reason or reasons one has for acting or behaving in a particular way.* It's important to be able to communicate the motivations for your actions—whether explaining your research to a community or devising an appropriate model for engagement.

- What is your personal motivation behind your project or research?
- Why do you want to engage with this community?
- What do you hope to achieve from engaging with this community?
- What do you hope to give back to this community, and why?

MEANING: Importance or value. Meaning in terms of why this is important, and meaning in terms of . . . the terms you use! It's important to avoid miscommunication and to identify the shared language you will use with your community partners.

- What are the values at the core of your research practice?
- What does engagement mean to you, to your community partners?
- Who does "community" include; how does this affect how you choose to design and communicate your research?
- Does everyone in your collaboration interpret the language you are using in the same way?

Make a list of three values you see as central to the project you are working on.
Next to each, identify <u>one</u> example or way your project enacts that value.
For example:
Respect—*I provide honoraria to acknowledge local participants' expertise and to compensate them for the time they spend working on this project in addition to their everyday work and responsibilities.*

MODEL: A way of doing something that can be used as an example.

- What models for collaboration and communication are appropriate to your practice?
- In what ways, or through what formats or media, do you want to engage with community members?
- What are appropriate models to do so, and why?

Communicate regularly to keep everyone informed.
What are the most appropriate formats to communicate and disseminate information about your project?

Write down one or two main stakeholders/communities you are engaging with for your project.

For each of these communities, write down four sample methods of sharing/communication (and note why you chose this format):

1. Considering alternative methods for informed consent, broadly construed
2. Sharing updates while the project is ongoing (which media is most appropriate to your project—for example, newsletters, email listserv, blog posts, Facebook posts, phone calls, YouTube channel)

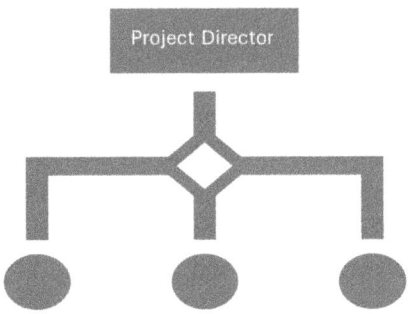

FIGURE C.1. Sample project organizational chart

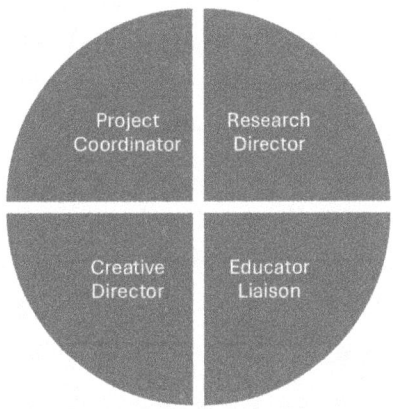

FIGURE C.2. Project organizational chart from Kumeyaay Visual Storytelling Project

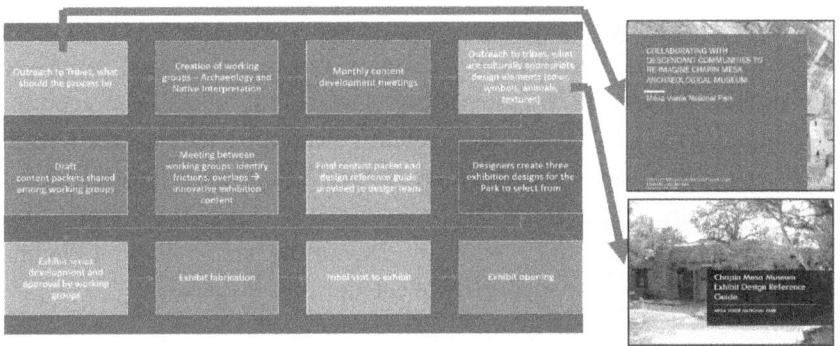

FIGURE C.3. Example from Mesa Verde National Park Chapin Mesa Archeological Museum redesign project, 2020. Green boxes are tribal decision points—where they make decisions and advise before the project can move forward.

3. Sharing outcomes of the project with participants
4. Sharing outcomes of the project with the wider community/public.

ENSURE THAT THERE ARE WELL-DEFINED AND CLEAR EXPECTATIONS.

What is the "organizational chart" for your project? Diagram the main roles and responsibilities for the community and university partners. Consider: how are responsibilities divided; where is authority concentrated? Would a community member create the same chart? (figures C.1 and C.2)

Diagram your project's time line/main steps, and circle or highlight the places where community members have decision, evaluation, or review responsibilities. Note tangible returns to the community. Consider the kinds of "decision points" that are baked into your project. Do the people you are collaborating with see the project in the same way? Would a community member be able to create a similar diagram (figure C.3)?

Appendix D

Sample Infographic and Grant Proposal

The Kumeyaay Visual Storytelling Project received two grants: a Whiting Foundation Public Engagement Fellowship to me and a California Humanities for All Grant awarded to the Campo Kumeyaay Nation. I include the latter below, which was developed in collaboration with Campo Kumeyaay Nation tribal historian Michael Connolly Miskwish, educator Jewyl Alderson, and comics creator John Swogger. For each collaborative project, I try to make a reference sheet that community partners and their contacts can use to explain and understand the project overview. This sheet was also good for early meetings as we set roles, responsibilities, and expectations for our work together. For more about the project, see https://kumeyaayvsp.weebly.com/.

For the project described in the proposal below, figure D.1 is a one-page resource I developed using PowerPoint. Due to the pandemic the time line shifted, and funders were supportive of extending grant periods.

Appendix D | 233

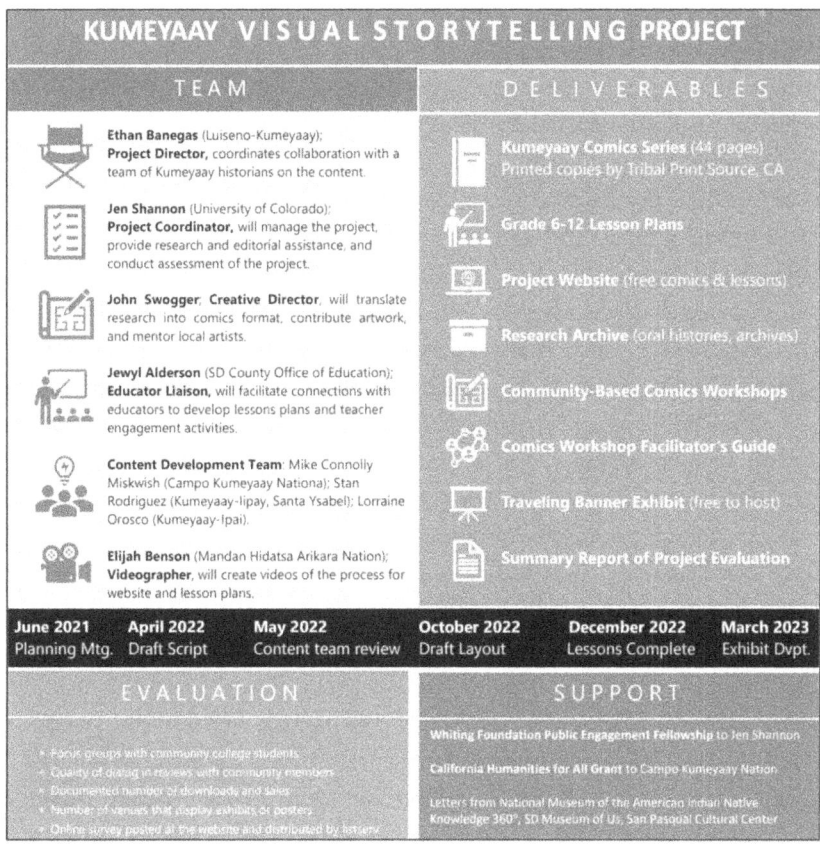

FIGURE D.1. Sample project infographic.

A. Proposal Narrative—Kumeyaay Comics: Indigenous Histories of California

1. PROJECT OVERVIEW AND RATIONALE

Why is this important? On June 18, 2019, California's governor, Gavin Newsom, issued an executive order (N-15-19) that apologized for atrocities against California Native Americans by the State and committed California to a Truth and Reconciliation process (State of California 2020). A key component to this process is recovering histories of the Indigenous peoples of California—including histories of Kumeyaay peoples from Kumeyaay perspectives.

Kumeyaay Comics: Indigenous Histories of California is a community-directed, arts-based research project initiated by Mike Connolly Miskwish, the tribal historian of the Campo Kumeyaay Nation (also known in the federal system as Campo Band of Missions Indians), a federally recognized tribe located about sixty miles east of San Diego. Connolly has enlisted the authors and producers of *NAGPRA Comics* to create a comic series about the Indigenous history of Southern California through collaboration with a team of Kumeyaay tribal historians.

The Kumeyaay Nation is represented in present day by twelve Reservations in the US and four Ejidos in Mexico. According to Connolly, historical presentations of the Native peoples of California have long been structured to present a simplistic account centered on a narrative of benign friars in Missions, pastoral Ranchos of the Mexican period, and the 49ers of the early American period. In all of these accounts, Native peoples were either eliminated or became backdrops to the dominant narrative (see also Fenelon and Trafzer 2014). The project will create a series of comics that illustrate lifeways before, during, and after Kumeyaay encounters with other peoples through a process similar to "community curating" practiced at the National Museum of the American Indian, which both Connolly and Shannon participated in during the early 2000s (Shannon 2014). Topics may include colonization, genocide, and resilience; relationships with the natural world; intergenerational learning; lifeways represented through material culture in collaboration with area museums; and more.

This project is sponsored by the Campo Kumeyaay Nation. It responds to the need for more accurate and Indigenous-centered accounts of California history—in mainstream schools and among Kumeyaay communities. This rigorously researched, and community authored and vetted, comic series will be widely accessible: available online for free as PDFs for the general public, to publish in local newspapers, or as exhibit panels in schools and museums and cultural centers; and, it will be supplemented with lesson plans for teachers to use in classrooms also available for free online. A traveling banner exhibit will be available to these venues as well at no cost. Printed copies of the comics will be available through Tribal Print Source, a tribally owned publisher in California that also prints *NAGPRA Comics*, which is the model for this project.

How does the project relate to the purpose and intent of the Humanities for All grant program? *Kumeyaay Comics* combines several areas of humanities including history, cultural anthropology, and the arts to increase our understanding and access to Indigenous histories and perspectives. This project is committed to and combines complementary research methodologies: decolonizing methodologies (Smith 1999) and arts-based research (Leavy 2018). The first comes from the field of Indigenous studies and is a critique of extractive research practice. Committing to decolonizing research methodologies means that the project is founded in respect and reciprocity, and Indigenous community partners determine the research questions, appropriate methods, and outcomes for the project (Shannon 2017).

Arts-based research is particularly useful for qualitative research. It utilizes creative arts, like comics and comics workshops described here, as part of the research process—for example for content generation, interpretation, and representation (Leavy 2018). Key strengths of this form of research include being participatory, raising awareness and empathy, challenging stereotypes and dominant ideologies, including marginalized voices and perspectives, and contributing to public scholarship (Leavy 2018:10). These strengths align with core outcomes of the project.

This project would provide a model in the new field of applied comics. Comics are a serialized form of illustrated storytelling that, despite popular conceptions, are well suited to addressing serious and culturally sensitive issues, as evidenced by *UNeducation: A Residential School Graphic Novel* (Eaglespeaker 2014), *7 Generations: A Plains Cree Saga* (Robertson and Henderson 2016), *Ghost River: The Fall and Rise of the Conestoga* (Francis et al. 2019; see also https://ghostriver.org/), and *NAGPRA Comics 1: Journeys to Complete the Work . . . and Changing the Way We Bring Native American Ancestors Home* (Atalay, Shannon, Swogger 2017). Comics can contribute to community healing and well-being as well (Borkent 2020:276).

In *The New Mutants* (2015), Fawaz discusses comics' role in facilitating space for dissenting voices to reshape the production and circulation of culture and imagine a more equal and plural society. In *Graphic Justice*, Giddens (2016) illustrates how comics can be teaching tools that engage active learning. There are rare examples like readingwithpictures.org and *Connecting Comics to Curriculum: Strategies for Grades 6–12* (Gavigan and Tomasevich 2011) that provide lesson plans for comics. *Kumeyaay Comics* would also provide a model in this medium for open educational resources.

What humanities-based learning experiences will it provide to participants/ audiences? Informal learning opportunities will include workshops and a traveling banner exhibit, and formal learning opportunities will be facilitated with lesson plans for classroom use. For schools, engaging with *Kumeyaay Comics* and the associated lessons, workshop exercises, and exhibit might be meaningful to them in terms of curriculum ambitions for art, literacy, creative writing, and oral history.

The project will engage creators and learners in history and arts based research, art making, storytelling, and illustrated educational resources founded in Indigenous perspectives. The comics will be a resource for members of the Kumeyaay Nation to learn about their history and engage in intergenerational dialogue. *Kumeyaay Comics* will also introduce the broader public to a largely "silenced past" (Truillot 1995)—absent from American mainstream education and popular media—regarding the experiences and histories of Native peoples in California.

Comics are a versatile medium. Once the stories are in comics format, sections can be formatted for exhibition panels, four-panel strips for newspapers, single-page posters, and books with full pages of added artwork from community members. In addition, the beauty of comics is that it is easy to insert alternative languages in the existing speech bubbles, so these comics can also be translated into the Kumeyaay language as a language program activity, or into Spanish should that be desired. While funding and labor for that is not a part of this project, it is certainly something that could develop once the comics are completed.

How will your Humanities Advisors contribute to the project? Humanities Advisors, Jen Shannon and John Swogger, co-produce *NAGPRA Comics*, a community-based, collaboratively produced comic series that tells true stories about repatriation from tribal perspectives. It is an applied/educational comic series, so it also explains what the law is and how it works. The demonstrated audiences for these comics are tribal community members and cultural centers, university classrooms, archaeologists, and the general public. *NAGPRA Comics*' "iterative editing process, and embedded layers of cultural interpretation, resulted in [tribal] leadership . . . feeling it was their story and that it was appropriately told, and they have distributed it widely" (Atalay and Shannon 2019).

Shannon contributes research, project planning, community engagement experience and scholarship, and writing and editorial skills to the project. Her work is committed to facilitating and disseminating more diverse and inclusive understandings of history and contemporary lives, particularly through collaboration with Indigenous peoples. She has four years of experience making comics with Native communities, and over 20 years of experience doing project management and collaborative research with Indigenous communities, including for oral history projects and museum exhibits. Based on this experience she brings skills essential to this project including collective leadership, project management, cultural sensitivity, flexibility, conflict mediation, community curating, and communicating history and anthropology to the public. Since working at the National Museum of the American Indian in 1999 to publishing a book about its "community curating" process, Shannon has engaged in, and critically reflected on, collaboration with Native peoples (Shannon 2014). She has led, managed, and written about collaborative projects with Native communities to create, for instance, culturally informed collections care (Shannon 2018), an oral history documentary (Shannon 2017, 2019b), community based filmmaking workshops (Shannon 2019a), citizen science curriculum (Wirfs-Brock 2015), and NAGPRA Comics (Atalay and Shannon 2017). She is currently facilitating a collaboration between Mesa Verde National Park and 26 Pueblos and Tribes to redesign an archaeological museum in the Park.

Swogger contributes comics workshop facilitation, creative direction, and comics layout, writing, and artwork skills to the project. He has been making archaeology, heritage, and informational illustrations and comics for over 20 years. According to Swogger (2020a) and exemplified in his work, comics can engage community collaboration and lead to impactful outreach. Comics are a "highly accessible medium for communicating with diverse public audiences," and comics he has created about archaeology and local heritage have "been used to speak with audiences across divides created by age, literacy and familiarity, enabling complex information to be communicated easily, quickly and successfully" (Swogger 2015:19). In his work, comics "are the principal means by which the project's public outreach is conducted in schools, tourism offices, museums, and local businesses" (Swogger 2015:19). Swogger began making comics to help local residents of Çatalhöyük, Turkey, to gain interest and understanding of the famous archaeological site nearby. He has gone on to create comics for education and outreach, including some bilingual issues, with diverse communities in places like Palau (2020b), Yap (2019a), Nicaragua (2019b), Wales (2019c), and the US (Atalay et al. 2017).

2. PARTICIPANTS AND AUDIENCES

Through this project we hope to engage Kumeyaay and other tribal communities in California, the general public, and students in California classrooms—including tribal youth. Kumeyaay teens and teens throughout California classrooms are considered an important audience to these comics, as connecting Kumeyaay and Indigenous histories to younger generations is a central interest for the Kumeyaay contributors. We plan to reach these audiences through a number of ways.

Native Communities: Comics workshops will engage youth and adult Kumeyaay Nation members. We will advertise a featured Indigenous comics artist talk to multiple tribal nations which will take place at the conclusion of the first workshop. **General Public**: The comics will be available free online as PDFs and to publish in local newspapers or as exhibit panels in schools and cultural centers, and a traveling exhibit will be available. Printed copies will be available through the tribally owned California company Tribal Print Source. We will market the comics through area news outlets, social media, and announcements in schools and at Kumeyaay Community College. **Educators and Students**: San Diego has an active community of educators who use comics in the classroom and beyond. Through the project's Educator Liaison Jewyl Alderson, we will coordinate with area teachers to explore ways in which *Kumeyaay Comics* and associated lesson plans can be utilized in their classrooms.

3. OUTREACH AND PUBLICITY

We will conduct comics workshops for Kumeyaay youth and adults, create a Facebook page and website with mailing list, aim to place the comics in local newspapers, create a traveling banner exhibit, and work with teachers to incorporate the comics into their units on Native Americans and California history. We will also give talks at local area schools and cultural centers, and present at conferences. In addition, the Project Director and Humanities Advisors will co-author a scholarly article about the process and outcome of the project, aiming for an academic audience as well (cf. Atalay and Shannon 2019).

To date, *NAGPRA Comics* has distributed more than 2000 copies at academic conferences and tribal cultural centers, and over 7000 print copies were purchased from Tribal Print Sources—all while free copies are available online as downloadable PDFs. *NAGPRA Comics* co-producers and community co-authors have presented at the American Anthropological Association and Society for American Archaeology annual meetings, Association of Tribal Archives, Libraries, and Museums, the Applied Comics Network, and San Diego Comic-Con. Given the numbers of issues we have distributed of *NAGPRA Comics*, which is a far more limited and specialized subject matter, we imagine 10,000 copies being distributed in digital and print formats to Native and non-Native people in California and throughout the United States and other countries such as Canada and New Zealand that have Indigenous communities who also engage in comics as a form of storytelling.

Kumeyaay Comics will have a dedicated website, similar to *NAGPRA Comics* (https://nagpracomics.weebly.com). Weebly.com is free and suitable for the purposes of this project. Comics issues, comics panels, exhibit posters, and lesson plans will be available at the project website. Similar to *NAGPRA Comics*, we will include an "about" page for the project and team, a blog for announcements about events and workshops and project updates, and a contact page for those who would like to receive an occasional newsletter about the project. We will also create a Facebook Page and share the links to download the comics and posters through social media. For wide distribution and sharing, we publish under a Creative Commons License: "You are free to make derivative, non-commercial works based on this comic, but you must attribute its original creators and must distribute it under a similar license."

The lesson plans will also be uploaded to the open educational resources website https://www.oercommons.org/. In addition, the director of the National Museum of the American Indian's Native Knowledge 360, which "provides educational materials and teacher training that incorporate Native narratives, more comprehensive histories, and accurate information to enlighten and inform teaching and learning about Native America" (SI 2020), has expressed interest in including *Kumeyaay Comics* on their online educational resources page as well.

4. ACTIVITIES

The timeline is a feasible plan according to the Project Director and Humanities Advisors who, throughout the duration of the project, will have monthly phone meetings, more frequently when needed. Because the project is community-directed through collaboration, the outputs and schedule are subject to change. The phases of the project include inception and planning, initial research and workshop preparation, team meetings and content development, comic layout and draft artwork, workshops, comic draft review and editing, distribution and assessment, and presentations and publications.

The core activities of the project are research, collaborative authorship, workshops, and dissemination. **Research** will include the project partners working together and delving into relevant archives, museum collections, historical documents, and literature and conducting oral histories with elders and tribal historians. These materials will be presented as a digital archive of resources for the Campo Kumeyaay Nation when the project is complete. **Collaborative Authorship** entails a cycle of brainstorming, researching, writing and illustration, reviewing and revising. Revising will be informed by tribal Elders meetings, community feedback after presentations, and focus groups with tribal college students. Final approval for publication rests with the Project Director and Tribal Historians. In addition, if a local artist(s) is identified and interested, they will be invited to contribute artwork to the series (alternative covers, particular sequences, full page layouts, whatever they prefer to do). Recently, Barona Cultural Center has been hosting community comics workshops through their own program and may suggest potential artists to be mentored by and/or contribute to *Kumeyaay Comics*. To develop lesson plans, collaborative work with area educators will be achieved through consultation, iterative drafts, and approval by Tribal Historians and the Educator Liaison. Successful examples of Indigenous centered curriculum from Washington State and elsewhere will provide additional insight to lesson planning for the comics (WOSPI 2020; NMAI 2020).

Workshops provide everything from basic introduction to the medium to making one's own comics. The nature and location of the workshops provided will be determined by the Project Director. The aim of the workshops is to develop participants' writing and drawing skills sufficient to enable them to create informational comics capable of communicating both historical information and contemporary experience. Each session is a stand-alone workshop, but participants can attend multiple sessions. *General Sessions* are 3 hours and get participants familiar with the story-telling language of comics. They serve as an introduction to comics and comics-making, and are open to the general community. They are informally-structured, and designed for all ages. Participants are led through a series of drawing and writing exercises that explore how comics work (Shannon and Swogger 2019). *Advanced Sessions* develop participants' practical skills in drawing, writing and composition, and give them an appreciation of comics' range and diversity. These sessions are more formally structured and are open to those high school age and up. *Mentored Sessions* are for those who will contribute to *Kumeyaay Comics* artwork and will focus on skills for creating their own comics. Participants are also introduced to comics as an industry, as a possible career, and as a field of academic inquiry. The focus for each participant throughout these mentored sessions is the completion of a comic they have designed, written, and drawn themselves—a work which will then be exhibited to the community. The first workshop will also include an event where a prominent Native comics creator gives a talk and meets with the community.

Dissemination of the comics in various formats entails managing and promoting the website, facilitating the traveling exhibit to be displayed in area museums and schools and cultural centers, creating presentations locally and at conferences, outreach to San Diego region teachers and schools, pitching to area newspapers and media organizations, and writing journal and blog articles.

5. PROJECT PURPOSE AND ASSESSMENT

The project purpose is, through decolonizing and arts-based research, to produce more accurate and inclusive understandings of California's Indigenous peoples' history in accessible and engaging formats.

Project Goals and Outcomes: Develop positive, collaborative relationships among all project participants; Raise awareness about the history of Indigenous peoples in California; Challenge stereotypes and dominant ideologies; Include marginalized voices and perspectives in mainstream education; Contribute to public scholarship about the colonial and Indigenous histories of California; Provide more accurate and inclusive representations of history for Kumeyaay students; and, Engage young people in learning about history.

Project Outputs: Archive of research documents, historical documents, and oral history recordings for project; *Kumeyaay Comics* series; Lesson plans for comics; Exhibit panels, posters, and traveling banner exhibit based on comics artwork; Free online PDFs; Free printed copies of comics available for Kumeyaay community members; Conference and area schools presentations; and, Scholarly articles.

Assessment of Project's Success: Feedback from tribal Elders and workshop participants; Focus groups with community college students; Documented number of downloads and sales; Quality of dialog in review sessions with community members; Successful application for additional grants to continue the series; and, Number of venues hosting traveling exhibit.

6. PROJECT PERSONNEL

The Project Director, tribal historian Mike Connolly Miskwish, is responsible for directing the entire project. The duties allocated to what the grant program calls "Project Director" will be enacted under the title "Project Coordinator" so that it is clear to community members and comics readers that the project is directed in all matters not related to logistics and project management by Mike Connolly Miskwish. Tribal Historians and Kumeyaay Elders will contribute to the content development of the comics. The organization of content—narratives of historical events and understanding past and present lifeways through archival research, oral histories, and material culture—into comic panel layouts is the responsibility of Humanities Advisors John Swogger and Jen Shannon. Local artists and Swogger will contribute artwork.

Project Director: Mike Connolly Miskwish (Campo Kumeyaay Nation) is the project and research director. He determines and directs the process of the collaboration, the comics' subject matter, and the budget allocations, and he coordinates with the Humanities Advisors and Tribal Historians to identify what stories to tell and how to do so in a culturally appropriate manner. Mike's formal education includes a Bachelor of Science in Manufacturing Engineering, a Master of Arts in Economics, and an Associate of Arts in Kumeyaay Studies. He is the author of *Kumeyaay: A History Textbook*, Vol. 1: *Precontact to 1893* (2006) and is an adjunct faculty member in American Indian Studies at San Diego State University. He served 17 years in elected office for the Campo Kumeyaay Nation. He currently consults with tribal governments and governmental agencies on topics of economics, resource management, taxation and education. He works directly with the Kumeyaay Diegueno Land Conservancy and Kumeyaay Community College. He was a co-curator for the Kumeyaay exhibit at the National Museum of the American Indian which opened in 2004 and continues to write and lecture on Kumeyaay history and culture.

Project Coordinator: Jen Shannon will fulfill the duties allocated to what the grant program calls "Project Director," preferring the title "Project Coordinator," for project management, coordinating logistics, and project communication and website management. Jen will keep track of the budget with guidance and coordination with the Project Director.

Humanities Advisors: Jen Shannon and John Swogger will provide guidance regarding storytelling through comics formats, research assistance, feedback on narrative development in preparation for the comics format, lead community-based comics workshops, and advise throughout the process. In addition, John will contribute artwork and apprentice local artists to do so as opportunity arises, and Jen will assist in locating and gathering archival, museum, and oral history materials.

Jen Shannon is a museum curator and cultural anthropologist at the University of Colorado who specializes in collaborative and public anthropology. She has a PhD in Sociocultural Anthropology, is the author of *Our Lives: Collaboration, Native Voice, and the Making of the National Museum of the American Indian* (SAR Press, 2014), is co-host of *SAPIENS: A Podcast for Everything Human*, and is a consultant for the National Museum of the American Indian.

John Swogger is an archaeologist, archaeological illustrator, and comics creator who specializes in informational, outreach and educational comics about archaeological excavation and research, anthropology, prehistory, community heritage and local history. He published an annotated anthology of four panel comics about a town in Wales titled *The Collected Oswestry Heritage Comics* which, along with *NAGPRA Comics*, is a model for the format of *Kumeyaay Comics*.

Tribal Historians: Mike Connolly Miskwish, Stan Rodriguez, Ethan Banegas, and Lorraine Orosco form the content development team, and they work with the Project Director to identify the topics and narratives for the stories that will be told in the comics and identify resources to tell those stories. They advise on the writing of the script to be translated into a comic format and review draft lesson plans.

Stan Rodriguez (Kumeyaay-Iipay, Santa Ysabel) is a Board Member and Kumeyaay Language Instructor at Kumeyaay Community College. He learned from his Grandmother and other Kumeyaay Elders the methods and culture. Stan has an MA in Human Behavior and received his doctoral degree at University of California San Diego.

Ethan Banegas (Luiseno-Kumeyaay) grew up on the Barona Reservation. He has a BA in History, Religious Studies and Political Science and an MA degree from the University of San Diego. He teaches Kumeyaay history courses at Kumeyaay Community College.[1]

Lorraine Orosco (Kumeyaay-Ipai) is a Board Member and teaches Kumeyaay humanities at Kumeyaay Community College. She is from the San Pasqual Ipai Band and grew up on the San Pasqual reservation. Her teachers (Kwechmuuyaaw) were family, tribal elders and community. She has a BA in Sociology and Ethnic Studies from UC San Diego and an MS in Education.

Educator Liaison: Jewyl Alderson is the Integrated Curriculum Coordinator, Innovation Division of the San Diego County Office of Education. She will facilitate connections with San Diego educators and curriculum developers to develop resources and lessons plans for the comics to be used in schools.

7. SPONSORING ORGANIZATION AND PARTNERS

The Sponsoring Organization and the organization represented by the Project Director is the **Campo Kumeyaay Nation**. The Nation's reservation was founded in 1893 and is 16,512 acres of tribally owned land. The Campo Kumeyaay Nation has no previous funding from a public humanities program like this, but it is a good anchor for the project because tribal histories should be directed and led by tribal leadership. The Nation intends to build relationships with area schools and cultural centers, as well as Indigenous comics artists and the leadership of San Diego Comics Fest, as a result of this project.

Partners in the project represented through the Humanities Advisors include the production team of **NAGPRA Comics** and the **University of Colorado Museum of Natural History**. *NAGPRA Comics* is three years old and is currently working with three tribes using three different collaborative models. There are three new issues underway, including one that is complete and awaiting a community visit for final approval from tribal partners when travel restrictions are lifted. UCMNH is a public museum in Boulder, Colorado, with exhibits, outstanding research collections, and a museum studies graduate program.

The Tribal Historians teach at **Kumeyaay Community College** in El Cajon, CA. The Mission of Kumeyaay Community College is "to promote a quality education for the Kumeyaay / Diegueño Nation, California Native American Indians, and other individuals interested in a unique and supportive educational experience." College archives are dedicated to "preserving the cultural knowledge of our ancestors and the knowledge of our current Elders."

San Pasqual Cultural Center, San Diego Museum of Man, and **Comic-Con Museum** are regional museums that have communicated to us support for the project and interest in hosting the exhibit.

NOTE

1. Mike Connolly Miskwish and Ethan Banegas decided to swap roles later in the project due to their relative workloads outside the project.

REFERENCES

Atalay, S., and J. Shannon. 2019. "Completing the Journey: A Graphic Narrative about NAGPRA and Repatriation" in *American Anthropologist* 121(3):769–772 and at multimodal online section.

Atalay, S., J. Shannon, and J. Swogger with S. Martin and Ziibiwing Center of Anishinabe Culture & Lifeways. 2017. *NAGPRA Comics 1: Journeys to Complete the Work . . . and Changing the Way We Bring Native American Ancestors Home.* https://nagpracomics.weebly.com/.

Borkent, M. 2020. "Seeing Histories, Building Futurities: Multimodal Decolonization and Conciliation in Indigenous Comics from Canada" in *Graphic Indigeneity: Comics in the Americas and Australia*, ed. Frederick Luis Aldama, 273–98. University Press of Mississippi.

Eaglespeaker, J. 2014. *UNeducation, Vol. 1: A Residential School Graphic Novel about Boarding School*. CreateSpace Independent Publishing Platform.

Fawaz, Ramzi. 2015. *The New Mutants: Superheroes and the Radical Imagination of American Comics*. New York: New York University Press.

Fenelon, J., and C. Trafzer. 2014. "From Colonialism to Denial of California Genocide to Misrepresentations: Special Issue on Indigenous Struggles in the Americas." *American Behavioral Science* 58(1):3–29.

Francis, L., IV, Weshoyot, A., and W. Fenton. 2019. *Ghost River: The Fall and Rise of the Conestoga*. Philadelphia: The Library Company of Philadelphia.

Gavigan, Karen W., and Mindy Tomasevich. 2011. *Connecting Comics to Curriculum: Strategies for Grades 6–12*. Santa Barbara, CA: Libraries Unlimited.

Giddens, Thomas, ed. 2016. *Graphic Justice: Intersections of Comics and Law*. London: Routledge, Taylor & Francis Group.

Leavy, P. 2018. "Introduction to Arts-Based Research" in *Handbook of Arts-Based Research*, ed. by P. Leavy, 3–21. New York: Guilford Press.

National Museum of the American Indian [NMAI]. 2020. "Native Knowledge 360: Lessons and Resources." https://americanindian.si.edu/nk360/resources.

Robertson, D., and S. Henderson. 2016. *7 Generations: A Plains Cree Saga*. Winnipeg: HighWater Press.

Shannon, J. 2014. *Our Lives: Collaboration, Native Voice, and the Making of the National Museum of the American Indian*. Santa Fe: SAR Press.

Shannon, J. 2017. "On Being a Tentative Anthropologist: Collaborative Anthropological Research with Indigenous Peoples in North America" in *Practicing Ethnography: A Student Guide to Method and Methodology*, ed. L. Mannik and K. McGarry, 58–65. University of Toronto Press.

Shannon, J. 2018. "Collections Care Informed by Native American Perspectives: Teaching the Next Generation" in *Collections: A Journal for Museum and Archives Professionals* 13(1): 205–224.

Shannon, J. 2019a. "Museum Mantras, Teachings from Indian Country: Posterity Is Now; Failure is an Option; and Repatriation is a Foundation for Research" in *Science Museums in Transition*, ed. H. McLaughlin and J. Diamond. Philadelphia: Routledge.

Shannon, J. 2019b. "Posterity Is Now" in *Museum Anthropology* 42(1): 5–13.

Shannon, J., and J. Swogger. 2019. "A guide for facilitating Comics Workshops." https://nagpracomics.weebly.com/project-updates/comics-workshops-at-mandan-hidatsa-arikara-nation.

Smith, L. T. 1999. *Decolonizing Methodologies: Research and Indigenous Peoples*. New York: Zed Books.

Smithsonian Institution [SI]. 2020. "Native Knowledge 360°." Americanindian.si.edu/nk360/about.cshtml.

State of California. 2020. "Truth and Healing Council," Governor's Tribal Advisor Office. Available at https://tribalaffairs.ca.gov/truth-and-healing-council/ (accessed 7/23/2020).

Swogger, J. 2020a "Prehistory, protest and public engagement: Using comics and cartoons to tell the Old Oswestry story," eds. T. Malim and G. Nash, *Old Oswestry and its Landscape*.

Swogger, J. 2020b. *Kedung el Chebud* (Good Grasshopper and Bad Grasshopper). Traditional Stories of Palau, Bureau of Arts and Culture with Sunny Ngirmang and Filly Collins.

Swogger, J. 2019a. *Footprints of the Ancestors*, U. Oregon/National Geographic. With M. Napolitano and E. Mietes. 28-pp. comic book about the archaeological survey of southern Yap island.

Swogger, J. 2019b. *Exploring Our Indigenous Past: Juigalpa Museum Comics 1*, J. Swogger with A. Geurds, University of Oxford/University of Leiden. Series about archaeology in Nicaragua.

Swogger, J. 2019c. *The Collected Oswestry Heritage Comics*, Qube/OCA/Heritage Lottery Fund. Anthology collecting the entire 2016–2018 Oswestry Heritage Comics.

Swogger, J. 2015. "Ceramics, Polity and Comics: Re-presenting formal publication in archaeology" in *Advances in Archaeological Practice* 3(1): 16–28.

Truillot, M. 1995. *Silencing the Past: Power and the Production of History*. Boston: Beacon Press.

Washington Office of Superintendent of Public Instruction [WOSPI]. 2020. "Since Time Immemorial: Tribal Sovereignty in Washington State, Ready to Go Lessons." https://www.k12.wa.us/student-success/resources-subject-area/time-immemorial-tribal-sovereignty-washington-state.

Wirfs-Brock, J. 2015. "Citizen Science On The Rez—Kids, Science And North Dakota's Oil Boom." *Inside Energy*. November 23.

Appendix E

Job Searching and Professional Development

This appendix is for those who are about to graduate, change jobs, or enter a new field. I teach a unit about professional development with assignments that include looking through job listings, writing a résumé, and doing informational interviews (see chapter 37, "Teaching Museum Studies and Professional Development"). Here are some activities that may help jump-start your next steps in seeking an internship, a job, or a new career.

Get to know the kinds of jobs and employers that are out there.

- What are the various job titles? ("Curator" can be part of a number of titles; "museum specialist" covers a lot of things in the federal system.)
- What skills are listed as required and ideal?
- What kinds of language and words are associated with these jobs?
- Write a sample job title and description that embodies your ideal position as a career. If you are starting out in the field, make sure to understand what kinds of entry-level positions are available.

Conduct informational interviews.

- I am always surprised at how few students know about the ingenious "informational interview." Do a quick online search about it!
- Be specific about what you are asking: an invitation for an informational interview.
- Let them know what is expected of them, how much time it will take, and whether it will be conducted in person, online, or on the phone.

Write a résumé.

- Typically one page front and back, but follow the conventions in your field (a CV, in contrast, can be fairly long and lists publications and grants).
- Be specific, consistent, and action-oriented in your writing.
- Use language from the job listing. If it asks for database experience, write how many years of that experience you have, list what databases you have worked with, and other relevant details.
- Attention to detail matters. Imagine that your job is correcting database records. It doesn't look good if you missed the fact that you failed to capitalize "chicago."
- In museum studies, volunteer experience counts the same as paid experience. Put it under relevant work experience.

Craft a cover letter.
- Each letter should be specifically crafted for each job application.
- Look up the hiring institution—what is its mission?
- The letter should demonstrate that you did some research and know about the institution.
- Many people don't know what anthropology is—make a list of the skills you have learned through your courses or experience. Explain how your degree is suited to the job; describe that connection in the cover letter.

After you get the job, keep learning!
- Find a mentor in your new institution.
- Go to conferences; discuss professional development opportunities with your supervisor.
- Visit other museums; view their exhibits, or talk to staff about their methods and practices.
- A culture of learning requires that we bring new ideas into our workplaces, and engaging with others in our fields in different institutions is a great way to do that.

After you get the job, pay it forward!
- If you are lucky enough to supervise interns or volunteers, consider this another way to continue to build a culture of learning and bring forward new ideas.

Appendix F

Guide to Thinking about Collaboration for Exhibit Planning

This guide was created for considering how to invite community into exhibition development. I created this document in 2016 for a cultural center that was in the process of development; the steering committee was planning to work with a design firm and was wondering how best to engage with the community so people would feel ownership over and support the outcome of the exhibition development process. Whether a tribal cultural center or a mainstream museum, these are some considerations to keep in mind for how to engage with communities in exhibition development. I include an excerpt from the guide here not as an exhaustive list or simply a resource to use but as an example of the kind of document you can create in service of community or organizational partners too, whether Native or non-Native.

The sections of the guide include:

- Introduction
    - Content Development Plan Overview
    - Introduction and Thank You
    - Why Community Participation?
    - Brief History of Collaborative Exhibit Making
    - Importance to the Center
    - Some Questions to Begin
- Managing Expectations
    - Working with a Design Firm
    - Time Line
    - Community Contributions
    - Decision Making
- **Models for Community Participation**
    - **Which Model Suits Your Project Best?**
        1. **Community-Wide Updates**
        2. **Advisory Board**
        3. **Community Curator Group**
        4. **Subject-Specific Curator Groups**
        5. **Individual Advisers**
        6. **Core Team / Extended Team**
        7. **Survey the Community**
- Recommendations
- Lessons Learned
- Contact

Which Model Suits Your Project Best?

In her introduction to part 3 of *Museums and Source Communities*, Ruth Phillips (2003) identifies two main kinds of collaborative exhibits: community-based and multi-vocal. Community-based exhibits are by and for the local community and emphasize their voices and perspectives. Multi-vocal exhibits include other voices, like perhaps a historian or an archaeologist, alongside the community perspective.

Consider these questions to guide your exhibit-making process:

1. Who is your primary audience?
2. Whose voice should be speaking to the audience?
3. What is your ideal relationship to the community in developing the exhibits?

The exhibit planning process you select depends on your resources (time, money, people), the reasons for community participation discussed above, and your mission. Review the models below with staff, and consider which is best for your organization. These are "ideal types," and a combination is possible if that meets your needs best.

1. COMMUNITY-WIDE UPDATES

This would include quarterly visits (every three months) to each region of the community to do presentations about the cultural center's progress. I recommend that this be a part of any effort, regardless of what kind of content development model you choose, because of the community's spread-out locations.

Ideally, the presentations would be audiovisual, allow questions and answers, and be well advertised (Facebook, local radio, local newspaper, and other media). Or instead of quarterly visits, you can do milestone presentations (introduction to the cultural center, preliminary content themes, final content themes, design mockup, final design, and the like).

Benefits: This is an excellent way to keep the community at large updated and show that you are interested in keeping it informed and are available to take feedback at these meetings. It also shows, through who repeatedly attends, those who are interested and invested in the project (potential contributors at another level).

Concerns: Different people will likely show up each time, so you may feel you have to start from square one at every update. However, that can be managed through the presentation content.

2. ADVISORY BOARD

This might be a group of six–twelve people; one exhibition had twenty people on the board, but that can get out of hand. The ideal size depends on your goals for this board. There are different purposes for advisory groups, and their membership can be composed of different kinds of people. Should members be elected or chosen? What criteria or categories might be important in selecting people (for example, age, gender, knowledge of particular histories, role in community, tourism experience)?

It is important to be very specific about the role of the advisory board: is it a source of preliminary ideas and themes, for informal brainstorming, for checking and approving plans, some combination? It is very important that you indicate whether the board has the responsibility for final approval. If not, its members need to know that they are advising and not making decisions. Avoid having members feel as though they are simply rubber-stamping already decided-upon content. If that's the case, why are you asking them to advise? It is best to engage with board members at the idea development stage, for brainstorming, and so on. They can also act as representatives to the wider community, helping to assure that all the materials developed are appropriate and acceptable (for example, they may raise red flags that others might not anticipate).

Benefits: Cultural center staff can validate that they are creating exhibits that have community member support and approval. Advisory board members also lend their reputations to the project; it is important that they feel utilized in a productive way.

Concerns: As in any community, there are diverse perspectives and opinions within a group, and divisions might occur. Set clear expectations for how differences will be resolved.

3. COMMUNITY CURATOR GROUP

Elected or selected? This would be a group of four–eight people who help deliberate on and determine the main themes of the cultural center's exhibits and may contribute content about those themes as well (or point you to community members who would be appropriate to contact for specific knowledge or objects). If you decide to have both an advisory group and community curators, the main difference is that the advisory group reviews content and gives feedback. The community curators develop the content the advisory group reviews.

Benefits: A smaller group is easier to work with in developing main themes. If chosen correctly, they may also lend credibility to the final product.

Concerns: Working with a group takes more time. If you intend for this group to feel empowered in decision making, its consensus may override the staff's or design firm's preferences.

4. SUBJECT-SPECIFIC CURATOR GROUPS

This might be a group of two–six people. They are selected for their reputation of having the authority to share specific stories or knowledge. For example, if you are interested in sharing an origin story, you might select several people to work on the best way to tell it so it is appropriate for an audience that is not from the community, determining what is appropriate to share publicly. Or you may want an exhibit on the importance of basketball in the community, so you select some starting players from both today and the past along with several coaches to determine the best way to tell that story (what objects are available, who has the best story to tell, what is most important for people to know).

Benefits: Having known experts in the community working on specific subjects lends credibility to the subject matter and broadens the number of community members contributing to the exhibit in easy-to-see ways (their names on text panels, for example).

Concerns: Working with multiple groups will take more time and may result (without good, clear oversight) in an overall exhibition that seems disjointed or uneven in its tone or treatment across different displays. It's important to have a project manager who attends meetings of all the different groups and ties their contributions together into a seamless whole.

5. INDIVIDUAL ADVISERS

Cultural center staff would select individuals in the community who have the authority to discuss specific kinds of content for exhibits themes that have already been developed. Or you may contact leaders in the community whose approval and participation is important to the cultural center's success.

Benefits: If the person is well-known for the kind of knowledge they are contributing, it lends credibility to the exhibit.

Concerns: Depending on who is selected, it may seem that some individuals are benefiting and others with relevant experience are not (especially if compensation is involved).

6. CORE TEAM / EXTENDED TEAM

You can have two teams that meet regularly—one more frequently, which is involved in the day-to-day activities and which may be the core team (likely the cultural center staff and designer), and the other, which includes the larger group of individuals involved in the project. In exhibition development, the core team might include the project manager, curator, designer, and educator. The extended team might be the core team plus the fabricator, mount makers, collections manager, and anyone else in the organization who is involved in the exhibit process overall but not in the day-to-day discussions. For content development, the core team may be the center's staff and a representative from the design firm, and the extended team may be an educator and two tribal historians. How you determine the "core" and "extended" teams necessary to your project is up to you. But this relationship is more within the institution—it is more formal and organization-minded.

Benefits: Community members are included in the organizational structure. In the other models, community members are external to the organizational structure, with a cultural center project manager/liaison connecting them to the institution. Members of the extended team are like extensions of the center's staff. They meet regularly, and roles are well defined. This is a business structure that implies a more formal relationship to the process, including team members in the organizational process and feeling more of a push for "milestones" and "deliverables."

Concerns: The formality, language, and regularity of meetings may not be amenable to community members' schedules and interests.

7. SURVEY THE COMMUNITY

For one of the exhibits at the National Museum of the American Indian, curators visited the community and hosted a meal. They asked all of those present to write down the top ten pivotal events in their community's history that they wanted on display at the museum. The ones most frequently recorded ended up in the history exhibit. Another way to survey the community for ideas is through an online or a paper survey. The survey can be a way to send everyone information about the cultural center while also seeking their feedback. As an example, you can ask: what top three things do you want to see in the center? Have a list of pre-selected options for them to rank as well (it has been shown that response rates are higher when pre-selected options are available). You can do a mail survey or use an online survey. I would not use Facebook, as the data are less reliable. I am happy to provide the use of the excellent survey software Qualtrics through my university for free.

Benefits: There are two good reasons for conducting a survey: first, you get ideas from people who might not stand up in a crowd or come to a meeting to share their thoughts; in other words, you hear from more people, often those you would not usually hear from. Second, a survey alerts a broader number of people in the community to what you are doing through the survey introduction, regardless of whether they complete it. It will reach more people than an event flyer at the community center (but post one there too). The survey can also be a way to recruit people (for example, a question might be: would you be interested in participating in content development for an exhibit at the cultural center).

Concerns: It is important to select a good survey instrument (well-written questions, easy to access) and to ask good questions so the data are useful. Otherwise, the survey may not produce useful feedback. Knowing what you want to learn from it, when in the process to use it, and how to administer the survey is important.

Appendix G

Guide to Creating Community-Engaged Comics

This is a guide I created with contributions from John Swogger for doing what he and I call "community-engaged comics." It is an example of how to shape a collaborative arts-based project and also how to create a guide to leave behind when you work with community. I have created several guides like this one, including one for how to conduct comics workshops and another for how to facilitate collaborative film workshops. The goal is that when you provide a training or teaching experience with a community, you leave something behind to support others in the community to continue on in your absence. The guides are provided as PDFs and Word documents, so community members can continue to edit and change them as needed. I created this document in 2022 following our work on *NAGPRA Comics* and the Kumeyaay Visual Storytelling Project.

The guide includes the sections named below, with those in bold provided in this appendix:

- **What Are Community-Engaged Comics?**
- Some Examples to Think With
- **Sample Process Outline**
- Products of Community-Engaged Comics Projects

- Sample Roles and Responsibilities
- Sample Budget Categories
- Publication and Exhibition of Comics
- Appendix I: Inspiration for True Story Comics
- Appendix II: Indigenous Comics Creators
- Appendix III: Additional Reading

See the full guide here: https://scholar.colorado.edu/concern/reports/sn00b026z.

What Are Community-Engaged Comics?

Community-engaged comics (CEC) are a form of collaboration where the result is a comic and so much more. The comics are a means for community engagement—a form of "arts-based research"—for community members to discuss and build together what they want to communicate about their past, present, and future. Community partners direct the project from conception to implementation to evaluation, and they are in control of content and distribution. Community-based workshops, presentations, and public events are part of CEC as well.

Sample Process Outline (see figure G.1)

Below I provide an outline of what a CEC project might include, along with answers to some common questions. The following pages provide additional ideas to determine the best course of action for a partnership.

Who participates? Participants include cultural specialists, youth, and comics creators. An established comics creator (Native or non-Native, depending on the project) can also take on a mentoring role to guide an artist who was identified in the community as promising during a workshop, a student recommended by a teacher, or perhaps someone who is new or just emerging in the comics field.

What is the role of museum collections? The museum collections, archives, and photographs can spark ideas for what kind of story you want to tell using comics. They can be the subject, or the starting point, of a story that gets told in comics. The collection items can be what the story is about, perhaps how they came to the museum or how to make them, their history or relevance

Seek Community Advising	Consider doing a community-based workshop prior to the first visit to collections, if possible. This can alert community members to the project and possibly identify community members with artistic talents who may want to participate as a mentee to a comics creator.
↳ **Ideas and Knowledge Gathering**	Community members determine what kind of story they want to tell—about the community, about museum collections or archives, or a story sparked by their engagement with collections.
↳ **Create a Team for the Comic Issue**	Seek out knowledgeable community members and museum collections, associated documentation, archives, and photographs to support the comic's story and accuracy.
↳ **Script Development**	Write a script and group reference images alongside story elements in a document for the comics creator to work from. (Comics creators may do the writing if they meet with a group regularly.)
↳ **Draft Layout and Artwork**	The comics creator will lay out the panels on the comic pages to tell the story in words and pictures.
↳ **Community Review**	Focus groups, elders' vetting sessions, classroom review, and others.
↳ **Distribution**	Free PDF and pay to print.

Comics, once created, can be distributed in many ways, including: with lesson plans to schools, in traveling banner exhibits, on posters, T-shirts, and similar items!

Example: Two elders who are language specialists, and a middle-aged individual, and a young person visit a museum basket collection with an established Indigenous comics creator from elsewhere and a young artist from the community. The artist sketches the process by which a basket is started based on the elders' discussion, which includes a story associated with the reawakening of basket practices in their community. The comics tell the story of the woman who brought traditional basket making back to their community. There are several double-spread pages of a basket and the Native language terms for its parts, as well as a diagram of how to start a basket and examples of symbols on baskets and what they mean. A second story in the comic is about a mother and her daughter gathering materials throughout the year to make baskets and talking about why they are important. The comics are distributed for free at the community cultural center during a demonstration/workshop on basket making. Posters made from comics images about the baskets and their parts identified in the local language are given to schools.

FIGURE G.1. Sample process outline.

to the community, the times in which they were taken or returned. They can also be a catalyst for remembering and teaching. Contact with collections can inspire stories about origins or families or cultural practices as well as language and heritage.

How do we develop the story we want to tell? This varies greatly from community to community and depends on the skills and interests of the project participants. Sometimes an adviser, like myself, will listen for weeks to community members discussing a topic and then organize the information into themes for discussion; eventually, a storyline will emerge through conversation and then be vetted by the collaborating group. Other times, as in the Kumeyaay project, a community member will take on the role of writing the script on their own, with feedback and guidance from John and me. Perhaps there is an existing account or testimony in the archives that can be translated into comics format.

Who lays the story out in panels? Who draws, colors, does the text lettering? Sometimes all these roles are performed by one person and sometimes not. For example, my collaborator John does all these things. For those who work in the comics industry at a place like Marvel, there are separate roles: writer (narrative story or description of what is on each page), layout (how many boxes per page, how big, and what is in each box according to the story), pencil (draw the images in the boxes), ink (make lines permanent), color (color in the drawings), and lettering (writing in the bubbles of text). Figuring this out ahead of time is important for budgeting purposes and to know who needs to be involved in the storytelling development process.

How do we get feedback on the draft comics? Community members will likely have suggestions for the appropriate way to get community feedback on the story, artwork, and text in the comics. It's important that the colors, symbols, and language are appropriate to them. Sometimes a review is conducted by an advisory board created for the comics project or by an elders' society or youth group; it can also be done by a class at a tribal college or a focus group of people of multiple ages. Whatever process is appropriate, be sure the artist knows that changes to their work will be required and that there is time to conduct reviews. In addition, share the revised version to ensure that the changes adequately and accurately reflect the guidance provided.

What kinds of engagement opportunities exist for this kind of project? There are so many ways to work with community members beyond the core team developing the comics—for example, creating lesson plans for use in tribal or mainstream schools, creating traveling banner exhibits or posters, gathering community members to review drafts or share final copies of the comics, hosting a speaker series of Indigenous comics creators, and conducting comics workshops (we have done this in K–12 classrooms, in community centers where families attended, and in a tribal government department with adults only). The comics themselves can foster engagement; for example, perhaps have a space on the page for the reader to draw a basket.

How do we distribute what we have created together? We often use a website to distribute free PDFs of the comics. We offer print copies through a tribally owned, nonprofit print company. Once the comics pages are created, they can be utilized in a number of media—on banners for a traveling exhibit, on T-shirts or posters, to inspire murals in community, or animated into a video using something like Adobe Character Animator (for language learning, this may provide audio to help learners hear how the written word is pronounced).

References

American Alliance of Museums. "Direct Care of Collections: Ethics, Guidelines and Recommendations." 2019. https://www.aam-us.org/wp-content/uploads/2018/01/Direct-Care-of-Collections_March-2019.pdf.

American Alliance of Museums. "Museum Facts and Data." *American Alliance of Museums* (blog). January 24, 2018. https://www.aam-us.org/programs/about-museums/museum-facts-data/.

American Alliance of Museums. "Museums and Trust 2021." 2021. https://www.aam-us.org/2021/09/30/museums-and-trust-2021/.

American Anthropological Association. "AAA Guidelines for Tenure and Promotion Review: Communicating Public Scholarship in Anthropology." 2017. http://www.americananthro.org/AdvanceYourCareer/Content.aspx?ItemNumber=21713&navItemNumber=582.

American Museum of Natural History. "Press Release: Historic Chief's Chest Journeys Back to Haida Gwaii from the American Museum of Natural History." July 2017. https://www.amnh.org/content/download/178641/2775275/file/historic-chief-s-chest-back-to-haida-gwaii-from-the-amnh.pdf.

Ames, Michael M. *Cannibal Tours and Glass Boxes: The Anthropology of Museums.* 2nd rev. ed. Vancouver: University of British Columbia Press, 1992.

Ames, Michael M. *Museums, the Public, and Anthropology: A Study in the Anthropology of Anthropology*. Vancouver: Concept Publishing, 1986.

Anderson, Jane, and Sonya Atalay. "Repatriation as Pedagogy." *Current Anthropology* 64, no. 6 (December 1, 2023): 670–91. https://doi.org/10.1086/727786.

Arts Council England. *Restitution and Repatriation: A Practical Guide for Museums in England*. September 2023. https://www.artscouncil.org.uk/supporting-arts-museums-and-libraries/supporting-collections-and-cultural-property/restitution-and-repatriation-practical-guide-museums-england.

Association of Research Libraries. "Land Acknowledgment." *Land Acknowledgment* (blog). No date. https://www.arl.org/land-acknowledgment/.

Association of Tribal Archives, Libraries, and Museums. "ATALM." No date. https://www.atalm.org/.

Association of Tribal Archives, Libraries, and Museums. "Locations of North American Native Nations and Cultural Institutions." September 29, 2023. https://www.atalm.org/locations-of-north-american-native-nations-and-cultural-institutions/.

Atalay, Sonya. *Community-Based Archaeology: Research with, by, and for Indigenous and Local Communities*. Berkeley: University of California Press, 2012.

Atalay, Sonya, and Alexandra McCleary, eds. *The Community-Based PhD: Complexities and Triumphs of Conducting CBPR*. Tucson: University of Arizona Press, 2022.

Atalay, Sonya, and Jennifer Shannon. "Completing the Journey: A Graphic Narrative about NAGPRA and Repatriation." *American Anthropologist* 121, no. 3 (2019): Multimodal Section Online.

Banegas, Ethan, Michael Miskwish Connolly, Lorraine Orosco, Stanley Rodriguez, John Swogger, Jen Shannon, and Jewyl Alderson. *Kumeyaay Comics 1: Beyond Gaming/Our Past, Present, and Future*. Boulder: University of Colorado, 2024. https://scholar.colorado.edu/concern/books/rf55z945w.

Baron, Nancy. *Escape from the Ivory Tower: A Guide to Making Your Science Matter*. Washington, DC: Island Press, 2010.

Bell, Catherine, and Melissa Erickson. *UNDRIP and Indigenous Heritage*. Canadian Museums Association, 2022. https://museums.ca/uploaded/web/TRC_2022/UNDRIP%20Indigenous%20Heritage_en.pdf.

Beloit College. "Center for Collections Care." https://www.beloit.edu/summer-programs/center-for-collection-care/.

Berlo, Janet Catherine, and Ruth Phillips, eds. *Native North American Art*, 2nd ed. New York: Oxford University Press, 2015.

Bernstein, Bruce, and Scott G. Ortman. "From Collaboration to Partnership at Pojoaque, New Mexico." *Advances in Archaeological Practice* 8, no. 2 (May 2020): 95–110.

Bourgeois, Rebecca L. *Repatriation in Canada: A Guide for Communities*. Edmonton: University of Alberta Libraries, 2024. https://doi.org/10.7939/R3-Z3BE-WF91.

Bowechop, Janine, and Jeffrey Mauger. "Tribal Collections Management at the Makah Cultural and Research Center." In *Living Homes for Cultural Expression: North American Native Perspectives on Creating Community Museums*, edited by Karen Coody Cooper and Nicolasa I. Sandoval, 57–64. Washington, DC: National Museum of the American Indian, Smithsonian Institution, 2006.

Brown, Patricia Leigh. "Relationships Carved from Clay Bring New Partners to Museums." *New York Times*, August 13, 2023. https://www.nytimes.com/2023/08/13/arts/design/museums-met-ceramics-pottery-native-americans.html.

Bruchac, Margaret M. *Savage Kin: Indigenous Informants and American Anthropologists*. Tucson: University of Arizona Press, 2018.

Canadian Museums Association. *More than Giving Back: Repatriation Toolkit, a Toolkit in Support of Moved to Action, Activating UNDRIP in Canadian Museums*. Ottawa: Canadian Museums Association, 2022.

Chari, Sangita, and Jaime M. N. Lavallee, eds. *Accomplishing NAGPRA: Perspectives on the Intent, Impact, and Future of the Native American Graves Protection and Repatriation Act: First Peoples (2010)*. Corvallis: Oregon State University Press, 2013.

Clavir, Miriam. *Preserving What Is Valued: Museums, Conservation, and First Nations*. UBC Museum of Anthropology Research Publication. Vancouver: University of British Columbia Press, 2002.

Clavir, Miriam. "Reflections on Changes in Museums and the Conservation of Collections from Indigenous Peoples." *Journal of the American Institute for Conservation* 35, no. 2 (1996): 99–107.

Collison, Jisgang Nika, Sdaahl K'awaas Lucy Bell, and Lou-ann Neel. *Indigenous Repatriation Handbook*. Victoria, BC: Royal BC Museum and Haida Gwaii Museum, 2019.

Colwell, Chip. "Collaborative Archaeologies and Descendant Communities." *Annual Review of Anthropology* 45, no. 1 (October 21, 2016): 113–27. https://doi.org/10.1146/annurev-anthro-102215-095937.

Colwell, Chip. *Plundered Skulls and Stolen Spirits: Inside the Fight to Reclaim Native America's Culture*. Chicago: University of Chicago Press, 2017.

Colwell-Chanthaphonh, Chip, and T. J. Ferguson. "Virtue Ethics and the Practice of History: Native Americans and Archaeologists along the San Pedro Valley of Arizona." *Journal of Social Archaeology* 4, no. 1 (February 2004): 5–27. https://doi.org/10.1177/1469605304039848.

Conaty, Gerald T., ed. *We Are Coming Home: Repatriation and the Restoration of Blackfoot Cultural Confidence*. Edmonton: Athabasca University Press, 2015.

Connolly, Michael. 2006. *Kumeyaay: A History Textbook*, Vol. 1: *Precontact to 1893*. Dehesa, CA: Sycuan Press.

Cornell Law School Legal Information Institute. "Duress." No date. https://www.law.cornell.edu/wex/duress.

Costales, Mikayla, and Scarlett Engle. "Collaborating with Descendant Communities to Reimagine Chapin Mesa Archeological Museum." Boulder: University of Colorado, 2019.

Danyluk, Stephanie, and Rebecca MacKenzie. *Moved to Action: Activating UNDRIP in Canadian Museums—a Response to the Truth and Reconciliation Commission's Call to Action #67*. Ottawa: Canadian Museums Association, 2022. https://museums.ca/uploaded/web/TRC_2022/Report-CMA-MovedToAction.pdf.

Darnell, Regna. *Invisible Genealogies: A History of Americanist Anthropology*. Lincoln: University of Nebraska Press, 2001.

Deloria, Vine, Jr. *Custer Died for Your Sins: An Indian Manifesto*. New York: Macmillan, 1969.

Demonstrational Lecture of the Collections Review Research. Osaka: Japan National Museum

of Ethnology, 2020. https://trajectoria.minpaku.ac.jp/articles/2020/vol01/01_2.html #film.
Denver Art Museum. "New Angles on Interpretation in the DAM's New Hamilton Building." Denver: Denver Art Museum, 2007. https://www.denverartmuseum.org/en/research-and-reports.
Doyle, Arthur Conan. "Chapter 1: The Science of Deduction." In *The Sign of Four*. Salt Lake City: Project Gutenberg, 2000. https://www.gutenberg.org/files/2097/2097-h/2097-h.htm#chap01.
Duwe, Samuel, and Robert W. Preucel, eds. *The Continuous Path: Pueblo Movement and the Archaeology of Becoming*. Tucson: University of Arizona Press, 2019.
Echavarri, Glenys Ong. "Decolonizing Museums: Perspectives from Indigenous Museum Professionals." *Museums Forward* 1 (2021): 1–23.
Edmiston, Paige. "What's Behind Match Day's Algorithm?" *SAPIENS*, March 16, 2021. https://www.sapiens.org/culture/match-day-matching-algorithm/.
Erikson, Patricia Pierce, Kirk Wachendorf, and Helma Ward. *Voices of a Thousand People: The Makah Cultural and Research Center*. Lincoln: University of Nebraska Press, 2002.
Errington, Shelly. *The Death of Authentic Primitive Art and Other Tales of Progress*. Berkeley: University of California Press, 1998.
Everything Was Carved. Oxford: Pitt Rivers Museum, 2011. https://vimeo.com/26104413.
Fine-Dare, Kathleen S. *Grave Injustice: The American Indian Repatriation Movement and NAGPRA*. Fourth World Rising Series. Lincoln: University of Nebraska Press, 2002.
First Archivists Circle. "Protocols for Native American Archival Materials." 2007. https://www2.nau.edu/libnap-p/.
First Nations Information Governance Centre. "The First Nations Principles of OCAP®." 2023. https://fnigc.ca/ocap-training/.
Fonseca, Felicia. "Law Protects Export of Sacred Native American Items from US." *AP News*, December 26, 2022. https://apnews.com/article/biden-new-mexico-paris-366ebbdedd8cd83ce238dee47fae25aa.
Global Indigenous Data Alliance. "CARE Principles." Global Indigenous Data Alliance, January 23, 2023. https://www.gida-global.org/care.
Goff, Sheila, Betsy Chapoose, Elizabeth Cook, and Shannon Voirol. "Collaborating beyond Collections: Engaging Tribes in Museum Exhibits." *Advances in Archaeological Practice* 7, no. 3 (August 2019): 224–33. https://doi.org/10.1017/aap.2019.11.
Greene, Candace. "Plant Fibers in Plains Embroidery." *American Indian Art Magazine* 40, no. 2 (2015): 58–71.
Hadley Toftness, Kate, and Lois Taylor Biggs. "In Good Relation: Reimagining the Grant Process for Community-Based Projects." *American Alliance of Museums* (blog). March 31, 2023. https://www.aam-us.org/2023/03/31/in-good-relation-reimagining-the-grant-process-for-community-based-projects/.
Hamdy, Sherine, and Coleman Nye. *Lissa: A Story about Medical Promise, Friendship, and Revolution*. ethnoGRAPHIC (University of Toronto Press). North York, ON: University of Toronto Press, 2017.
Harjo, Laura. *Spiral to the Stars: Mvskoke Tools of Futurity*. Tucson: University of Arizona Press, 2019.

Hollinger, R. Eric, Edwell John, Harold Jacobs, Lora Moran-Collins, Carolyn Thome, Jonathan Zastrow, Adam Metallo, Günter Waibel, and Vince Rossi. "Tlingit-Smithsonian Collaborations with 3D Digitization of Cultural Objects." *Museum Anthropology Review* 7, no. 1–2 (2013): 53.

Horse Capture, Joe. "Native People Have a Story to Tell—Their Own." *ICT News*, September 13, 2018. https://ictnews.org/archive/horse-capture-native-people-have-a-story-to-tell-their-own.

Intellectual Property Issues in Cultural Heritage. "Intellectual Property Issues in Cultural Heritage: Theory, Practice, Policy, Ethics." 2016. https://www.sfu.ca/ipinch/.

Isaac, Gwyneira. *Mediating Knowledges: Origins of a Zuni Tribal Museum*. Tucson: University of Arizona Press, 2007.

Jacknis, Ira. *The Storage Box of Tradition: Kwakiutl Art, Anthropologists, and Museums, 1881–1981*. Smithsonian Series in Ethnographic Inquiry. Washington, DC: Smithsonian Institution Press, 2002.

Jacobs, Christine, Holger Pfaff, Birgit Lehner, Elke Driller, Anika Nitzsche, Brigitte Stieler-Lorenz, Jürgen Wasem, and Julia Jung. "The Influence of Transformational Leadership on Employee Well-Being: Results from a Survey of Companies in the Information and Communication Technology Sector in Germany." *Journal of Occupational and Environmental Medicine* 55, no. 7 (July 2013): 772–78.

Jacobs, Julia, and Zachary Small. "Leading Museums Remove Native Displays amid New Federal Rules." *New York Times*, January 26, 2024, sec. Arts. https://www.nytimes.com/2024/01/26/arts/design/american-museum-of-natural-history-nagpra.html.

Janes, Robert. "The Blackfoot Repatriation: A Personal Epilogue." In *We Are Coming Home: Repatriation and the Restoration of Blackfoot Cultural Confidence*, edited by Gerald T. Conaty, 241–62. Edmonton, AB: Athabasca University Press, 2015.

Johnson, Jessica S., Susan Heald, Kelly McHugh, Elizabeth Brown, and Marian Kaminitz. "Practical Aspects of Consultation with Communities." *Journal of the American Institute for Conservation* 44, no. 3 (2005): 203–15.

Kenaitze Indian Tribe. "DNA Project Connects Dena'Ina Past and Present." April 12, 2016. https://www.kenaitze.org/dna-project-connects-denaina-past-and-present/.

Kimmerer, Robin. *Braiding Sweetgrass: Indigenous Wisdom, Scientific Knowledge, and the Teachings of Plants*. Minneapolis: Milkweed Editions, 2013.

King, Donald, and José-Marie Griffiths. "InterConnections: The IMLS Study on the Use of Libraries, Museums, and the Internet, Museum Survey Results." Washington, DC: Institute of Museum and Library Services, 2008. http://www.interconnectionsreport.org/reports/IMLSMusRpt20080312kjm.pdf.

King, Madison. "The John Marr Collections from Nunavik at the University of Colorado–Boulder Museum." *Arctic Studies Newsletter* 28 (2021): 60–62.

Kopytoff, Igor. "The Cultural Biography of Things: Commoditization as Process." In *The Social Life of Things: Commodities in Cultural Perspective*, edited by Arjun Appadurai, 64–92. Cambridge: Cambridge University Press, 1986. https://doi.org/10.1017/CBO9780511819582.004.

Kreps, Christina F. *Museums and Anthropology in the Age of Engagement*. New York: Routledge, 2020.

Kreps, Christina F. "On Becoming 'Museum-Minded': A Study of Museum Development and the Politics of Culture in Indonesia." Unpublished dissertation, University of Oregon, Eugene, 1994.

Krmpotich, Cara. "Teaching Collections Management Anthropologically." *Museum Anthropology* 38, no. 2 (September 2015): 112–22. https://doi.org/10.1111/muan.12087.

Krmpotich, Cara, and Laura Lynn Peers. *This Is Our Life: Haida Material Heritage and Changing Museum Practice*. Vancouver: University of British Columbia Press, 2013.

Kuhlthau, Carol. "Information Search Process." No date. https://wp.comminfo.rutgers.edu/ckuhlthau/information-search-process/. 2018.

Kuhlthau, Carol, Jannica Heinström, and Ross Todd. "The 'Information Search Process' Revisited: Is the Model Still Useful?" *Information Research* 13, no. 4 (October 18, 2008): 45.

Laguna Resource Services, Inc. "Kumeyaay Heritage and Conservation (HC) Project: Learning Landscapes Educational Curriculum." 2016. https://www.parks.ca.gov/pages/663/files/LearningLandscapes_Edited_20201120v1c%20REMEDIATED.pdf.

Lassiter, Luke E. *The Chicago Guide to Collaborative Ethnography*. Chicago: University of Chicago Press, 2005.

Lempert, William. "Palya Futures: The Social Life of Kimberley Aboriginal Media." PhD dissertation, University of Colorado, Boulder, 2018. https://www.proquest.com/openview/70caa0906c5e71426b712955cab8ab4e/1?pq-origsite=gscholar&cbl=18750&diss=y.

Linenthal, Edward Tabor. *Preserving Memory: The Struggle to Create America's Holocaust Museum*. New York: Viking, 1995.

Local Contexts. "Grounding Indigenous Rights." 2024. https://localcontexts.org/.

Lonetree, Amy. *Decolonizing Museums: Representing Native America in National and Tribal Museums*. Chapel Hill: University of North Carolina Press, 2012.

Macdonald, Brandie. "Pausing, Reflection, and Action: Decolonizing Museum Practices." *Journal of Museum Education* 47, no. 1 (2022): 8–17. https://doi.org/10.1080/10598650.2021.1986668.

Macdonald, Sharon. *Behind the Scenes at the Science Museum: Materializing Culture*. Oxford: Berg, 2002.

Mapp, Lauren. "Comic-Con 2023: Indigenous Panelists Seek to Dispel Myths through Visual Storytelling of Local Kumeyaay History." *San Diego Union-Tribune*, July 22, 2023. https://www.sandiegouniontribune.com/entertainment/story/2023-07-22/comic-con-2023-indigenous-panelist-seek-to-dispel-myths-through-visual-storytelling-of-local-kumeyaay-history.

Marsh, Diana E. *Extinct Monsters to Deep Time: Conflict, Compromise, and the Making of Smithsonian's Fossil Halls*. New York: Berghahn Books, 2019.

McCarthy, Conal, and Awhina Tamarapa. "Teaching a Master's Course on Museums and Māori: Decolonising and Indigenising Museum Studies in Aotearoa New Zealand." *Decolonising Museology* 3 (Decolonising Curriculum) (2022): 67–79.

McCloud, Scott. *Understanding Comics: The Invisible Art*. New York: William Morrow, 1994.

McGregor, Deborah, Jean-Paul Restoule, and Rochelle Johnston. "Introduction: Relationships, Respect, Relevance, Reciprocity, and Responsibility: Taking up Indigenous Research Approaches." In *Indigenous Research: Theories, Practices, and Relationships*, edited by Deborah McGregor, Jean-Paul Restoule, and Rochelle Johnston, 1–21. Toronto: Canadian Scholars, 2018.

McKeown, C. Timothy. *In the Smaller Scope of Conscience: The Struggle for National Repatriation Legislation, 1986–1990*. Tucson: University of Arizona Press, 2012.

McMullen, Ann. "The Currency of Consultation and Collaboration." *Museum Anthropology Review* 2, no. 2 (2008): 54–87.

Mimiaga, Jim. "Burials, Sacred Objects Returned to Tribes." *The Journal* (Cortez, CO), May 21, 2015. https://www.the-journal.com/articles/burials-sacred-objects-returned-to-tribes-2/.

Monteagudo, Luis, Jr. "At Comic-Con, Kumeyaay Tribe Reveals Plans to Counter the 'Romanticized Lie.'" *Times of San Diego*, July 22, 2023. http://timesofsandiego.com/arts/2023/07/22/at-comic-con-kumeyaay-tribe-reveals-plans-to-counter-the-romanticized-lie/.

Montiel, Anya. "Respect, Reciprocity, and Responsibility: A Way Forward." In *This Present Moment: Crafting a Better World (Exhibition Catalog)*, edited by Mary Savig, Nora Atkinson, and Anya Montiel, 171–79. Washington, DC: Renwick Gallery of the Smithsonian American Art Museum, in association with D. Giles Limited, 2022.

Moorehead, Warren. *The American Indian in the United States, Period 1850–1914*. Andover, MA: Andover Press, 1914. https://www.loc.gov/item/15005358/.

Musqueam Indian Band. *Musqueam: A Living Culture*. Vancouver: Coppermoon, 2006.

Nash, Stephen E., and Chip Colwell. "NAGPRA at 30: The Effects of Repatriation." *Annual Review of Anthropology* 49 (October 21, 2020): 225–39.

Nasser, Latif. "The World's Biggest Scavenger Hunt: A Guide to Finding Stories." Transom, 2018. https://transom.org/2018/latif-nasser/.

National Association of Tribal Historic Preservation Officers. "NATHPO Directory." No date. https://members.nathpo.org/thpodirectory.

National Park Service. "Museum Renovations—Mesa Verde National Park (U.S. National Park Service)." No date. https://www.nps.gov/meve/museum-renovations.htm.

National Park Service. "Native American Graves Protection and Repatriation Act." No date. https://www.nps.gov/subjects/nagpra/index.htm.

National Preservation Institute. "Trainings." 2024. https://www.npi.org/trainings.

Nicks, Trudy. "Museums and Contact Work: Introduction." In *Museums and Source Communities: A Routledge Reader*, edited by Laura Peers and Alison Brown, 19–27. London: Routledge, 2003.

Odegaard, Nancy, Alyce Sadongei, and Associates. *Old Poisons, New Problems: A Museum Resource for Managing Contaminated Cultural Materials*. Washington, DC: Rowman and Littlefield, 2005. https://rowman.com/isbn/9780759105157/old-poisons-new-problems-a-museum-resource-for-managing-contaminated-cultural-materials.

Ogden, Sherelyn. *Caring for American Indian Objects: A Practical and Cultural Guide*. St. Louis: Minnesota Historical Society Press, 2004.

O'Hanlon, Michael, and Robert Louis Welsch, eds. *Hunting the Gatherers: Ethnographic Collectors, Agents, and Agency in Melanesia, 1870s–1930s*. Oxford: Berghahn Books, 2001.

O'Neil, Cathy. *Weapons of Math Destruction: How Big Data Increases Inequality and Threatens Democracy*, vol. 39. New York: Crown, 2016.

Pacers, Megan. "Kenaitze Tribe Allows DNA Testing on Dena'ina Remains." *Alaska Journal of Commerce*, September 30, 2015.

Peers, Laura, and Alison K. Brown, eds. *Museums and Source Communities: A Routledge Reader*. London: Routledge, 2003.

Peers, Laura, and Alison Brown. *Visiting with the Ancestors: Blackfoot Shirts in Museum Spaces*. Edmonton: Athabasca University Press, 2016.

Phillips, Ruth B. "Community Collaboration in Exhibitions: Toward a Dialogic Paradigm; Introduction." In *Museums and Source Communities: A Routledge Reader*, edited by Laura Peers and Alison Brown, 155–70. London: Routledge, 2003.

ProPublica. "The Repatriation Project: The Delayed Return of Native Remains." *ProPublica*, January 11, 2023. https://www.propublica.org/series/the-repatriation-project.

Rowley, Susan, Dave Schaepe, Leona Sparrow, Andrea Sanborn, Ulrike Radermacher, Ryan Wallace, Nicholas Jakobsen, Hannah Turner, Sivia Sadofsky, and Tristan Goffman. "Building an On-Line Research Community: The Reciprocal Research Network." Toronto: Archives and Museum Informatics, 2010. https://www.archimuse.com/mw2010/papers/rowley/rowley.html.

Ryker-Crawford, Jessie. "Towards an Indigenous Museology: Native American and First Nations Representation and Voice in North American Museums." PhD dissertation, University of Washington, Seattle, 2017.

Schein, Edgar H., and Peter A. Schein. *Humble Leadership*. New York: Penguin Random House, 2018.

School for Advanced Research. "Guidelines for Collaboration." No date. https://guidelinesforcollaboration.info/.

School for Advanced Research. "Indigenous Collections Care Guide." 2023. https://sarweb.org/iarc/icc/.

School for Advanced Research. "Standards for Museums with Native American Collections." June 2023. https://sarweb.org/iarc/smnac/.

Serrell, Beverly. *Judging Exhibitions: A Framework for Assessing Excellence*. Walnut Creek, CA: Left Coast, 2006. https://www.routledge.com/Judging-Exhibitions-A-Framework-for-Assessing-Excellence/Serrell/p/book/9781598740325.

Shakespeare, Amy. "Routes to Return: Working Towards International Repatriation." Routes to Return, 2023. https://routestoreturn.com/.

Shannon, Jennifer. "'Dear Concerned about Consent' (Response to 'Yours Sincerely, Concerned about Consent')." *Yours Sincerely an Uncertain Anthropologist*, Edited by Paige Edmiston and Alexandra Dantzer (blog). June 15, 2022. https://americanethnologist.org/online-content/collections/yours-sincerely-an-uncertain-anthropologist/yours-sincerely-concerned-about-consent-replies/.

Shannon, Jennifer. "Drawing Together: Comics and the Return of Museum Collections to White Earth Nation." *Ohio History Connection* (blog). October 3, 2022. https://www.ohiohistory.org/drawing-together/.

Shannon, Jennifer. *Guide to Creating Community Engaged Comics*. Boulder: University of Colorado, 2022. https://scholar.colorado.edu/concern/reports/sn00b026z.

Shannon, Jennifer. "Informed Consent: Documenting the Intersection of Bureaucratic Regulation and Ethnographic Practice." *PoLAR: Political and Legal Anthropology Review* 30, no. 2 (November 1, 2007): 229–48. https://doi.org/10.1525/pol.2007.30.2.229.

Shannon, Jennifer. "Museum Mantras, Teachings from Indian Country: Posterity Is Now; Failure Is an Option, and Repatriation Is a Foundation for Research." In *Science Museums in Transition: Unheard Voices*, edited by Hooley McLaughlin and Judy Diamond, 28–36. London: Routledge, 2019.

Shannon, Jennifer. "My Cry Gets up to My Throat: Dysplacement, Indigenous Storywork, and Visual Sovereignty in the Mandan Hidatsa Arikara Nation." *Collaborative Anthropologies* 14, no. 1 (2021): 44–73.

Shannon, Jennifer. "On Being a Tentative Anthropologist: Collaborative Anthropological Research with Indigenous Peoples in North America." In *Practicing Ethnography: A Student Guide to Method and Methodology*, edited by Lynda Mannik and Karen McGarry, 58–65. Toronto: University of Toronto Press, 2017.

Shannon, Jennifer. *Our Lives: Collaboration, Native Voice, and the Making of the National Museum of the American Indian*. Santa Fe: School for Advanced Research Press, 2014.

Shannon, Jennifer. "Posterity Is Now." *Museum Anthropology* 42, no. 1 (2019): 5–13.

Shannon, Jennifer. "The Professionalization of Indigeneity in the Carib Territory of Dominica." *American Indian Culture and Research Journal* 38, no. 4 (January 2014): 29–56.

Shannon, Jennifer, Jim Kambeitz, and Chris Hammons. *MHA Collaborative Filmmaking Project Workshop Guide*. Boulder: University of Colorado, 2016. https://scholar.colorado.edu/concern/defaults/6w924d73w.

Shannon, Jennifer, and Jack Piephoff. "Facebook: Bougainville Museum Collections Abroad." No date. https://www.facebook.com/profile.php?id=100072151452569.

Shannon, Jennifer, Madeline Polmear, and Bailey Duhe. *MHA Citizen Science Curriculum*. 2016. https://scholar.colorado.edu/concern/defaults/hm50tt44f.

Shannon, Jennifer, Claire Quimby, Chip Colwell, and Scott Burg. "Anthropology, Empathy, and the Need for Social Science Communication." *Science Communication* 43, no. 4 (August 1, 2021): 529–37. https://doi.org/10.1177/10755470211018812.

Shannon, Jennifer, and John Swogger. *A Guide to Facilitating Comics Workshop*. Boulder: University of Colorado, 2019. https://scholar.colorado.edu/concern/reports/sn00b026z.

Shenandoah, Chief Leon. "Haudenosaunee Confederacy Announces Policy on False Face Masks." *Akwesasne News* 1, no. 1 (1995): 39.

Silverman, Raymond, ed. *Museum as Process: Translating Local and Global Knowledges*, 1st ed. London: Routledge, 2014.

Simpson, Leanne Betasamosake. *Dancing on Our Turtle's Back: Stories of Nishnaabeg Re-creation, Resurgence, and a New Emergence*. Winnipeg: Arbeiter Ring, 2011.

Smith, Linda Tuhiwai. *Decolonizing Methodologies: Research and Indigenous Peoples*. New York: Zed Books, 2021 [1999].

Smithsonian Institution. "Shared Stewardship and Ethical Returns." Smithsonian National Collections Program, Washington, DC, 2022. https://ncp.si.edu/SI-ethical-returns.

Stein, Arlene, and Jessie Daniels. *Going Public: A Guide for Social Scientists*. Chicago: University of Chicago Press, 2017.

Strong, Pauline Turner. "Exclusive Labels: Indexing the National 'We' in Commemorative and Oppositional Exhibitions." *Museum Anthropology* 21, no. 1 (1997): 42–56. https://doi.org/10.1525/mua.1997.21.1.42.

Tran, Andrew Ba, Claire Healy, and Nicole Dungca. "Search the Smithsonian's Records on Human Remains." *Washington Post*, December 15, 2023. https://www.washingtonpost.com/dc-md-va/interactive/2023/human-remains-database-smithsonian-museum/.

Trouillot, Michel-Rolph. *Silencing the Past: Power and the Production of History*. Boston: Beacon, 1995.

Turner, Hannah. *Cataloguing Culture: Legacies of Colonialism in Museum Documentation*. Vancouver: University of British Columbia Press, 2020.

UCLA/Getty Interdepartmental Program in the Conservation of Cultural Heritage. "Andrew W. Mellon Opportunity for Diversity in Conservation." No date. https://mellondiversityconservation.org/.

United Nations. "United Nations Declaration on the Rights of Indigenous Peoples." 2007. https://www.un.org/development/desa/indigenouspeoples/wp-content/uploads/sites/19/2018/11/UNDRIP_E_web.pdf.

United States Department of the Interior. "Press Release: Interior Department Announces Final Rule for Implementation of the Native American Graves Protection and Repatriation Act." December 6, 2023. https://www.doi.gov/pressreleases/interior-department-announces-final-rule-implementation-native-american-graves.

University College London. "Conference: Heritage, Participation, Performativity, Care." History of Art, February 23, 2021. https://www.ucl.ac.uk/art-history/events/2021/mar/conference-heritage-participation-performativity-care.

Wheeler, Ryan, Jaime Arsenault, and Marla Taylor. "Beyond NAGPRA/Not NAGPRA." *Collections: A Journal for Museum and Archives Professionals* 18 (March 1, 2022): 8–17.

Wilson, Shawn. *Research Is Ceremony: Indigenous Research Methods*. Black Point, NS: Fernwood, 2008.

Worth, Sol. *Through Navajo Eyes: An Exploration in Film Communication and Anthropology*. Edited by John Adair. Bloomington: Indiana University Press, 1972.

Younging, Gregory. *Elements of Indigenous Style: A Guide for Writing by and about Indigenous Peoples*. Edmonton, AB: Brush Education, Inc., 2018.

Index

Page numbers followed by f indicate figures. Page numbers followed by n indicate notes.

AAA. See American Anthropological Association
Aboriginal Australian, 16n1, 48, 138, 174–75
Adair, John, 169
Aguilar, Joseph "Woody," 22, 29
Ah-Tah-Thi-Ki Museum, 228
Alaska Native, 48
Alderson, Jewyl, 207–8, 210, 212, 238f, 244
Alutiiq Museum, 228
American Alliance of Museums, 6, 8, 71, 139, 157, 186, 229
American Anthropological Association (AAA), 198–99, 206, 214n18, 239
American Indian Center in Chicago, 189
American Indian community of Chicago, 46
American Indian Religious Freedom Act, 62
American Institute for Conservation, 157
American Museum of Natural History (AMNH), New York City, 125

American Philosophical Society Center for Native Americans and Indigenous Research, 228
Ames, Michael, 1, 44; *Cannibal Tours and Glass Boxes*, 44; *Museums, the Public, and Anthropology*, 101n2
AMNH. See American Museum of Natural History
Anderson, Jane, 124
Anishinaabe, 128, 205
anthropology, collaborative and public, 198–203
anthropology, cultural, 43, 192; changes in, 48; courses, 83, 85–98; curator, 57, 87; ethnography, 44
Apache, 96, 144–45
applied comics: 205–6, 235
Applied Comics Network, 239
Arapaho, xiii, 141, 144–45
Arctic Studies Newsletter, 97
Arsenault, Jaime, 56, 62

assimilation, 62
Association for Social Anthropology in Oceania, 162
Association of Tribal Archives, Libraries, and Museums (ATALM), 11, 157, 159, 165, 206, 239
Association on American Indian Affairs, 11
Atalay, Sonya, 27, 59, 205
ATALM. *See* Association of Tribal Archives, Libraries, and Museums
Autry Museum of the American West in Los Angeles, 22, 69

Banegas, Ethan, 207–10, 212f, 243
Barona Cultural Center, 210, 211, 212f, 240
Basso, Keith, 213n5
Begay, Tim, 28, 37f
Beloit College Center for Collections Care, 159, 221–22
Beloit College's Logan Museum of Anthropology, 222
Berkshire Museum, 137
Bernstein, Jan, 61, 136f, 216
Biggs, Lois Taylor, 186
Blackfoot, 5
Black Panther (movie), 60
boarding schools, 62
Bougainville Island, 160–64
Bougainville Primary Source Book, 160–64, 163f
Bunch, Lonnie, III, 60–61, 216
Butcher, Georgia, 202

Cain, Christina, 57, 120, 136f
California Humanities for All Grant, 207
Campo Kumeyaay Nation (Campo Band of Missions Indians), 207, 232, 234, 240, 242, 244
Canadian Museums Association, 8
Catlin, George, 76–78
Catlin Cubes, 76–78, 77f
Center for Braiding Indigenous Knowledges and Science, 27
Chapin Mesa Archeological Museum. *See* Mesa Verde National Park
Chavarria, Ben, 37f
Cherokee, xv

Cheyenne, xiii, 6, 141, 144–45
Christen, Kim, 124
collection practices. *See* collections, private; museum collections
collections, private, 64, 68, 106, 143
Collins, Kayci Cook, 30
Collison, Vince, 109
Colorado-Wyoming Association of Museums, 157
community curating, 72–75
community-engaged comics, 255–58, 256f
Cornell University, xvi
Costales, Mikayla, 34, 38
Crow Canyon Archaeology Center, 32
Crows Breast, Elgin, 136f, 136–37

Darnell, Regna, xiv, 171
Data Sovereignty, 146
Denver Art Museum: Catlin Cubes, 76, 77f; Indigenous Arts of North America galleries, 69
Denver Museum of Nature and Science, 109, 161–62
digitizing collections, 135, 140, 144–47, 160–61, 200–203
Dillon, Jennie, 164
Dublin Core, 139

Edmiston, Paige, 202–3
Engle, Scarlett, 31, 34, 36, 37f, 38, 203
Enote, Jim, 37f, 113, 166n2
Enright, Kristen, 202
Erikson, Patricia Pierce, 45, 179
Errington, Shelly, 138
ethnocide, 20, 62
ethnography: approach to anthropology, 44; of collaborative exhibition, 42, 44; early, 44–45; museum, 45, 83, 154–55; National Museum of the American Indian, 44, 46; outcome of cultural anthropology, 44; participant observation, 31, 192; of science museums, 45
Everything Was Carved (video), 107, 107f, 109, 166
exhibition development, 68–69; content development, 69–71
exhibition interpretation, 75–80; Catlin Cubes, 76–78

exhibitions: *Future Imaginaries: Indigenous Art, Fashion, Technology*, 69; *Grounded in Clay: The Spirit of Pueblo Pottery*, 73; *Indigenous Futurisms: Transcending Past/Present/Future*, 69; iShare, 71; *Our Lives*, 46; *Our Peoples*, xiv; *Questions in Culture*, 94, 103n48; *The Secret Life of Objects*, 95, 103n49; *To Feel the Earth: Moccasins in the Southwest*, 70; *Weaving the World into a Basket*, 96

Ferreira, Manuel, 164
Field Museum of Chicago, 60
First Nations Principles of OCAP (ownership, control, access, possession), 9

genocide, 20, 62, 234
Gilmore, Stephanie, 28, 136f
Glenbow Museum, 5
Global Indigenous Data Alliance, 146
Goff, Sheila, 34, 35, 36
Gover, Calton, 202
Gover, Kevin, 60, 216
Grant to Return Indigenous Knowledge to Pacific Island Communities (GRIKPIC) program, 162
Greene, Candace, 67, 86–87, 92, 103n51
GRIKPIC. *See* Grant to Return Indigenous Knowledge to Pacific Island Communities
Grinnell, Calvin, 21, 76–78, 136f, 136–37
Guidelines for Collaboration from the School for Advanced Research, 9
Gwin, Lyle, 78

Haaland, Deb, 59; Federal Indian Boarding School Initiative, 101n19
Hadley Toftness, Kate, 186
Haida, 107–8, 109, 166
Haida Gwaii, 125
Haitian revolution, 44
Hakala, Jim, 93
Hammons, Christian, 179
Haudenosaunee, 97, 119
Heald, Susan, 129
Heye, George Gustav, 57
History Colorado, 79
Holocaust, 44

Hopi, 70, 97, 141–42
Horse Capture, Joe, 22, 23
Howe, Craig, xiv

Indigenous Collections Care Guide (School for Advanced Research), 9, 228
Indigenous Comic-Con in Albuquerque, New Mexico, 206
Institute of American Indian Arts, 69, 221
Institute of Museum and Library Services (IMLS) grant, 144
institutional review board (IRB), 188–91
intellectual property rights, 145–46
Inuktitut (language), xv, 222; *Atanarjuat: The Fast Runner* (video), xv
iPINCH, 159
Iqaluit, 92
IRB. *See* institutional review board
Isaac, Gwyneira, 45, 214n18
iShare, 71, 79
Isuma Productions, xv

Jacka, Jerry, 161–62
Jacknis, Ira, 53–54
Janes, Robert, 5
Joe, Tony, 28
Johnson, Barbara, 164
Johnson, Conrad "Bud," 160–64

Kainake Project, 161, 164
Kalinago (Island Carib), 46, 63f
Karp, Ivan, 214n12
Kenny, Jesse Dutton, 96
King, Madison, 97, 143
Kociolek, Pat, 30
Kopytoff, Igor, 66
Kramer, Jennifer, 101n3, 214n18
Kuhlthau, Carol, 91
Kumeyaay Comics, 212, 234, 235–36, 238–41, 243; perspective, 168f
Kumeyaay Community College, 207, 211, 238, 244
Kumeyaay Nation, 206, 210, 211, 233, 236, 238, 241, 244
Kumeyaay Visual Storytelling Project (KVSP), 207–12, 254; project personnel, 209f, 242–44; sponsoring organization and partners, 244

Kunuk, Zach, xv
KVSP. *See* Kumeyaay Visual Storytelling Project
Kwakwa̱ka'wakw (Kwakiutl), 53–54, 70

La Jolla Historical Society, 212
Lakota, 67, 127–28
Lamar, Cynthia Chavez, 70
LaMaskin, Aaron, 97
Lambrecht, Mona, 164
Lempert, William, 174–75
Lexicon Task Force of the American Alliance of Museums, 139
Library of Congress, xiv–xv
Local Contexts (project), 124, 141
Loring, Stephen, 97

Makah Cultural and Research Center, 117, 139. *See also* Erikson, Patricia Pierce
Mandan Hidatsa and Arikara Nation (Three Affiliated Tribes), xv, 7, 21; Calvin Grinnell, 76–78; institutional review board documents, 188; oral history documentary, 52, 195; repatriation, 136, 160, 177–79, 181, 206
Martin, Shannon, 18f, 205–6
Matteliano, Melanie, 202
Meister, Nicolette, 222
Memorandum of Affiliation between the Musqueam Indian Band and the University of British Columbia, 228
Memorandum of Understanding between the Penobscot Nation and the University of Maine, 229
Mesa Verde National Park (MVNP), 12, 22, 29, 32, 38, 203, 231f, 237; Chapin Mesa Archeological Museum (Chapin Mesa Museum), 29, 36, 37f, 38, 231f

Miskwish, Mike Connolly, 206, 207–12, 212f, 232, 234, 242, 243; *Kumeyaay: A History Textbook, Volume 1: Precontact to 1893*, 210, 242
Montiel, Anya, 172
Morgan, Lynn, 200
Moutu, Andrew, 162–63
museum anthropology: anthropology of museums, 42–46; areas of research, 15; changes in, 68–69, 214n18, 217–21; collaboration with Native communities, 14, 41, 171, 177, 217–21; collections research course, 85–98; Colorado University Museum Anthropology Section, 97, 160; *Museum Anthropology* (journal), 89; practiced in museums, 47–52; section, 41–104; teaching, 83–85. *See also* museum anthropology courses
museum anthropology courses: Collections Research in Cultural Anthropology, 83; Exploration of a Non-Western Culture–Native North America, 83; Introduction to Museum Anthropology, 83–85; Introduction to Museum Studies, 83, 153; Practicum: Collections Research in Cultural Anthropology, 87; Research Methods in Cultural Anthropology, 86–87
Museum Anthropology (journal), 89, 100, 201
museum collections, 15, 24, 28, 115; accession, 49, 55–56, 145; active and passive, 54–55; associated documentation and archives, 134f, 142–43; catalogs and online databases, 138–42; changing language (terms), 214n7; collections management policy and shared stewardship, 104f, 148–50; collections stewardship, 104f, 221; conservation, 126–29; cultural care, 64, 121f, 125, 140, 145, 151–52, 195; deaccession, 49, 55, 56, 58, 135; early, 53–55; policy, 149; digitization and digital return, 143–46; housing, 114–18; loans to communities, 124–26; Native community visits to, 107–14; plan, 56; repatriation consultations, 129–37, 134f; researcher access, 146–48; welcoming workplace, 151–52
Museum of Us in San Diego, California, 216
Musqueam First Nation, 25, 37, 78, 101n3, 108
MVNP. *See* Mesa Verde National Park

Nacotchtank (Anacostans), 221
NAGPRA Comics 1: Journeys to Complete the Work . . . and Changing the Way We Bring Native American Ancestors Home (Atalay), 205, 235; relationality, 18f

Index | 273

NAGPRA Comics 2: Trusting You Will See This as We Do: Tribal Sovereignty and the Return of Sacred Objects and Objects of Cultural Patrimony, 206; Chapin Mesa Museum Exhibit Design Reference Guide, 37f; repatriation, 404f
NAGPRA Comics project, 58–59, 204, 206, 214n18, 236, 238–39, 243, 244, 254. See also applied comics
National Association of Tribal Historic Preservation Officers, 165
National Museum of African American History and Culture, 60, 216
National Museum of Taiwan, 71
National Museum of the American Indian (NMAI): collaboration, 22; community curating, 72–75, 234; conservation, 128; cultural care, 118; cultural thesaurus, 139; exhibit labels, 83; Igloolik exhibit, 27; indoor ceremonial room, 108; Native Knowledge 360, 80, 239; NMAI Act, 57, 68, 129; Our Lives, 46; shared stewardship, 104f, 215–16
National Park Service (NPS), 30–38, 101n19
National Preservation Institute, 159
National Science Foundation, 27, 199–200
Native American Graves Protection and Repatriation Act (NAGPRA), 48, 97; cultural care practices, 64, 118, 140, 149; Duty of Care, 59, 98, 102n30; grants, 65; law, 58, 60, 67–68, 148–49; repatriation, 57, 70–71, 129–33, 136–37; STOP ACT (Safeguard Tribal Objects of Patrimony Act of 2021), 60; training, 159; United States Department of the Interior, 59. See also NAGPRA Comics
Native Hawaiian, 60
Navajo, 101n12, 169
Navajo Nation, 28–29, 37f, 71, 87, 121, 169, 197
Navajo Nation Museum, 71
Newland, Bryan, 59
Newsom, Gavin, 233
NMAI. See National Museum of the American Indian
Noro, Jeffrey, 161–64, 167n26
Northern Science Award, 27

Novera, Junior, 161–64
NPS. See National Park Service
Nunavut (Canada), 92, 97, 98

Odegaard, Nancy, 129
O'Hanlon, Michael, 53–54
Ohio History Connection, 148
open educational resources, 239
Orosco, Lorraine, 207–9, 209f, 211, 212f, 243

Paiwan Cultural Center, 71
Pamunkey, 221
Papua New Guinea, 161–62
Papua New Guinea (PNG) National Museum and Art Gallery, 162, 163f
Parzen, Micah, 216
Penobscot Nation, 229
Phillips, Ruth, 249
Piscataway, 221
Pitt Rivers Museum, University of Oxford, 54, 108
Podlasek, Joe, 189
Poon, Elysia, 73–74
"Posterity Is Now," 5, 8, 10
Powdermaker, Hortense, 213n5, 214n5
Prairie Public, North Dakota public radio, 178
Prairie Rose Seminole, xvi
professional development, museums, 153–54; informational interviews, 154–55; internships and mentoring, 157–59; job searching and professional development, 247–48; professional development, 155–57; reviewing exhibitions, 154, 166n2
Protocols for Native American Archival Materials (First Archivists Circle), 9, 229

Radiolab, Border Trilogy, 200
Ramaswamy, Robert, 222–23
research, collaborative, 169–70; grant writing, 182–87; interviewing and recording, 192–97; research design, 175–82; review and informed consent, 188–91; sharing results, 197–98; values-centered research practice, 171–75
Richardson, Jane, 161

274 | INDEX

Robert S. Peabody Institute of Archaeology, Phillips Academy (Peabody Andover Museum), 56, 62, 68
Rodrigeuz, Stanley, 206, 207–8, 210–11, 243
Rowley, Sue, 61, 91–92, 101n3
Roybal, Gary, 32
Ryker-Crawford, Jessie, 127–28, 221

Sadongei, Alyce, 129
San Diego Comic-Con, 206, 208, 210, 239
Sands, Charles, III, 101n19
San Ildefonso, 22, 32, 70
San Pasqual Ipai Band, 243
Santa Clara Pueblo, 37f, 70
Schein, Edgar, 10
Schein, Peter, 10
School for Advanced Research (SAR): "Grounded in Clay: The Spirit of Pueblo Pottery" (exhibition), 73; Guidelines for Collaboration from the School of Advanced Research, 9, 17n8, 50, 52, 109
Science Museum in London, 45
Shannon, Jennifer, 63f, 214n18, 242–43
Sholly, Kristy, 30
Silverman, Ray, 214n12
Smithsonian Institution: Lonnie Bunch, 60-61, 111, 216; National Museum of the American Indian, xiv, xvi, 6, 22, 42, 44, 57, 78, 108, 125, 139, 215, 220, 221, 234, 239; National Museum of Natural History, 45, 67, 86, 119; National Museum of Natural History's Summer Institute in Museum Anthropology (SIMA), 67, 85–88, 103n51; (course materials), 102n41; Shared Stewardship and Ethical Returns Policy, 9, 60-61, 215-16, 228, 229; Traveling Exhibit Service, 94
Society of American Archaeology, 206, 239
Sparrow, Leona, 37, 101n3
Standards for Museums with Native American Collections (SMNAC), 9, 229
St. Regis Mohawk Tribe, 55
Strong, Pauline Turner, 94
Swogger, John, 40f, 206, 207–10, 212, 212f, 237, 242–43, 254; artwork, 18f, 37f, 104f, 111f, 121f, 134f, 168f
Sycuan Cultural Center, 206, 210

Tallmadge (Tryhane), Kendall, 70
Tax, Sol, 213n5, 214n5
THPO. *See* tribal historic preservation officer
Tlingit Dak̲l'aweidi, 119
Treaty of New Echota, xv
tribal historic preservation officer (THPO), 13, 98, 122, 218; advice to museums, 109, 112; national association, 165
Tribal Print Source, 204, 234, 238
Trouillot, Michel-Rolph, 44

UNDRIP. *See* United Nations Declaration on the Rights of Indigenous Peoples
Ungalak, James, xv
United Nations Declaration on the Rights of Indigenous Peoples (UNDRIP), 9, 59, 100, 101n16
United States Capitol building, 46, 221
United States government, 30, 58, 62, 193
University of British Columbia Museum of Anthropology: example policies, 228; loans, 125; Memorandum of Affiliation between the Musqueam Indian Band and the University of British Columbia, 228; Michael Ames, 44; Miriam Clavir, 126; Multiversity Galleries, 69–70; Musqueam 101, 78; Reciprocal Research Network, 145; shared stewardship, 215; Sue Rowley, 61; terminology, xvi, 25
University of Colorado, xvi, 14; American Indian Law Program, 204; Center for Native and Indigenous Studies, 204; Graduate Program in Museum and Field Studies, 29–38, 178; Heritage Center, 164. *See also* University of Colorado Museum of Natural History
University of Colorado Museum of Natural History, xiii, 7, 244; Anthropology Section, 87–88, 97, 120, 141, 156, 160–64; Bougainville Island items, 160–62; collaboration with National Park Service, 30; collection information system, 147; Conrad "Bud" Johnson collection, 160–64; iShare, 71, 79; Mandan, Hidata, and Arikara Nation oral history documentary, 52, 86, 177; Museum and Field Studies program, 153–54; NAGPRA

grants, 65; repatriation consultation, 57, 64, 129–37; storage mounts, 116; University of Colorado museum studies program, 47
University of Massachusetts Amherst, 27
Ute, xiii, 79, 141, 144–45
Ute Mountain Ute, 61–62

Vanuatu, 116
Vinsonhaler, Isabella, 96, 160–61

West, Paige, 161–62
West, W. Richard, Jr., 6, 78
Wheeler, Eric, 56
White Earth Nation, 56, 62, 137, 143, 148

Whiting Foundation Public Engagement Fellowship, 207, 232
Wilbert, Claire, 130
Willie, Mikael, 70
Wilson, Shawn, 28
World War II, 161
Worth, Sol, 169

Yazzie, Sam, 169

Zibiwing Center of Anishinabe Culture and Lifeways, 206, 228
Zuni, 45, 70, 97, 113–14
Zuni A:shiwi A:wan Museum and Heritage Center in New Mexico, 45, 113–14

About the Author

Jennifer Shannon is a museum curator and associate professor of cultural anthropology at the University of Colorado (CU) Boulder. She has a bachelor's degree in biology and anthropology from Bowdoin College, a master's in social science from the University of Chicago, and a PhD in sociocultural anthropology from Cornell University. She was a postdoctoral teaching fellow at the University of British Columbia before joining the faculty at CU in 2009. Jen's commitment to collaborative research methods and public scholarship was recognized through a 2021–2022 Whiting Foundation Public Engagement Fellowship. She co-produced *Kumeyaay Comics* and *NAGPRA Comics*, and she was the co-host of the first three seasons of *SAPIENS: A Podcast for Everything Human*.

Jen began her museum career as a curatorial research assistant for the National Museum of the American Indian's inaugural exhibitions and is the author of *Our Lives: Collaboration, Native Voice, and the Making of the National Museum of the American Indian* (SAR Press, 2014). From 2017 to 2022 she served as a consultant for the NMAI, and in 2022 she took a leave of absence from CU to manage the NMAI's Community Loans Program. In 2023, Jen helped design and establish the NMAI's Outreach and Engagement Planning Office, dedicated to developing and supporting collaborations with Indigenous communities and allied organizations to support the museum's mission.

Jen, originally from Chicago, loves spending time with her fluffy pup, Ellie. She has been playing ultimate frisbee and enjoying the Spirit of the Game for over thirty years by captaining teams, coaching high schoolers, and competing at local, national, and international events.

www.ingramcontent.com/pod-product-compliance
Lightning Source LLC
Chambersburg PA
CBHW051529020426
42333CB00016B/1847